An Introduction to the Greek World

An Introduction to the Greek World

PETER D. ARNOTT

Macmillan

LONDON · MELBOURNE · TORONTO

St Martin's Press

NEW YORK

1 9 6 7

MACMILLAN AND COMPANY LIMITED
Little Essex Street London WC2
also Bombay Calcutta Madras Melbourne

THE MACMILLAN COMPANY OF CANADA LIMITED
70 Bond Street Toronto 2

ST MARTIN'S PRESS INC
175 Fifth Avenue New York NY 10010

Library of Congress catalog card No. 67-10699

PRINTED IN GREAT BRITAIN

Contents

List of Illustrations

Preface

IN recent years the decline of interest in formal classical studies has been answered by a surge of enthusiasm for classics in translation. Almost every Greek or Latin work of merit, with some of very little merit, is now available in English, and the major authors are retranslated with increasing frequency. This activity, together with the growing popular interest in archaeology and successful novelistic treatments of ancient history, testifies to the fact that a public which may no longer have time to educate itself in ancient languages is no less aware of its debt to ancient society. Universities have recognized this need — with initial reluctance, to be sure — by offering courses in Classical Literature in Translation, or Ancient Civilization. In American universities this is now standard procedure and their British counterparts are rapidly following suit. The purists may weep, but it is not altogether an unhealthy sign. There are surely two sides to the coin here : while it is possible, with Eric Bentley, to argue that all translation is by definition bad, it is also permissible to suggest that if the great Greek poets owed as much to their *language* as the purists say they do, they would not be as good as in fact they are. Translation, as most would now admit, is a process of judgement : the stature of the original is measured by the amount that comes through in a foreign tongue. By the same token, many classical scholars have found the new pressures on their discipline to be an asset rather than a liability. Forced to emerge from behind the covers of erudite specialist journals, they must now expound and defend their subject before an audience of critical and intelligent laymen. The success with which this can be achieved is a measure both of the scholar and of his subject.

It is for this sort of public that this book is written — for the student unversed in classical languages who wishes to acquire an elementary knowledge of the ancient world ; for the traveller who wants something a little deeper than a guidebook ; for those who know nothing and want to know something, or for those who have a smattering and want a little more. It is planned somewhat along the lines of my earlier *An Introduction to the Greek Theatre*, and, in the main, attempts to illuminate certain features of ancient life by discussion of specific works in their literary and historical context. This does not mean that the book will tell the story of the *Iliad*, or summarize Thucydides' *History*. The student can read the books for himself. The present study merely aims to offer certain relevant background material in an interesting and cogent way. Inevitably this entails much condensation and simplification, with their attendant dangers. This will be particularly apparent in the historical survey offered in Chapter Two, and I would say in defence here that this is intended as a skeleton only, to provide the reader with a framework giving coherence to the various particular discussions that follow. It may also be objected that much of what appears here is too elementary, even for a survey of this nature. Here I would mildly suggest that a professor's notion of what is elementary may differ from his pupil's. My own initial explorations in the classics were bedevilled by this fact ; a great deal of basic information was considered so elementary that no one bothered to mention it, let alone write it down. I am anxious not to repeat this process with anyone who reads this book.

While on the subject of basic information, it may be appropriate to mention the matter of names and dates, which often puzzle the tyro. There are in many cases at least two acceptable ways of spelling a given Greek name. As scholarship came to Greece by way of Rome, the Latinized spellings became customary, and have endured in use for centuries. Aischulos became Aeschylus. The Greek diphthong *ai* became Latin *ae*, the Greek termination *-os* became Latin *-us*, Greek *k* became Latin hard *c*, for *k* does not exist in Latin. Sometimes the changes were more fundamental, as in the name of the Homeric hero Aias, better known in the

Latin form Ajax. In addition, custom anglicized certain well-known place names. It would be simply pretentious to talk of Athenai when we mean Athens, or Korinthos when we mean Corinth. More recently, however, there has been a determined movement to restore the consistency of Greek spelling. This is admirable in intention, but cumbersome in practice. Odysseus' son becomes the rather fearsome Telemakhos, and the seductive sibilants of Circe become the spiky Kirke. There are other possible combinations and variants : the Greek letter *ksi*, usually transliterated by *x*, sometimes appears as *z*, so that one book may talk of Xenophon, another of Zenophon. There is the same problem with names of works. Some are more familiar in their English form, some in Latin, some in Greek. In this book I have taken the coward's way out and used whichever form seemed most familiar. Thus the more common Greek names appear in Latinized or anglicized versions, and the less familiar in a closer approximation to the original spelling. As for dates, newcomers are often confused by the system of double dating that must be used — for example, 425/424 B.C. This is necessary because the Greek year overlapped the modern, and unless we know the month of a particular event, the two dates have to be cited. In this book, incidentally, it is normally assumed that dates are B.C. unless otherwise noted.

Throughout the book certain important themes recur, and the illustrations are designed to support these. It has not been thought necessary to include pictures of already well-illustrated monuments. Anyone desiring a close-up picture of the Parthenon sculptures, or a long-range view of the theatre at Epidaurus, need only open any one of five thousand books. The pictures here, some of ancient sites and some of modern, are designed to evoke a mood, and to present the reader with an illustration of the realities of the Greek countryside.

P. D. A.

Athens – Mykonos – Iowa City
December 1965

Acknowledgements

THE author and publishers acknowledge their thanks for permission to reproduce passages from the following :

From Sophocles' *Oedipus the King* and *Antigone*, translated and edited by Peter D. Arnott. Copyright 1949 by Appleton-Century-Crofts Inc. Reprinted by permission of Appleton-Century-Crofts, Division of Meredith Publishing Company.

From Aeschylus' *Agamemnon, The Oresteia* : Part I and *The Libation Bearers* and *The Eumenides, The Oresteia* : Parts II and III, translated and edited by Peter D. Arnott. Copyright © 1964 by Meredith Publishing Company. Reprinted by permission of Appleton-Century-Crofts, Division of Meredith Publishing Company.

Chapter One

Land and People

THE course of Greek history is often obscure. For the crucial, formative years we must rely almost entirely on archaeology. This emerged as a serious study only in the latter part of the nineteenth century, and, like most new discoveries, was greeted with sometimes excessive enthusiasm. There was a new insistence on the value of material objects, and a feeling that only what the excavator's spade could uncover was historically valid. Growing familiarity with archaeological methods and problems, and the more sober assessments of hindsight, have brought the realization that archaeology, like any other way of exploring the past, is necessarily fallible. In recent years serious controversies have arisen over archaeological findings, one of which affects our whole concept of the beginnings of Greek civilization and will be discussed at greater length below.

When literary and epigraphical evidence begins to appear, this may be incomplete or, worse, contradictory. The writer's particular bias must be sought and kept in mind, and his judgements evaluated on this basis. Often, the same bare facts lend themselves to equally convincing but mutually incompatible interpretations. For example, Pericles' legislation has been interpreted by one scholar to prove that he was an oligarch, by another to show that he was a democrat. Of course, this sort of historical problem is not peculiar to Greek studies. Similar conflicts have arisen over the acts and deeds of (for example) Charles II, Abraham Lincoln and Adolf Hitler. In Greek history, however, the problem is multiplied by the remoteness and unfamiliarity of the material, by the fact that we are dealing with an alien temperament (a fact which European and American scholars often forget) and by the tendency of the Greeks themselves to confuse poetry and history, allegory and fact.

In one respect at least the historian finds solace. Greek history divides itself fairly neatly into periods. Here there is an immense contrast with the history of Rome. In Italy one is always conscious of the interplay of epochs, the continuity of history. Classical buildings stand cheek by jowl with modern neighbours. An early imperial structure may have the Renaissance on one side and the twentieth century on the other. The buildings themselves have usually taken on new shapes and functions through the ages. On the bank of the Tiber, the Castello Sant' Angelo was built as a tomb and became in turn a fortress, a summer residence both sacred and secular, a prison and a museum. It has equally strong associations with Hadrian, who was buried there, Benvenuto Cellini, who was imprisoned there, and Giacomo Puccini, whose operatic Tosca jumped to death from its ramparts. The Piazza Navona began as an imperial racecourse and was transformed to an aristocratic promenade. In the centre of St. Peter's Square, watching the entrance to the Basilica, stands an obelisk that once overlooked the pagan splendours of Nero's circus. In Italy it is only the freaks of history that have escaped this process, like Pompeii, covered by volcanic eruption and artificially preserved from time.

In Greece, the dividing of history into neat compartments is the rule rather than the exception. It is not enough that Lord Byron's signature, real or spurious, should be scrawled upon a pillar of the temple at Sunium. Where modern cities bear ancient names, the new have often shifted significantly from the old. This is true of Athens, where the city centre has moved north from the old Acropolis, leaving the memorial of its earlier greatness largely untouched until recently. It is almost unbelievable that the Odeum of Herodes Atticus, holding five thousand people and now used annually for the Athens Festival of music, drama and ballet, should have been largely buried until the nineteenth century, only the top tiers of its outer wall visible above earth ; or that the famous bull, monument to a dead Dionysios, which towers above the Cerameicus cemetery, was likewise below ground until the German scholars uncovered it. Similarly Corinth, though an attractive city, has none of the prestige of its illustrious predecessor. The ancient city, Palaia Korinthos, lies some miles away, and owes its present state largely to American excavators. Sometimes the present, blind to the past, has obliterated what is old and potentially valuable. Oedipus' city of Thebes is submerged beneath a modern township of little interest or charm. The Greeks themselves, though aware of their heritage, have sometimes been resentful of it ; they have felt, justifiably, that it is unfair to compare them to Greeks of Pericles' time and expect them to live up to an impossible ideal. This public annoyance has been matched by private indifference. One area of Delphi, the oracular shrine of Apollo, acquired the sinister name Marmoria, 'the marble quarry'. Here peasants could find good finished stones for building, or for turning into quicklime. Limekilns were similarly established on the island of Delos, Apollo's legendary birthplace : the god was as much persecuted by builders as in former years he had been glorified by them. The same thing, of course, happened in Italy — there were limekilns in the Forum too — but the damage was not so vicious. Even now losses can occur. Stones recorded by archaeologists thirty or forty years ago are no longer to be seen. In such an atmosphere the depredations of European scholars and collectors such as Lord Elgin, who removed the famous marbles from the Parthenon to the British Museum, were justifiable. In more recent years the Greeks have shown a new awareness of their past — an awareness partly mercenary and inspired by the tourist trade, but in great measure altruistic and representing a real desire to atone for years of neglect. Many of the important classical sites are now models of accessibility and preservation.

This separateness of past and present reveals itself in various ways within the context of Greek history. Changes have been violent, and have brought with them obliviousness of the old ways. The coming of the Indo-European invaders marked the end of Cretan power, and an empire that had once dominated the Mediterranean was almost entirely forgotten. Its highly sophisticated legal system survived only in myth : Minos, King of Crete, and his brother Rhadamanthys, became judges in the Underworld. On another level, the Cretan system of domestic sanitation was not to be equalled in Europe for centuries. The mainland cities, led by Mycenae and Tiryns, next became dominant, but after their demise they were as good as forgotten. Later generations wondered at the monumental architecture of Mycenae and called the walls Cyclopean, conjecturing that they could have been built only by Cyclopes, giants. King Nestor's city of Pylos, one of the more important sea-powers of the Mycenaean era, vanished so completely that in the fifth century B.C. jokes about its inaccessible location were already old. In the interplay of city-states that followed, one city after another changed the political structure of the country ; Alexander's conquests altered all, and gave the fourth-century world a new complexion. Then came the Romans, to reduce Greece to a cultural annexe of Roman domains, and ultimately the Turks, who brought the beginning of the long night of Greek history. When the Turks occupied the Athenian Acropolis they did not so much re-order it as obliterate it, and the same is generally true of the effects of Moslem domination on the classical heritage.

This separation of history is matched by that caused by geography. The country, to a large extent, determined the character of its inhabitants. Greece is a land which makes its own terms, and which imposes certain requirements on those who come to live there. First, it is mountainous. The merest glance at the map will show how the terrain is divided by mountain barriers into small, isolated pockets of cultivable land. Here small settlements could grow up apart from and oblivious of their neighbours. As new waves of immigrants moved in from the north, they settled in these valleys ; often, one wave would not intermingle with another but pass it by, kept off by the barrier mountains. Thus the country developed as a collection of separate and distinct small settlements, with different origins, different customs, constitutions, religions and ways of life. It is false to speak of Greek history as though it were the history of a nation. It was no such thing. Rather, it was the history of an agglomeration of small and quarrelsome political entities, first one and then another predominating. This was not entirely a matter of geography ; the small-settlement pattern was acceptable to the Greek temperament for other reasons, but geography created the mould wherein such a pattern might be shaped.

Only on three occasions, in the period we are considering, can the Greek states be said to have acted in any degree collectively. The first of these was the famous Trojan War, traditionally dated at 1184 B.C., when the Greek cities fought under the leadership of Mycenae ; the second was during the Persian invasions of the late sixth and early fifth centuries B.C., when the states were joined by fear, seeing they must unite or be destroyed ; and the third was a unity imposed by force in the person of Alexander the Great, who in the fourth century thrust some sort of cohesion on the cities that he conquered, reversed the pattern of Mediterranean history and led Greece to the conquest of Asia Minor. On none of these occasions, however, was the union successful or long-lasting. The Homeric poems and associated legends contain many references, open or explicit, to the unwillingness of cities to submit to Mycenean leadership. Achilles was hidden among the women by his mother, and Odysseus feigned insanity ; even in the Heroic Age military conscription was unpopular. During the Persian Wars the cities still bickered while striving to offer a united front to the invader. Sparta was only too happy to see Athens destroyed, and Athens employed the successful outcome of the war not as a foundation of panhellenism but to further her own imperialistic ends. In the fourth century Alexander conquered and passed on, and the cities immediately resumed their quarrelling behind him, devising plots and stratagems against him and against each other.

This lack of unity endures. It is represented today at its best in the fierce, possessive pride which a Greek feels for his own community — in the spirit, for example, which will make a trainload of Athenians burst spontaneously into song as they come in sight of the Acropolis. It took its ugliest shape in the years after the

B

Second World War, when history repeated itself and the story of the Persian Wars was retold. United against the Germans, the Greeks were fiercely divided against themselves. Even before the Occupation had been lifted, this factionalism turned to civil war, with individual groups pursuing their own interests and often shifting allegiances alarmingly during the course of the fighting. The chaos of these war years is, in heightened form, the story of Greek politics through the ages. Even the traditional barriers still have their deterrent effect : the mountains, historically the great impediment to land communication, now affront modern technology and obstruct the creation of a national television network. In the cities, now so much larger than they used to be, Greeks will often confine their interest to their own immediate neighbourhood. In the country, one village may affect complete ignorance of the whereabouts of the next ; in the city, a taxi-driver may need directions if he travels more than a few streets from home.

This, then, is one of the constants of Greek history. It must be remembered, for it manifests itself continually. The society which evolved under these conditions has been compared to that of the American West in its pioneer days. Although this comparison may easily be overworked, there is much truth in it. In both periods one sees the same factors operating : the growth of small, self-contained settlements, isolated in the one case by mountains, in the other by distance. In such a society the stranger is a person of importance. He must be treated with caution, for he is unknown and thus potentially dangerous, of different stock and therefore, until proved otherwise, of dubious morality. At the same time, he is one of the few links with the outside world, and a good source of information if handled with care. Thus there grows up an elaborate code of hospitality in which visitors fall into a definite category. They may expect welcome and special privileges. In return for this they must expect to be pumped. Just as the sheriff, in the archetypal Western film, sidles up to the stranger in the saloon and asks what his name is, where he is from and how long he expects to remain in town, so

Homeric personages ask, and expect to be asked, for long accounts of family background and personal history. The code makes its mark in language. The Greek words for stranger and guest are the same, *xenos*. The host–guest relationship, *xenia*, was a social obligation supported by religion. Zeus, King and Father of the gods, was invoked as protector of the stranger within the gates. This too is a concept which has far from disappeared in Greece today, where the hospitality, particularly of country people, is proverbial, and where each visitor is expected as a matter of course to deliver a lengthy account of himself.

For all this the Greek possessed some sense of a common ancestry, for which they sought mythic sanction in various ways, and a feeling that the inhabitants of their country were different from those of other countries. As always, different was taken to mean superior. They looked down on foreigners as inferior beings, calling them *barbaroi* — a name said to originate from the way foreign languages sounded to the Greek ear, a meaningless ba-ba-ba. Although the word can have the purely neutral meaning of *foreigner, non-Greek*, it acquires the derogatory connotations that produce the modern *barbarian*. This racial arrogance is one of the ugliest features of the Greek character. It reveals itself, for instance, in the comedies of Aristophanes, which read on occasion like the most class-conscious nineteenth-century British farces. Aristophanic comedy is full of jokes about comic foreigners. Anyone who cannot speak Greek, or who speaks it badly, or who has a foreign name, is automatically funny. The comic Persian in Aristophanes is the comic Frenchman of English farce or the comic Italian or Swede in American popular comedy : the racial arrogance that produces such characters is the same. A similar attitude reveals itself, in more sinister ways, in Aristotle. It is he who, discussing slavery, makes the distinction between natural and unnatural slaves. It is wrong for one Greek to enslave another, for they are equals. Certain foreign nationalities, on the other hand, are naturally inferior, and *ipso facto* fit to be enslaved if the occasion arises. Such pernicious doctrines were, much later, to be quoted as justification for slavery in America. Such attitudes existed not merely between Greek and non-Greek but internally, between one city and another. Athens was particularly prone to this, boasting that its people were indigenous and never polluted by admixture of other races. This was fictionalized in the story of an earth-born king from whom all subsequent Athenians descended. This is the uglier side of patriotism, and reveals itself in the passionate, often obsessive identification of individual with city that reveals itself throughout Greek history. For a Greek, and particularly for an Athenian, to be banished was a punishment almost as bitter as execution.

In connection with the attitude of Greek to foreigner, the relationship of the Greeks towards their Eastern neighbours needs further exploration here, for it is another of the constants of ancient history. The earlier civilizations were Eastern — Babylon, Egypt, and the various powers of Asia Minor. Compared to these, Greece was an upstart newcomer. Greece lies within tempting sea-reach of Asia Minor. The waters are dotted with its islands, some large, like Lesbos and Chios, some tiny, like Delos and the volcanic speck that ancients knew as Thera, moderns as Santorini. Geographers argue that these were once part of a land-bridge which later submerged, leaving only the mountain tops visible to form the present islands : what is now Athens is seen as the western end of this chain. Some would go further, connect the submersion with the volcanic activity still apparent around Santorini, and suggest that this sunken land was the lost continent of Atlantis. Be that as it may, the islands show themselves like stepping-stones across the sea ; singly, they are easy objects of conquest by a hostile fleet. Greece was thus, from its earliest times, sensitive to Eastern influence, whichever form it happened to take. The Phoenicians, great colonizers of the early Mediterranean, gave the Greeks their alphabet. Oriental patterns and motifs appear in early Greek pottery. One may take pottery as an epitome of history here, for soon the orientalizing tendency vanishes to be replaced by indigenous geometric designs. When oriental patterns reappear in Greek art, it is when the influence has turned the other way — in the later fourth century B.C. when Alexander's armies were pushing eastward and the returning soldiers brought home Eastern patterns to be copied, and Eastern stories to be retold and embedded in Greek literature. In the long interim Greek art pursues independent paths. The Eastern powers observed the growing strength of Greek cities with alarm ; they recognized a different culture at work, and a possible antagonist. This led to the great wars of the late sixth and early fifth centuries, with Greece emerging the surprising, and surprised, victor ; to the subsequent involvement of Greeks in Persian politics, and Greek harassment of Easterners on their own ground ; and to the wars of Alexander, ending with the diffusion of Greek culture over wide stretches of Eastern lands. This antagonism did not subside with the ending of the classical era. It appears again in the Middle Ages, when Greece, now the centre of Christendom, was attacked by the Turks and lost its capital, Constantinople, in 1453. Athens itself, occupied by Franks and Catalans since 1204, fell to the Turks three years later, leaving Austria as the next bastion of the Western world against the Eastern. It revives in the Greek War of Independence, culminating in the escape from Turkish domination in 1827. It has reappeared, sporadically but cruelly, in our own time, in the conflict over the island of Cyprus, where Greek still lives at enmity with Turk just as in ancient days, on the coast of Asia Minor, Greek colonists lived in nervous proximity to Persians. To this day the Greeks recognize their position on the fringe of the Western world. When a Greek takes a trip to Italy he will often speak of 'going to Europe', and in the very vegetation of the country, palm and cactus speak of the East while the buildings look to the West. Throughout Greek history, whether Greece was free or dependent, subject or conqueror, she could never ignore the East, and particularly the Persians. Their near presence was a constant menace, a factor to be reckoned with in Greek affairs.

As the mountains divided the cities from one another so they took greedily from the soil. Cultivable land in Greece has always been scarce. Harsh conditions were imposed by the

terrain on any community that wished to survive — grow enough
to feed yourselves, or be strong enough to bring food in from
elsewhere. The farmer-poet Hesiod, writing in the ninth century
B.C., sums up the lot of the Greek smallholder in a few bitter lines :

> *Have but a single son, to feed his father's*
> *House ; so wealth will multiply within your doors.*
> *But if you leave a second son, you had better*
> *Be old before you die. But Zeus can easily bestow*
> *Great wealth on greater numbers. More hands, more work*
> *And greater increase. If your spirit pants for riches*
> *Do what I tell you : work, and on top of that put more work.*[1]*

The Greek farmer adapted himself as best he could to his conditions, and so he continues to do. To select a striking though
unclassical example, the island of Mykonos, though possessing a
minimum of cultivable land, is able by skilful terracing to produce enough food for its population of four thousand.

In the best of circumstances, however, crops were scarce, and
had to be worked for. The common pattern of ancient warfare
was for the attacking army to aim for the crops and the defenders
to come out to protect them. This is how the Peloponnesian
War began ; the Spartans' first act after declaring war on Athens
in 431 was to march into Attica to ravage the harvest. If the
crops were saved, there could be a respite, and if not the community would die. This accounts, too, for the emergence of
harvest festivals as a natural time of celebration, perhaps more
vividly in Greece than in gentler countries. When the grain was
gathered or the grapes brought in the village could relax a little
and allow itself some brief self-indulgence. Out of these rustic
acts of thanksgiving develop some of the major festivals of
the Greek calendar. The religious year is firmly rooted in the soil.

When demands became too great for resources expedients had
to be found. Colonies drained off the surplus population. If
enough food could not be grown, more had to be imported from
outside. Often, what began as trading expeditions ended as a
colonizing process. Ships went out for grain, for minerals.

* See p. 17. Notes appear at the end of each chapter.

Legend gives us some of these early mercantile activities in colourful form. Jason's fabulous expedition to fetch the Golden Fleece
has been rationalized on this basis. In the story the hero is sent
to Colchis, on what is now the Black Sea, to fetch the fleece
gleaming with gold. It has been suggested that the quest represents primitive merchant adventures in search of gold, in an area
of the world that the Greeks eagerly exploited for its mineral
resources, or, more specifically still, that the Golden Fleece was,
prosaically enough, a real fleece used in the panning process.
Gold-laden water would run over the wool and minute particles
of gold would adhere to it. There are many examples of
Greek legends lending such colour to a workaday process, and
transmuting a fact of history or economics into something
magical.

In short, it may be said that early Greek history was the history
of merchant seafaring. Sailing was a part of life, and influenced
many other aspects of life. Religious centres often become commercial centres, because traders use the religious amnesties to sail
in and market their goods. In an age without the protections of
international law, traders had to find protection where they
could. Thus the island of Delos, for example, achieves immense
importance not only as the centre of worship of Apollo but as one
of the great markets of the ancient world : on this island, the
sacred and the commercial harbours lie side by side. The city
which controlled the trade-routes was not only secure itself, but
could impose its will on others by cutting off supplies and closing
markets. It was to such superiority that Athens was later to owe
her own supremacy.

In the early days merchants and pirates were virtually synonymous. They were concerned to find trade and profit where they
could, and however they could ; they were adventurous and not
unduly scrupulous. In the *Odyssey*, when Odysseus and his
companions present themselves at the cave of the monster
Polyphemus, he asks them :

Strangers, who are you?   What land sent you on the sea roads?
Is it for trade you come, or do you wander at a venture

Like pirates on the briny sea, who roam haphazard
Staking their lives, and bringing trouble where they touch?[2]

The historian Herodotus on one occasion mentions merchants who were not pirates, with a touch of surprise, as if this were worthy of special note. Such pirates were to survive the establishment of organized society and become, by Roman times, a major threat to travel in the Mediterranean, and even a force in politics. They were to interfere in the wars which marked the end of the Roman Republic ; they flourished under Byzantine rule, using Mykonos, now a tourist centre, as one of their strongest bases ; they were to earn respect by fighting for their country in the Greek War of Independence. Both the farmer and the merchant-pirate represented the Greek response to the challenges of nature : the one with toilsome patience worked a bare living from the stony soil, the other faced unknown perils in the hope of rewards and a better life. This constant struggle hardened the character and gave the Greek his patience in adversity, fortitude against attack and his often incredible self-discipline. Conversely, the Greeks did not take easily to prosperity. With the easier life that later developed in some cities came weakness and softening. In the later fourth century, when society became increasingly urbanized, the Greeks looked nostalgically towards the rugged virtues of the countryside, just as the Romans were later to idealize the sturdy virtues of their young Republic and, later still, modern America hankers after the time of its pioneers and loves to recreate dramatically the values of a sterner epoch in its history.

With trade and sea-faring so important to their livelihood, the Greeks lived on familiar terms with the water. No Greek lived far from the sight of the sea. It was an element as natural to him as the air he breathed. One of the most vivid passages in Greek historical writing is the description by Xenophon, in his *Anabasis* (*The March Up Country*), of a small Greek force cut off in Asia Minor, landbound for months and struggling to regain their home waters. When they at last come within sight of the sea, they run down to the beach shouting *Thalassa ! thalassa !* — The sea! The sea! — so glad are they to see the dear water again. The Romans, by contrast, never took naturally to the water. Necessity forced them to become a maritime power, but they ventured out with distrust and trepidation. Roman literature is full of nervous testimonies to the sea's malice, and awe-stricken tributes to the first man who was foolhardy enough to build a boat. Greek literature plays on this theme too, but there is an air of greater confidence. For the Greeks, as for the Romans, the sea could be malicious, but this was a fact of life. In a chorus of his tragedy *Antigone* Sophocles sounds the note of danger, but also of triumph that the danger has been overcome :

> *The world is full of wonderful things*
> *But none more so than man,*
> *This prodigy who sails before the storm-winds,*
> *Cutting a path across the sea's gray face. . . .*[3]

From the sea the Greeks took many of their artistic motifs — the octopus, the dolphin, the shell, which serve as symbols on coinage or decorations on vases. From the sea they took part of their language ; it is their most prolific source of verbal imagery. Around 600 B.C. Alcaeus, poet and politician of the island of Lesbos, wrote of a storm at sea :

> *Where blows the wind I cannot tell :*
> *Over on one side rolls a wave*
> *And on the other ; we between*
> *Are swept in our black ship along*
> *Sore in the storm, so great it is.*
> *The bilge is over the masthold now,*
> *The sail shows daylight through, there are*
> *Great rents the length of it. . . .*[4]

We are told that this is metaphorical, and that Alcaeus is writing of his city and the rough political seas in which it was wallowing. Over and again Greek writers use this metaphor of the Ship of State. For us it is a stale political cliché, so weary that even politicians shrink from using it. For the Greeks it was a perfectly natural, fresh and vivid figure, drawn from the element which was so vitally important to them.

On land the Greeks lived an open-air existence. Their climate forced them outdoors. Under the sun they conducted their political discussions, both formal and informal ; their theatres were uncovered, they slept on their rooftops in the summer — and still do. A public existence was the only possible one. In more northerly climates the temperature imposes privacy ; one is forced to spend much of the time within walls, under a roof. In Greece most of the day was spent in the streets. Men knew their neighbours well, and indeed knew nearly everyone in the city well. It is the same today ; in modern Greece the parks are popular meeting places, and in the cool of evening householders take chairs into the street to greet their neighbours as they stroll by. In ancient Greece such a public life brought its usual consequences, notably the strict segregation of women, who were expected to stay at home and take no part in men's affairs. Aristophanes based two comedies on the notion, obviously hilarious to the Greeks, that women could exercise political power. Custom and climate could change history. In 405 the Athenians lost their fleet at Aegospotami — 'Goat River' — in the Troad because the Spartans had the effrontery to attack at siesta time. A Western reader sees this as a shocking piece of Athenian mismanagement. Seen in terms of Greek habits, however, it reveals itself as a Spartan blow struck with as much psychological shrewdness as the attack delivered by Japanese forces on Pearl Harbour on a Sunday.

The Greeks lived in the sun, and relished its brightness and warmth. All the sensations are strong in Greece — particularly smell, for better or worse, and sight. For the Greeks, quite literally, light was life. The living were *hoi blepontes*, those who see. Zeus, the bright god, ruler of the heavens, was the deity of the living. Hades, God of the Dead, was his opposite : the name means 'he who makes dark' or 'he who is blind'. In drama, when a tragic hero dies, he makes his last farewell to the sun. When Oedipus, in the myth and in the play, blinds himself by his own hand, he is inflicting upon himself a punishment worse than death, for it is death in life : the body continues to function but

the vital sense, the faculty of sight, is destroyed. Modern Greek
continues the association. Darkness is *skotadhi, skotono* to kill.

The Greeks also loved the things that light showed them : they
were keenly sensitive to visual stimulation, delighting in colour
and ornament. The modern world, which still tends to see
Greece through French and German intermediaries, has somehow
acquired a monochrome view of the country and its monuments.
We tend to think of Greece as a land of bleached columns reared
against a blue sky, because that is how the monuments appear to
us now. It was not always so. In the Cerameicus Museum of
Athens, where relics from the ancient cemetery are preserved,
there stands a sphinx, a bird-woman, which once crowned a
pillar over someone's grave. It is almost drained of colour now ;
but when it was erected the wings were brilliantly striped and the
breast was a patchwork of red and blue. Faint traces of these
colours can be seen on the stone — enough to allow the original
coloration to be restored. A reconstruction of the fully painted
original hangs in the museum beside the sculpture, and the contrast is startling : it is the difference between Greek art as it was,
and the pale marbles beloved of the Romantics. At one end of the
Stoa of Attalus in the Athenian Agora stands a column the paint
on whose capital is likewise visible. Once again the colours were
strident. To imagine the Parthenon thus calls for a substantial
act of imagination. The colour sense of the ancients was gaudy.
There is an interesting allusion to the process in Plato's *Republic*.
Socrates, who had probably himself been a sculptor, finds an
example from his old profession :

> Now suppose we were painting a statue, and some critic came
> along and said 'Why don't you use the loveliest colours on the
> loveliest parts of the body ? There's nothing more lovely than
> eyes ; they should be purple, and you've made them dark.'[5]

The coloration implied by this story, and borne out by the
smudged and fading examples in the museums, is not naturalistic,
but reveals a great love of colour for its own sake. It is a good
remedy, perhaps, to step into a modern Greek Orthodox church.

You will be confronted at once by a mass of colour — vividly painted ikons, mosaic and paintwork, lavish and indiscriminate use of precious and pseudo-precious metals. The total impression will come rather closer to the reality of the classical world than does the cool, muted interior of a museum.

The Greeks went to excess in their other senses also. They loved to talk, and talked a great deal too much. Some of the talk was wonderful, flowering into the dialogues of Plato and the speeches of Demosthenes, but some was merely tiresome. Athenians particularly had a reputation for the love of argument : they were always debating, always in the courts. But this love of debate was a natural consequence of the open-air life, and of being thrown together under the hot sun. The Greeks were temperamentally volatile, inclined to emotional excesses. It is no accident that drama was born on the shores of the Mediterranean, where a mild protest becomes a public outcry and the smallest accident is exaggerated into earth-shaking catastrophe. But what helped to produce vivid theatre was not necessarily useful in diplomatic negotiation, or in political discussion, where cool heads were worth more than hot tempers. The Greeks were well aware of their own failings in this regard. Their perception of the need to curb these weaknesses accounts for a great deal of Greek philosophy, and for some of the less easily comprehensible acts of Greek legislation. It has been well said that the Greeks told themselves so often to avoid excess because they had to : they were so prone to it in every direction.

We have, then, a people frantically busy, both because they had to be and because they wanted to be. Life was short, and its brightness cried out to be enjoyed to the full before the shadows of Hades closed over. Hard work was a necessity of life. Each city was striving and thrusting ; the history of Greece is a record of the various collisions that ensued, between city and city and individual and individual.

NOTES TO CHAPTER ONE

1. Hesiod, *Works and Days*, 376.
2. Homer, *Odyssey*, IX. 252.
3. Sophocles, *Antigone*, 332.

4. Loeb Classical Library, *Lyra Graeca*, vol. i ; Alcaeus, fr. 37.
5. Plato, *Republic*, IV. 420c18.

Chapter Two

The History

To find the beginnings of Greek civilization we must look not to Greece itself, but to its southern neighbour, the long, narrow island of Crete. Some believe that Crete was once part of Africa. Certainly the eastern tip of the island still displays African vegetation, and this is seen as evidence of a prehistoric land-connection ; the lack of such survivals elsewhere on the island is attributed to the destructive effect of the earthquakes and tidal waves to which Crete was notoriously susceptible. Others would argue that the vegetation has been accidentally transmitted, and that there was never any such connection. All agree that the shape of the coastline has changed considerably since ancient times. What were once harbours are now submerged, and gradually being rediscovered by submarine archaeology. What are now islands were once part of the shore.

Crete commanded a favourable position on the waterways of the ancient world. It was a convenient stopping place between the Nile and the Aegean. The already ancient civilization of Egypt had established a thriving trade. When merchants wished to extend their voyages to the northern seas, Crete became important as a centre. Thus the island grew up as head of a considerable empire with a powerful fleet. The trade with Egypt gives us valuable historical data. Egyptian artifacts can usually be dated with reasonable accuracy, and the Egyptian monarchical system encouraged strict dating and record-keeping. When excavations uncover Egyptian objects of a certain period in Crete, the relevant stratum may be dated accordingly. This is by no means the only example of Eastern chronology being called in to aid Western. The first Greek historians were compelled to use the same techniques and date Greek events by Asian references, as we shall later see. This Cretan empire, known as Minoan from the name Minos — traditionally Crete's most famous king, and probably a regularly occurring royal name — endured in its fullest form from roughly 3000–1400 B.C. Excavations have uncovered the remains of an overwhelmingly impressive civilization. The most important single monument is still the great palace at Cnossos, just outside the modern city of Irakleion. This was the island's capital and home of its kings ; built and rebuilt, subject to various seismic shocks, its ruins today reveal a bewildering though deliberate complexity. They include a grand staircase which is a marvel of ancient engineering, massive storerooms testifying to the palace's material prosperity, and royal suites of great elegance and sophistication. Around the palace stand other buildings, smaller but no less luxurious : a lesser palace, a royal villa, houses of the aristocracy, and a caravanserai for the merchants who brought Cnossos her wealth.

Cnossos was the chief but by no means the only palace. Others have been uncovered elsewhere in the island, the residences of tributary princes. Normally we do not know what the ancient names of these townships were ; they are identified now by modern names. East of Irakleion along the coast stands Mallia, where a palace of considerable size is still being excavated. It is built on substantially the same pattern as Cnossos, though less complex ; the large central courtyard which was a feature of these palaces is clearly visible, and a similar tangle of rooms surrounds it. Mallia has been less productive of artifacts than Cnossos, though the large numbers of fishing-net weights found on the site and now to be seen in the adjacent museum testify to the township's reliance on the sea. Further east still is Gournia, whose discovery is a story in itself and well illustrates the rôle of luck and chance survival in archaeology. *Gournia* literally means 'the pot place', from *gournes*, 'pots'. The local people of later centuries gave it that name from the great jars they found here, relics of a vanished civilization whose importance they did not even begin to comprehend. The name stuck, and at the beginning of the twentieth century attracted the attention of

American archaeologists. Excavations revealed a whole town, with palace, houses, temples and shops, the home of an independent monarch who seems to have lived on closer terms with his people than was the practice at haughty Cnossos. On the shore were fishermen's huts and more shops. This is the only Minoan town to have been excavated. Much more is still buried, waiting for time and money to bring the work to completion.

South of Irakleion, overlooking the fertile plain of Messara, is the palace of Phaistos, traditional home of Rhadamanthys, Minos' brother. There were buildings here from 2000 B.C. Like Cnossos, the palace was destroyed by earthquake and subsequently rebuilt. It must have been equal in magnificence to the capital, though this is difficult to appreciate today, as Phaistos has not been restored to the same extent. There is a 'theatral area' — a large rectangular courtyard with steps around it, used for some sort of dance ritual or processions — a grand staircase, elaborate royal suites, and, as in all Minoan settlements, a number of lustral areas, places for the ritual ablutions which accompanied prayer and sacrifice. For the Cretans cleanliness was not merely next to but an essential part of godliness. Two miles from Phaistos lies another, smaller palace, known by the name of an adjacent village, Aghia Triadha (Holy Trinity). All these settlements (with the strange exception of Phaistos) have been rich in art works, notably in huge frescoes which once decorated the palace walls and many of which have been conjecturally restored. These show, hardly unexpectedly, a strong Egyptian influence. The hieratic rigidity of Egyptian art is reproduced in Crete, though with a freer hand and a more liberal choice of subject-matter. The multiplicity of sea motifs, particularly the octopus, show how, at the very beginning of the Greek world, salt was in the Cretan blood.

All these cities were destroyed at about the same time. Cnossos fell about 1400 B.C. How they fell is a matter of dispute. According to one theory, it was by conquest from the mainland ; they were subjugated by the immigrants who were the first true

Vines and olives surround an outdoor oven in this Cretan village

Olive press in the shape of an olive: Palace of Phaistos, Crete

Vineyards near the Palace of Cnossos . . .

. . . where wine was once stored in jars like these

Fishing-boats off Marathon. The sea is still part of the Greek way of life . . .

*. . . as in the past,
when it inspired this
mosaic on Delos*

Volcanic Santorini

Mycenae, warrior city on the bleak hills: excavations in progress

Athens: the Stoa of Attalus gives necessory shade

Cretan plumbing: water channels, Aghia Triadha

Athens, watergate in Cerameicus, with the shrunken River Eridanus

Merchants' footbath, Palace of Cnossos

Greeks. According to others, the disaster was due to earthquake
which, originating from Santorini (still actively volcanic), carried
the shock and a tidal wave to Crete. Whatever the cause, the
ruins still carry traces of the fall. At Phaistos, stones are still
black with burning. At Gournia, the end seems to have come
less predictably. During the excavations a cache of tools was
discovered hidden under a large flat stone. It has been conjectured that they belonged to a carpenter who, watching the
waves grow higher and higher, thought it might be safer to leave
his livelihood, retreat and come back afterwards. There was no
afterwards. The death of the Cretan empire may have been due
to natural causes, but the process of decay had set in long before.
This rich and ultimately decadent civilization, so secure in its
prosperity that its cities were built without walls, had already
yielded to the influence of a new power emerging from the North.
Successive waves of migrants had moved down into Greece and
established cities there. These were the people we call Indo-
Europeans. There origins are still much disputed, though it is
clear that they came of different racial stock from the earlier
inhabitants of the Mediterranean. They spoke a language which
was the parent of Greek, Latin, Sanskrit, Celtic and so ultimately
of English, German and the Romance languages. None of this
language was written down — we are talking here of a pre-
literary society — but it can, by a quasi-algebraic process, be reconstructed at least in outline from its known offspring. The
people also brought new deities, and new customs.

Thus mainland Greece, which had earlier been probed by
Cretan colonizers, fell under this new influence. The immigrants
built strong cities ; their language developed into what we now
know as Greek, and they eventually began to write this language
down. It is this writing which has caused one of the great
archaeological controversies of our time, involving the precise
balance between Cretan power and that of the newcomers.
When Sir Arthur Evans, the great pioneer of Cretan excavation,
was working at Cnossos, he discovered a quantity of clay tablets inscribed with a system of writing known to specialists as Linear B.

c

Evans argued that they had been stored in offices on an upper floor, and at the time of the destruction had fallen through into store-rooms below. In later excavations at Pylos, on the mainland of Greece, other deposits of such tablets were discovered. After years of experiment, and through a combination of shrewd guesswork and expert cryptography, the language of the tablets was finally identified as Greek, written in a syllabic script — that is, with each sign representing a syllable and not an individual letter. First proposed by the English architect and amateur cryptographer Michael Ventris in 1953, this decipherment is now generally accepted. Most resistance to the solution was offered by Greeks themselves — perhaps annoyed (and understandably so) that tablets so long in their possession should be revealed by foreigners to be in their own language. From the literary point of view the tablets are disappointing. They are inventories, dockets, mere lists of men and materials. They testify to the power and complex organizational problems of the cities of this time, and permit certain inferences about Greco-Cretan relations. If the palace of Cnossos used the Greek language for its record-keeping, this would seem to posit one of two things : either the mainland newcomers had taken over the palace administration, or their influence was so strong that their system of record-keeping, and scribes trained in the mainland manner, were imported into Crete.

To measure the extent of this influence, it is obviously important to know the date of the Cretan tablets. Evans, whose enthusiasm for the civilization he had discovered reached at times the point of obsession, saw Crete as the dominant power of the early Mediterranean. He recognized no other claims, and saw the mainland cities as mere colonies or Cretan offshoots. He argued that the power of Cnossos ceased with its destruction, and that after 1400 the site was occupied by squatters only. It has more recently been held that this view is false ; that even after the destruction of the palace, the Cretan system continued to operate, though in new hands ; and that far from being dated before the palace's destruction, the Linear B tablets come from some considerable period afterwards, showing that there was no real break and that things continued to go on much as they had done before. This is an involved argument, and probably an insoluble one ; we can do no more than set down the outline here. Many Cretan records remain to be deciphered. An earlier Cretan script, known as Linear A, still defeats the interpreters — it can be said with certainty, however, that this is *not* Greek ; and some still hope that vestiges of Cretan literature may yet be discovered, arguing that inventories of the palace stores would not necessarily be kept in the same place as the palace poetry. Time alone will show this.

What were these cities of the mainland ? The most important were in the Argolid. Mycenae stood on a commanding position overlooking the fertile plain of Argos, and the overland trade route from the south to the Gulf of Corinth. It is a warrior baron's town ; one may easily imagine the armed horsemen assembled on the hilltop, massing to swoop down on the merchants beneath. Such a city could grow rich on tribute from those passing ; it needed no natural resources. The remains of Mycenae reveal a Bronze Age city with massive fortifications. Where Cnossos shows the softness and self-indulgence of peace, Mycenae is hard and built for war. The Cretan palace had noble architecture, rich paintings, places for sports and dancing ; at Mycenae and Tiryns, its near neighbour, the building is done in huge, rough stone blocks, keeping position by their own weight and almost impregnable against assault. Entering Cnossos you pass across a broad courtyard, or up wide flights of stairs between columns and painted walls. Entering Mycenae you move through a passage-way to a massive fortified door, so situated that those approaching it are under fire from three sides. In Crete the dead were interred in painted sarcophagi, doubled up in the foetal position, returning to the womb of Mother Earth who was so important in Cretan religion. In Mycenae the dead were laid in deep shaft graves or outside the city walls in great beehive-shaped tombs, surrounded by their rich possessions ; the entrances to the tombs were then filled with earth and allowed to blend with the enclosing hillside. The lords of Mycenae, plunderers themselves, took precautions against similar tendencies in others. It says much for their forethought and ingenuity that these tombs were still untouched when the modern excavators came to them, and have yielded information of incalculable value about the city and its times.

Mycenae was strong enough to impose its will on other communities. The Trojan War is a case in point. According to the tradition, Paris, prince of Troy, abducted Helen, wife of King Menelaus of Sparta. Menelaus' brother Agamemnon, King of Mycenae, led an army from the combined cities of Greece to subdue Troy and reclaim the errant woman. Legend, as has already been mentioned, testifies to the unwillingness of some of the lesser kings to join the war — but also to the fact that they went, regardless. Homer tells of one Euchenor, son of Polyidos of Corinth, whose prophetic father told him that he was fated to die of disease if he stayed at home, or in battle if he went to war. Therefore he went to battle, says Homer, 'to avoid the heavy warfine'. This implies both the dependence of Corinth on Mycenae, and a strict feudal relationship existing between overlord and subject : Euchenor has to contribute his services or pay a penalty.

Many things about the Trojan War are in dispute. Greek tradition represents it as a glorious victory over a strong hostile power. It may have been. Alternatively, it may have been not a major war but a raid, or a series of raids ; it may not have been a victory at all. It has been suggested that the victory of tradition is simply Hellenic propaganda, and that the truth of the expedition is revealed in the associated stories about the return of the heroes from Troy : almost all of them meet disaster, in some shape or form. Troy itself has been excavated, first by Heinrich Schliemann, who, using Homer as a guide-book, found what he considered to be Homer's city. In fact there are a series of cities, one built on top of another. Subsequent excavations have corrected and refined Schliemann's conclusions and suggested that the city of the *Iliad* is that known as Troy VII A, whose marks of destruction seem to show the results of war and ravaging.

These excavations have also suggested that the traditional date of the war, 1184 B.C., may be approximately correct.

In the next stage of Greek civilization, the power of Mycenae declines and other cities, originally subordinate, become independently powerful. To call these settlements 'cities' is misleading. The Greek word, *polis*, means at once city and state. Each was a separate political entity. Each created its own laws and evolved its own form of government independently of the others. Each was a state in its own right, looking on men from other states with suspicion, as foreigners. As the hold of Mycenae slackened, these places grew up vigorous and powerful. For the moment we need note only the most important. There was Athens, near the coast. There had been a settlement here from about 4000 B.C. Archaeologists have found traces of Mycenaean fortifications, including a watchtower ; part of a Mycenaean wall may still be seen on the Acropolis. It was a good site, possessing an easily fortified hill and two fine natural harbours. Near by, on the coast at Laurion, were silver deposits, destined to be important in the later Athenian economy. Further south was Corinth, holding an ideal trading position on the narrow isthmus separating northern Greece from the Peloponnesus. It could thus command trade routes by land and water. Ships sailing the east–west route would be hauled the short distance overland, saving the delay and danger of rounding the Peloponnesus. Remains of the old shipway have been discovered. Ancient attempts to cut a canal through the Isthmus were unsuccessful : traces of these attempts were found by modern workers who finally achieved what is now known as the Corinth Canal. Corinth was the Port Said of the ancient world, both in its commercial importance and in the doubtful moral reputation which hangs around great ports. The legends of Theseus, subsequently King of Athens, tell that he was born in Troezen and travelled on foot up the Isthmus, meeting and defeating various picturesque robbers as he passed. These are but colourful versions of the importance of that narrow neck of land to trade, and the dangers that continued to threaten the ancient traveller.

Other cities grew and flourished : Thebes, in Boeotia, the
'cow country' : Argos, on the fertile plain near old Mycenae and
Tiryns ; Sparta, destined to be, for a time, the most powerful
military state in Greece and to bring Athens to her knees. All
these cities sent out colonies as the older Eastern powers had done
before them. Pressure of space, the needs of a growing population, the acquisitive instinct and sheer thirst for exploration sent
parties out in all directions. Greek cities were already established
on the coast of Asia Minor, in the region known as Ionia. Prominent among these was Miletus, a great centre of mercantile life
and culture. Trade flourished across the Aegean. Other colonies
were founded on the Black Sea coast, with access to the grain- and
iron-producing regions ; eastwards, to the toe of Italy, where
Greek influence soon became all powerful ; from there to Sicily,
the South of France and Spain. These colonies were regarded as
children of the mother city, not as separate ventures. A regular
procedure for colonization came into being. Fire from the altar
of the mother city was kept alive to burn in the new foundation,
a visible symbol of the tie between parent and child. Thus the
mainstream of Greek life was continued abroad. Colonies in
turn sent out their own colonies, and by the sixth century B.C.
Greek influence had spread along the northern shores of the
Mediterranean, growing constantly more powerful and facing
the established Semitic colonies — result of Phoenician infiltra-
tion — on the southern shore. Two cultures, one ancient and
one a newcomer, stared at each other across the dividing sea. It
was clear that before long this opposition must come to a head.

Asia Minor was meanwhile undergoing changes of its own.
The Ionian colonies on the coast were in a precarious position.
Greek in population, they were separated from their motherland
by the sea, and so became tributary to whichever power was
strongest in Asia at the time. For a while they had formed part
of the empire of Lydia, whose king, Croesus, was well disposed
towards the Greeks and treated them fairly. But a new power
was rising — that of Persia, under King Cyrus, who conquered
Lydia in 546. The Ionians thus fell under a harsher master, and

the Persians began to move against Greece itself. In 512 Darius
led an expedition into Thrace, to the north of Greece. In Athens
feeling was divided. There was by no means a clear anti-
Persian policy. Some wished to offer opposition to Persia, others
temporized and counselled less adventurous courses. The Alc-
maeonids, one of the most glorious families of Athens, seem to
have been prominent among the appeasers. The history of this
period reads very like the prelude to the Second World War ;
the Athenians nervously debated about the menace across the
sea, embassies came and went, treaties were proposed and rejected.
In Persia, the home of lost causes in the ancient world, dissatisfied Athenian exiles attempted to use Persian influence to
regain their lost position. In 499 Aristagoras, a citizen of Miletus,
initiated a revolt of the colonists against their Persian overlords.
He sought help from Sparta, and was refused. Coming to
Athens, he was given twenty ships. Historians differ as to the
value of this force. Was it a sizeable navy, or a mere token ?
It may well be that Athens' honest indecision led her into a
dangerous middle course, like the United States in the Bay of
Pigs fiasco in 1962 ; she sent a force which was large enough to
give offence, but too small to do any real harm. She saw the
revolt crushed, and herself drawn willy-nilly into the imbroglio.
The colonists won a few victories by surprise, and actually
succeeded in penetrating inland and burning the Persian capital,
Sardis. Persia, however, was bound to win by sheer weight of
numbers. Miletus burned in revenge for Sardis.

This was more than the destruction of a city. Miletus had
been a rich centre of cultural life. It had produced the first
philosophers of the Greek world, the first geographers, the first
scientists. From this time on, the focus shifts from Asia Minor
to mainland Greece as a centre of learning, and particularly to
Athens, favourably situated to absorb trade and ideas. With
regard to the Persians, Athens still frantically temporized. The
choice was between all-out war and appeasement. In 496
Hipparchus was elected archon — one of the city magistrates —
a significant figure because insignificant, pushed into prominence

to avoid the election of anyone who might show more conspicuous opposition to Persia. None the less, the voice of the war
party grew louder. In 493 Themistocles became archon. He
saw the danger clearly, and also where Athens' safety lay — in
ships. Through him the city embarked on an ambitious ship-
building policy that was to ensure her hegemony for the better
part of the next century. In 493 too the tragedian Phrynichus
produced his *Capture of Miletus*, dealing with the late calamity.
Political collusion, or straws in the wind ? There was no longer
any opportunity to choose. Persia made a token demand of
submission from the Greek cities, and was refused. In 490 a
Persian fleet crossed the Aegean and landed an army at Marathon,
on the coast about twenty miles from Athens. The Spartan army
was summoned but did not attend. Athens was forced to face
the Persians alone and surprisingly won, in a battle which has
passed into history as a classic example of the triumph of a small,
well-organized force over larger numbers. Driven back from
the shore the fleet sailed round the coast to Athens, only to find
that the army had anticipated them by a forced march and was
already in position. The Persians retired, disgraced and defeated,
to await a more favourable opportunity.

There was no doubt in Greek minds that Darius would avenge
Marathon. Such an insult to the Great King could never, they
knew, be forgotten ; the only doubt was when retribution would
come. Fortunately for the Greeks it came later than expected,
postponed first by the revolt of Egypt from Persian rule and then
by Darius' death in 486. Xerxes, Darius' son, succeeded to the
throne, settled the internal dissensions of his empire and prepared
for attack. An army was gathered, a northern route selected —
the ships to follow the army along the coast, through a protective
canal dug across the promontory of Mount Athos — and stores
accumulated along the line of march. The army wintered in
Sardis and Xerxes began his march in the spring of 480.

Herodotus the historian and Aeschylus the poet dwell on the
size of the invading army. Aeschylus represents Persia as being
drained of men, while Herodotus, venturing into precise figures,

numbers the host at a grand total of 5,283,220. Modern historians agree that this is an outrageous exaggeration, and settle for something nearer 180,000 fighting men — still a great force. At a conference in 481 the Greek cities had recognized the danger and foreseen that the enemy would invade this time by the longer, overland route. Local animosities were temporarily forgotten. Sparta presided, and at Themistocles' urging it was decided to offer resistance at the pass of Thermopylae, to the north, where a small force might stand a fair chance of defeating a large one. The combined Greek forces probably numbered no more than 10,000 men. In the meantime, the Greek navy engaged the Persian ships. There was success on sea, defeat on land. The Greek fleet retired to Salamis, and the broken army fell back to the Isthmus of Corinth. This was the next logical place where resistance could be offered, with only a narrow front to protect. Athens had to be left defenceless, but this was an unfortunate necessity of war, secretly delightful to the Spartans. Evacuation took place ; a copy of the decree authorizing this has been discovered. Athens itself was twice sacked by the Persians.

Themistocles' creation, the new Athenian fleet, saved the day. In enclosed waters the heavy Persian ships were slow to manœuvre, and useless. Once lured into the confined waters of the Bay of Salamis they were an easy prey to the lighter and more mobile Greek vessels. Deprived of his fleet and thus of his supply line, Xerxes was forced to retreat. His huge forces now proved an embarrassment. What ultimately defeated the Persians was their inattention to logistics. Inadequate arrangements had been made for supplies, and so large an army could not live off the country — so poor a country, and in winter besides. The bulk of the Persian forces retreated, suffering heavy losses. An expeditionary force remained in Greece but was finally defeated at the battle of Plataea in 479. Once again the Persian menace had been subdued. Simultaneously with Xerxes' invasion the Phoenician colony of Carthage, on the north coast of Africa, had attacked the flourishing Greek cities in Sicily. We may see this as part of a concerted Eastern movement to crush the young power of Greece. But in Sicily too the Greeks were victorious ; Syracuse, that island's most important city, drove the invaders out.

So far we have seen the pattern of Greek culture as mainly local and sporadic. Each city developed its own traditions, art forms and ways of living. Writers composed in their own dialects. Sparta, in the early stages of its development, had produced beautiful local pottery and iron work ; Miletus had its geographers and philosophers, Samos its school of poetry and science ; Corinth was a prominent patron of the arts. Centres of cultural importance tended to shift with political changes. Now, the destruction of Miletus gave a new importance to Athens. Throughout the fifth century Athens' swift rise to power gave her not only political but cultural supremacy, so that when in this period we speak of Greek art, drama, sculpture, it is nearly always Athenian that we mean ; most of the enduring products of Greek civilization have come from Athens in the fifth century B.C.

The Persian wars had brought Athens to the fore as champion of Greece, displacing Sparta. Sea power was now seen to be more vital than land power, and it was sea power that Athens conspicuously possessed. She had taken the initiative in facing the Persians by sea ; responsibility for the victory, and the consequent prestige, were almost entirely hers. Athens lost no time in capitalizing on her new position. The Persian wars, though causing great havoc and loss, had given Greece something never enjoyed before, a measure of unity. External pressure had imposed on this collection of small autonomous states, loosely knit confederacies and shaky alliances a spirit of cohesion in adversity which would never have resulted from other means. The elation arising from so great a triumph was not soon to be dispersed, and Athens profited from the prevailing euphoria.

Sparta contributed unwillingly to this process. Her commander, Pausanias, conducted himself in a singularly tactless way, going so far as to adopt Persian manners and customs, behaviour hardly calculated to increase his own or his city's popularity. The allies, led by the important islands of Chios, Samos and Lesbos, swung into the Athenian orbit. A league was formed to secure the Greek states against future Persian retaliation. Oaths were sworn, a common treasury was set up in the sacred island of Delos, and meetings were held to determine policy. States could contribute money or ships. Money was preferred, as being less trouble, and the first assessment brought in the considerable sum of 460 talents. League meetings were held at Delos, and it is safe to assume that the states were initially autonomous, each having an equal vote. Sparta, though by no means a spent force, was surprisingly quiet.

The League grew in size, largely owing to the Athenian general Cimon, who forced a series of uprisings against the Great King. Military force and compulsory recruitment to the League were justifiable in view of its programme, but the fact that these victories were won under an Athenian general pointed an ominous finger towards the future. Thucydides the historian gives the extent of the alliance in 431 : Chios, Lesbos, Plataea, the Messenians in Naupactus, most of Acarnania, Zakynthos, the coast of Caria and the Dorian colonies thereon, Ionia, the Hellespont and the Greek towns on the Thracian side, the islands lying between the Peloponnesus towards the east, and all the rest of the Cyclades except Melos and Thera. Even this does not represent the League at its fullest extent, which according to another historian was reached in 455–454 ; by 431 there had already been a few defections.

All this while power had been shifting into Athenian hands, and the erstwhile autonomous allies were being transformed into Athenian subjects. Secession, repressed by Athens on the pretext that it brought danger to the League, was tantamount to rebellion. In 454 the treasury was transferred, on the grounds of safety, from Delos to Athens. At this time, if not before, the board of treasurers was transformed into an Athenian magistracy. In 449 came the death blow to the hopes of all who still claimed to see the original policy at work in the League. Athens made a peace treaty with Persia. There was no longer any pretext for the

League's continuation, no common enemy. Nevertheless it continued, transformed into an Athenian empire in fact if not in name. Sparta was still strong enough to interfere, at least sporadically. After peace was officially declared Athens announced a conference to discuss the rebuilding of temples destroyed in the Persian wars. Sparta announced that it was not interested; the other cities took their cue from Sparta and nobody came. This fiasco showed Athens that her position was not yet secure.

Athens was dependent on the tribute paid by the allies for her own resurgence. This was now her principal source of income. We possess the tribute lists for these crucial years, graven upon stone, and they are among our most important historical evidence. Painstakingly reconstructed by modern scholars, they show who paid, and how much ; perhaps more important, when the states did not pay, and when the assessment was raised to correspond to Athens' growing need. States which proved unruly, as Samos did in 440, were smacked down. To reject Athenian control was to invite interference. Ships appeared in harbour to discourage thoughts of independence. Athenian settlers were moved into others' lands. The money raised was used in Athens for an elaborate building programme, ostensibly to repair war damage but in reality going far beyond this, to create a new and marvellous city. Under the guidance of her great statesman Pericles Athens grew and flourished. As so often in world history, colonial expansion went hand in hand with cultural advancement : the initiative and enterprise which led men to strike out into new worlds and consolidate their political power were paralleled by similar advances in the arts. Sculptors and architects worked to make the city beautiful. On the Acropolis, ancient citadel of Athens, new buildings rose on the old destruction, notably the Parthenon, Athena's majestic temple containing her gold-hung statue, work of Pheidias. In literature fifth-century Athens, like Elizabethan England, found its most vital expression in the drama. To this period belong the tragedies of Aeschylus, Sophocles and Euripides, and the comedies of Aristophanes. Athens' cultural supremacy made itself felt throughout Greece. Athenian poets were invited abroad and visitors from other cities came to pay their respects. Herodotus, a native of Caria, was honoured to stay there. Gorgias, the Sicilian orator, came on an embassy and gave new impetus to the study of rhetoric. Philosophers came to work and teach in this eager, busy city. As well as producing its own writers and artists Athens attracted what was best from abroad, and Athenian standards came to be those by which the work of others was judged.

Sparta and the other Peloponnesian states were gradually being forced into a position where they had to take action or see their own eclipse. Athens was acquiring an economic stranglehold. In 431, after the usual exchange of pretexts, war was declared. Athens' financial position was strong, but not so strong as it might have been. The amount of money transferred from Delos to Athens is given, in the lowest estimate, as 5,000 talents. Building on the Acropolis had cut heavily into these reserves, and the war against Samos had been expensive. Nevertheless, Athens was secure enough to fight the initial stages of the war on her own terms. King Archidamus of Sparta led his troops into Attica, and Pericles' reply was brilliantly unconventional. Instead of meeting them in open battle he withdrew the population within the city walls, let the Spartans waste their strength on the empty air and concentrated on harrying the Spartan bases, behind their backs, with the superior strength of the Athenian fleet. During the consequent overcrowding of the city, however, plague broke out, and rapidly spread. Pericles died, and his successors were less gifted. After ten years of costly campaigning — the tribute had to be raised in 425 — both sides were ready for peace. In March of 421 Aristophanes presented his comedy *Peace*, in which the farmers and the little folk were represented as being ground down by war, using Athenian and Spartan generals as pestles to crush them in his mortar. A fifty-year peace was declared, on the basis of a return to the *status quo*. This was easier to say than to do. In Thrace, cities were in revolt against Athens and did not want to be restored. Corinth considered herself robbed by cities officially outside the scope of the peace treaty. Thebes, not included in the negotiations, refused to enter into any long-term arrangements at all, looking only to further her own advantage. Swayed largely by the other states, the principal combatants reopened hostilities in 419.

From this point the tide turned against Athens. A misguided attempt to recoup her fortunes by a costly expedition against Sicily ended in disaster. Mismanagement and suspicion at home were matched by weakness and incompetence at the front. Dissatisfaction with the government led to an abortive oligarchic revolution in 411. Persia, like other adjacent powers, speculated on the outcome of the war, her nobles divided among themselves and offering support to both sides. At last, in 404, Athens succumbed, after nearly thirty years of conflict which cost her not only her power but also the distinctive qualities which she had used that power to foster. It is a thankless task attempting to apportion blame for this defeat, but prominent among the causes we must list the Athenians' fickle temperament and their vanity. On several occasions during the war they ruled their best men out of office, on the most trivial pretexts. Nor did they ever realize how much they were hated, until it was too late. Athens seems to have been prepared for most contingencies except that which did her most harm, the revolt of the allied, or rather subject, states. These defections cost her more money than she could afford and dangerously distracted her attention from immediate problems.

In the constant ferment of Greek politics Athens could not remain subdued for long, but she was never to regain the power she had attained in the fifth century. Nevertheless, she was firmly established as a cultural centre, and for centuries was to be the recognized fountainhead of learning, of art, of philosophy. Her lost power was not long to remain in the hands of her rivals. A new force was rising in the north, shortly to descend on the cities of Greece and impose a new pattern on Greek civilization. This was Macedon, a country on the fringes of the civilized world, rough, uncultured and preserving a way of life long abandoned in the southern cities.

None the less Macedon had made great advances in the art of warfare, and pursued now a policy of expansion. King Philip had enjoyed a Greek education; he knew the Greeks and how best to exploit their weaknesses. His gradual progress down the country, annexing and overcoming, met with mixed feelings in Athens. There was already some movement towards Hellenic unity — thinkers who could transcend the narrow limits of local patriotism and saw the advantages of combining all Greece under one leader, recognizing in Philip the man to do it. But civic pride was too strong to countenance this ideal. Demosthenes, mouthpiece of the patriotic party at Athens, urged his fellow citizens to resist. The outcome was inevitable. After a long period of hostilities Philip defeated the Greek forces at the battle of Chaeronea in 338, and established himself as head of all the Greek states except Sparta, which still held out against him. Two years later Philip was murdered, but his power passed into the hands of his son Alexander, who continued and expanded his father's policies. With a united Greece behind him, Alexander saw himself as the champion of Greece against Asia. Before this, Greece had not interfered extensively in Persian affairs, being content to maintain a defensive position and keep her own cities and civilization safe from the Persian menace; only rarely had war been carried into the Persian territory. Now Alexander was powerful enough to take the offensive. His armies marched into Asia Minor and defeated the Persian king at the River Granicus in 334. Marching southward, Alexander freed the Greek cities of Ionia; another pitched battle was fought at the Gulf of Issus, and the King offered terms, proposing that the River Euphrates should be the new boundary, Alexander to hold undisputed dominion over the whole of western Asia Minor. Alexander, however, saw no limits to his conquests. He pushed first into Egypt and then further into Persian territory, finally defeating the King at the battle of Arbela, 331. The whole Persian Empire, including the Nile Valley and Mesopotamia, centres of the world's earliest civilizations, were now in Greek hands, and the younger civilization had finally established its supremacy over the old.

Alexander even penetrated India; his ambitious projects were cut short only by his premature death in 323.

An empire so widely spread and so quickly won could not be expected to hold together for long. It was impossible to police the new territories adequately. Even during Alexander's lifetime there was intrigue, treachery and open rebellion. On his death-bed Alexander cynically bequeathed his empire to the strongest of his generals, with the inevitable result. After a period of dispute and war, the empire was divided into three kingdoms — Macedon, comprising not only the Greek territory itself but the other subject cities of Greece; Antioch, broadly speaking the old Persian empire; and Egypt. These continued to be ruled by Greek dynasties who imposed the pattern of Greek culture on their conquered countries.

Alexander had achieved what no man had done before. He had unified Greece, and carried Greek civilization to the limits of the known world. The importance of these conquests was enormous. We have seen how Greek culture began by being local and diversified; then Athens established herself as a centre of the arts and sciences, setting a standard by which other places were measured. Thus, Athenian civilization became the basis of the new empire. Local variations and traditions were ironed out, and subordinated to a general pattern of Greek culture that held good for the new, enlarged Greek world as a whole. The language of this Hellenistic age, as it was known, was Attic Greek, the local dialect of Athens, simplified and popularized. This was the official language of the empire. Whatever tongue might be spoken locally, Greek was always used for matters of state and official business. It was the international language of trade and scholarship, and one which every educated man had to know.

The great age of literature had passed with Athens' decline. The Hellenistic age was the age of scholarship. In Alexandria, the new city founded by Alexander in Egypt and one of several throughout the empire to carry his name, the Ptolemies, the reigning Greek dynasty, established a library of more than half a million volumes. Scholars accumulated the works of the past,

studied, edited and preserved them. Important texts were prepared in new editions. The works of Homer and Herodotus, the
Greek dramatists and others were thus edited and circulated in
'Alexandrian editions', from which most of our extant manuscripts survive. We owe a great debt to these Alexandrian
scholars for preserving works of the utmost value that might
otherwise have perished. Study of the old texts created the need
for a scientific study of language, for grammars and dictionaries.
The first Greek grammar was composed in Alexandria in 120 B.C.,
and formed the foundation for subsequent studies of the language.

The Greek influence on Asia was to some extent reciprocal.
Soldiers and travellers returned home with new ideas and strange
tales. New patterns and designs were introduced into Greece
from abroad. But these tended to debase, not stimulate, the
existing tradition. The Hellenistic culture lacked vitality;
spreading it so far had spread it thin, and new impetus was
lacking. Writers and artists sought to offer entertainment or
sensation rather than inspiration. Sculpture cultivated perfection
of technique, as opposed to content. In the drama, tragedy
became violent and spectacular, while comedy lost its old vitality
to become an innocuous comedy of manners. The literature of
the period is perhaps typified by the poems of Theocritus —
pastoral idylls in an elegant and artificial style, sophisticated but
remote. The reason for this decline is not hard to find. Art and
literature of the classical age had been considered as strictly
functional, and as closely associated with civic life and with
religion. The most important building of the city was its temple,
and the drama was part of an act of worship. In the Hellenistic
Age the gods had been deposed and kings put in their places.
Architecture now concerns itself with public buildings and
offices; the purpose of literature and the visual arts is to entertain,
not to edify. Alexander, in the later stages of his career, had
entertained ideas of self-deification. He wished to establish himself as a god, and this principle was followed by some of his
successors. The elevation of the monarch was followed by the
increasing servitude of his subjects. Without the stimulus that

D

had formerly led them on to higher things, the Greeks declined into a race of self-conscious dilettanti, content to rework what had been done in the past and lacking the power to strike out in new directions.

Science, however, flourished. Alexander's conquests placed a wealth of new material at the scientist's disposal. Aristotle had been tutor to the young king, and his biological researches benefited immeasurably from his former pupil's forethought. In Alexandria Euclid laid the foundations of geometry; in Sicily Archimedes discovered basic principles in mathematics and engineering. As the Greek world expanded, geographers were able, by travel and report, to compile more complete records than had yet existed. Eratosthenes, also working in Alexandria, calculated the size of the earth, and prepared a map of the known world using lines of latitude and longitude, thus founding the study of scientific geography.

Yet for all these discoveries the Greek spirit, which had reached its zenith at Marathon and Salamis and in the noble years that followed, was waning. In the remaining years of independence the history of Greece reveals little but petty squabbling, domestic bickering and shifting of alliances with little real object. We may partly blame the orientalizing influence, deliberately encouraged by Alexander and his successors and infiltrating insidiously into every walk of Greek life. Life in early Greece had been hard. Men had to work and fight for a living, and scheme against their neighbours if they were to have more than a bare subsistence. This constant struggle of man against man and man against nature produced vigorous and independent minds, adaptability to new circumstances and resilience in times of misfortune. These qualities were dissipated in fashionable weariness and Eastern languor. Greece was never again to rise to the status of a world power.

Chapter Three

The Greeks and Their Gods:
(1) The Twelve Olympians

THE Greek religion is a subject that must come first in any study of the Greek accomplishment. Religion played a vital part in Greek life and culture, and the finest flowering of that culture was inextricably interwoven with the worship of the gods. We cannot hope to comprehend classical art and literature without some knowledge of the nature of these gods and of the complex mythology associated with them.

Firstly, some general characteristics. Greek religion was polytheistic; it believed not in one god but in many, each with his own functions and attributes. In this respect Greece followed the almost universal pattern of the ancient world. The religions of the earlier civilizations, those of the Near East and of Egypt, were all polytheistic. We may discount here the attempt of Amenhotep III, Pharaoh of Egypt, to establish a monotheism, worshipping only the Sun-god: the experiment was in advance of its time and lasted only as long as Amenhotep himself. Secondly, the Greek religion was non-credal. The believer today, be he Christian, Moslem or Orthodox Jew, is brought up in the understanding that his religion implies a definite pattern of behaviour. It imposes social and moral ordinances which govern every aspect of his daily life. The devout believer will accept this code, and endeavour to follow the commands of chastity, of honesty, of kindness that are given him. Although these moral codes may differ considerably in substance, they are alike in that they are an essential part of the religion. The Greeks had nothing like this. They believed that it was necessary to appease the gods if they were to obtain something they wanted; they believed that it was

39

possible in some ways to offend the gods, and bring divine retribution on their heads; but the worship of the gods implied essentially only a series of ritual observances, not adherence to any moral code. There was no general belief, for example, that to lead a good life would bring rewards, either in the present or in the afterlife. The gods would help, if approached in the right way, but they could be bribed or even deceived. Thus it was possible for a man to lead a grossly immoral life by modern standards and still be genuinely accepted as a true believer. Religious belief and a moral code were two distinct and separate things.

One respect in which the Greek religion differed both from its predecessors and from Christianity was in its failure to recognize a positive power of evil. The earlier civilizations saw in their gods a conflict between two groups, the Powers of Light and the Powers of Darkness, the good and evil spirits. Christianity evolved its own Prince of Darkness, the Devil. Greece had nothing of this. It is true that there were monsters. Some of the earlier creations of Greek mythology are dark and terrifying. Generally speaking, however, there was only one set of gods who could be good or bad, friendly or hostile, according to their mood and the way they were approached. Even Hades, the God of Death, does not fill the devil's rôle, although he is frequently referred to as a god who stands alone, shunned by the other deities. But he represents an absence of life, of the desirable things, rather than a positive force for bad. Perhaps the nearest that the Greeks came to devils was in their myth about the mischiefs lurking in Pandora's jar who were loosed to bring misfortune on mankind. Zeus, angry with the Titans Prometheus and Epimetheus, fashioned the latter a wife out of clay, and sent her with a jar that she was instructed not to open. Feminine curiosity got the better of her and she disobeyed. Hope remained at the bottom of the jar,

> But the others wander among men, plagues numberless.
> Full is the earth of troubles, and the sea is full also.
> By day there come, and come by night, diseases

On men uninvited, without sound or signal bringing
Harm upon mortals : for Zeus in his foreknowledge took
Their speech : so is his purpose unescapable.[1]

Certain other general characteristics of Greek religion may be
mentioned here. These are not unique to Greece, but common to
other types of religion, particularly in their early stages. Firstly
there is a tendency to see gods in everything, particularly in
objects which seem to defy natural explanation. The primitive
mind sees supernatural forces inside natural phenomena — in
mountains and trees (hence the nymphs of various sorts who play
so picturesque a part in Greek mythology), in meteorites and
strangely shaped stones, in rivers and streams. The latter are
particularly susceptible to such interpretation, for a river behaves
to some extent like a human being. It can move fast or slowly
and grow bigger and smaller; it can be calm and friendly or
rough and hostile. Early man imagined a god in the river itself,
and we find in myth and literature stories of how these river-gods
fought with mankind. In the twenty-first book of the *Iliad*
Achilles is represented as fighting so with the River Skaman-
dros. These stories are no more than picturesque enlargements
of man combating flood, or striving to ford a river in full
spate.

As well as this there is another phenomenon, again not unique
to Greek religion: the idea among believers that there exists,
somewhere in the universe, some potent force, inaccessible to
mankind in general but accessible to certain sorts of being —
gods, spirits and the occasional outstanding human. Men attempt
to influence this power to help themselves, by way of religion or
magic. This pattern is also observable in Homer. Warriors with
divine connections may have a watchful deity who restores their
strength and fighting spirit. So Athena restores Diomedes, *Iliad*,
x. 366; so does Apollo restore Hector in *Iliad*, xv. 262: 'So he
spoke, and breathed great might into the shepherd of the host.'
So even does Zeus restore exhausted warhorses, *Iliad*, xvii. 456.
The *menos*, Homer's word for this sort of power, comes upon
them and they return to the battle renewed.

Against this background we may plot some of the principal steps in the development of the Greek religion. It has been noted that Greek culture derived from the fusion of two distinct racial groups, the earlier settlers of the Mediterranean — represented by the Cretans — and the later Indo-European invaders. The difference between them was not merely racial but in their whole way of life. The earlier peoples were settled, free from fear of invasion and prosperous. They cultivated the soil and reaped their crops in peace. Any religion must answer the particular needs of its adherents, and it is hardly surprising that in these circumstances the deities should be goddesses, emblematic of fertility. As a woman bears children, the earth brings forth crops. This type of fertility goddess, known generally as the Great Earth Mother, was worshipped widely across the Mediterranean in many guises and under a variety of cult-names. In Cretan religious iconography, where there is a male figure he is represented very small — either a sacred child or a god given the size his importance warrants. Snakes were important in the Cretan religion. The familiar Minoan fertility goddess has snakes coiled on her wrists. These too were fertility objects, and continued to have a sacred significance for long afterwards. Snakes live in holes in the earth, and earth secretes the growing corn. In Crete also the snake would have had another, and more immediately practical, function: to give warning of earthquakes. Even in the present century workmen excavating Cretan sites have learned that it is safest to leave the dig when they see the snakes leaving their holes. It is a sure sign that a tremor will follow.

One aspect of Cretan ritual involved the famous bull-dance, in which trained athletes swung themselves over the bull's horns and pirouetted off his back. The details of the ritual are no longer known. Modern bullfighters claim that such a feat could never have been accomplished, and no classical scholar has yet made the experiment. In outline, however, the ancient testimony seems clear enough. One of the finest treasures of the Irakleion Museum is a fragmentary ivory statuette of such a matador, showing him at the moment of the leap; it dates from 1600 B.C.

He originally formed part of a group which included the bull and the jumper's assistants. One of the frescoes from the Palace of Cnossos shows a similar bull-dance; the fresco itself, now restored, is also in the Museum, and a copy has been erected in the north entrance to the palace. The bull motif is frequently used in other ways — in the great stone horns, cult-objects found at Cnossos, and in the rhytons, or libation vases, also in the Irakleion Museum and shaped like bull's heads. These were presumably intended to hold blood from the slaughtered animal.

Later imagination played productively with the stories of the Cretan bulls. It was said that King Minos had caused Daedalus, the architect, to build a labyrinth under his palace in which was housed the monstrous Minotaur, half bull and half man. Captives were annually fed to this beast until Theseus, Prince of Athens, killed it and escaped. This familiar story probably owes its origin to a number of sources. First, there would have been distorted memories of the actual bull-dance, in which prisoners may well have been trained to perform just as the Romans were later to train slaves to become expert gladiators. The Minotaur himself probably recalls a priest in bull's mask. Survival of the bull-fight fresco would have reinforced these tales, though in the controversy over the archaeology of Cnossos its date and position have been questioned. The labyrinth itself arises out of semantic confusion. *Labrys* in Greek means 'double axe' — it is originally a foreign word — and refers to the type of axe used as a familiar Cretan decorative symbol, with a blade on each side of its shaft. Such axes stood on pedestals around the palace and masons carved their shape, apparently at random, into the walls and pillars. One has even been found — though some prefer to call it a dagger — in England, on a pillar at Stonehenge, thus giving rise to intense speculation about the extent of Cretan influence. *Labyrinthos* thus means literally 'the place of the double axes' and acquires its modern meaning by association with the complex structure of King Minos's palace.

From the goddess, or goddesses, who were the mainstay of the Cretan religion derive the goddesses of the later Greek pantheon.

What seems to have happened is that the general fertility-figure, worshipped in different places under a variety of names, came to be departmentalized. Out of one goddess, responsible for fertility in general, derived several, each responsible for one particular aspect of fertility. This will be apparent in the roster of Homeric deities below.

The Indo-European invaders lived a vastly different life. They were not settlers but nomads, moving from place to place with their herds, hunting where they could and passing on. Thus their deities are masculine, exemplifying the qualities which their worshippers had to possess if they were to survive — strength of arm, fleetness of foot, cunning of mind. When the two races mixed, their religions fused, and in the Homeric pantheon the gods, with some important exceptions, may be traced back to the Indo-Europeans and the goddesses to their predecessors. This fusion is represented in mythology by a series of divine marriages, such as that between Zeus and Hera : the new god mates with the old goddess and becomes the dominant partner. The same sort of change is deduced in contemporary society : an original matriarchal system, in which descent was traced through the mother, yielded to the patriarchal system we still employ. Needless to say, given the nature of the country and the people, there were numerous variant traditions. The isolation of one group from another produced a diversity of religious beliefs. Each city had its own patron god or spirit, either indigenous — under an old or a new name — or imported, regarded as having the people under his protection. A wealth of stories were woven around them. This diversity persists in later mythology. Try to construct a family tree of the Greek gods and you will face enormous complications. For example, was Demeter the wife, sister or daughter of Zeus ? There are different answers depending on the sources consulted.

Nevertheless the Greek religion was eventually codified, at least to some extent, and this was due to the works of Homer. These poems, as we shall see, drew on a wide range of existing poetic material and worked the earlier poems into finer shapes.

They collected the various traditions of the gods and imposed some sort of unity upon them, presenting the gods as a divine family with more or less clearly defined inter-relationships. Hence arose the description of Homer as 'father of the gods'. The universal popularity of the poems superseded earlier variants and provided a familiar pattern to which later writers could adhere. In listing these various Homeric gods and their functions, it is important to realize that, because of the way in which the gods came into being, these functions often overlap. Often several primitive deities have combined to make one Homeric deity, with the result that their spheres of influence cannot be exactly defined, and may at times be self-contradictory. The gods themselves are as follows:

Zeus was king and father of the gods, lord of the bright sky, of the thunder and the lightning. His common Homeric epithet is 'cloud-gatherer'. He is an Indo-European deity, as his name shows. It appears in Latin as deus, 'god'; the Roman Jupiter is simply diu-pater, 'god the father'. A different tradition of the coming of Zeus was preserved in Crete. Zeus, it is said, was the son of Cronos, who had been warned that one of his children would supersede him and thus developed the unpleasant habit of eating them as they were born. His wife gave birth to Zeus in secret, and in order to protect him substituted a stone for the newborn child. This Cronos swallowed, and vomited up the children he had previously devoured. These, with Zeus, became the new generation of gods. Cronos' fate was no more than he deserved, for he had overcome his own father. Zeus emerges as the ultimate victor, representative of the third generation of gods. Aeschylus sums up this bloody history:

> He who at time's beginning stood
> Supreme and terrible
> Has passed and is as nothing.
> And he who came after met his match
> And is gone ; but let a man cry 'Hail
> To Zeus Omnipotent' and he
> Shall not fall short of truth.[2]

The cruelty inherent in this story is always present in the Greek religion, though often in muted form. Critics of the religion make such stories their first point of attack, and apologists feel the necessity for explaining them away. It may be remarked here that in Greek the name Cronos is only an aspirate away from *chronos*, 'time'; and once we begin to talk of god as the child of time, we are moving in the world of allegory.

Hera, wife of Zeus, was originally a fertility goddess especially associated with the city of Argos, though she tends to lose these functions when she becomes consort of Zeus. She is represented as a jealous lady and had cause, for Zeus had a roving eye.

Poseidon was in classical times god of the sea. Usually represented as brother of Zeus he may have come, like him, from the North, and it seems clear that he was not a sea-god from the start. He has some more earthly characteristics. In Homer he is the earthshaker, the spirit of earthquake, and bulls were sacrificed to him. It seems likely that he was originally a god living inside the earth and associated with springs and rivers — fresh, not salt water: the bull is a familiar image for a river. When the nomads moved south and saw the sea for the first time, Poseidon, by a natural transference, assumed his marine functions. It is significant that there is no Greek (i.e. Indo-European) word for 'sea': the noun *thalassa* is pre-Greek, and the other common words are really adjectives which have come to function as nouns — *hals* 'the salt element', *pelagos* 'the broad element'. Linguistic researches into the Linear B tablets have suggested a meaning for Poseidon's name — 'husband of the earth' and, possibly, a different origin for this deity. This merely goes to prove, however, how complex are the origins of the Olympian gods, and how wary one must be of making any definite pronouncement concerning them.

Hermes is most familiar as the divine messenger. We may find his origins, perhaps, in naturally deposited heaps of stones to which the primitive mind attributed supernatural significance. The stones lay in what appeared to be an orderly manner and it was therefore believed that some god must have put them there. We may observe the same sort of superstition today in connection with the Scottish cairns, stone-heaps of indeterminate origin to which it is politic, the locals believe, to add another stone in passing, and which may not be disturbed with impunity. Upright stones were added to distinguish the heaps; these then came to be used as milestones, or boundary marks, and the god inherent in them transferred his interest to the roads so posted. There is evidence that monuments of this form were worshipped in Mycenaean times, and we may suppose that when the Indo-Europeans came they gave this friendly spirit a Greek name. Even in classical times the god's statue retained much of its primitive form, a head and other attributes being added, but the rough rectangular shape, reminiscent of the original pillars, remaining.

As Hermes resided in the boundary stone he naturally became the god of roads and travellers, and hence the messenger of the gods, taking messages from heaven to earth and conducting the souls of the dead to the underworld. His virtue lay in his speed and wits rather than in his strength, and hence he became the patron of merchants and, by a natural extension to the early Greek mind, of thieves and robbers also : it is appropriate to recall here the remarks made earlier about the connection between trade and piracy. The word *hermaion*, derived from his name, means 'a windfall, a godsend'. Several myths tell of his quick-wittedness and mischievous escapades. According to one, no sooner was he born than he stole the cattle of Apollo and hid them in a cave. When Apollo came suspiciously enquiring, he found Hermes lying innocently in his cradle :

> Then Hermes answered him with crafty words :
> 'Why, Leto's son, what angry words are these ?
> And is it cattle that you come to seek ?
> I've not seen or heard of them from anyone
> And couldn't tell you even if you paid me.
> Do I look strong enough to be a cattlethief ?
> That's not my mistake. I have other pleasures —

Napping, and milk drawn from my mother's breast,
And blankets tucked up round my neck, and bath-time.' 3

Hermes finally appeased Apollo's wrath by giving him the lyre
which he had just invented; thus, through Hermes, Apollo
became god of music. Stories like these preserve dim racial
memories of clashing cultural traditions, and of one race trans-
mitting its ideas to another. Classical art often gave Hermes the
more elaborate form of a man with winged cap and sandals, and
a winged staff as befitting a messenger of the gods; he also wore
a broadbrimmed traveller's hat. His statue in its cruder pillar
form, the Herm, was a familiar sight in the streets of a Greek city.

Demeter is the clearest example of an early fertility goddess
surviving in the Greek system. Her name means 'earth-mother':
she is the goddess of growing things, but eventually becomes
associated with a cult of rather wider importance, for which
reason it will be more appropriate to postpone discussion of her
nature until later.

Artemis seems originally to have been another aspect of the
fertility goddess, concerned particularly with birth, both in
humans and in animals. We find this aspect of her cult particularly marked in Asia. Greek influence stripped away some of
these old associations and transformed her into the patron deity
of wild things, and, by apparent contradiction, into the patroness
of hunters. This contradiction is not so real as it appears, for
both hunters and hunted are regarded as partaking in the delight
and ritual of the chase. Some aspects of the ancient fertility cult
did, however, survive; Artemis remains in classical times the
guardian spirit of childbirth.

Aphrodite is another example of the fertility goddess who survives in transmuted form. Her cult seems to have been centred
on Cyprus, an ancient trade-centre, and where Artemis became
the patroness of childbirth Aphrodite remained in classical times
as the embodiment of the passion of love. Ancient tradition
made her the mother of Eros, the familiar winged Cupid. *Eros*
as a common noun is usually translated 'love' but really means
'sexual desire'; the concept of romantic love was slow to

develop in the ancient world, and appears regularly in literature only in the fourth century B.C. When classical writers speak of *eros* they mean something more carnal.

Athena was almost certainly a pre-Greek goddess, protector of the princes of Mycenae. One of her attributes is the snake — as we have seen, a regular fertility symbol — though this is less familiar as her companion than the owl, emblem of the city of Athens to which she gave her name. Her sacred olive tree grew on the Acropolis; in modern times a new tree has been replanted on the old site.

Hephaistus probably began as god of volcanic fires, an instance of the primitive tendency to attribute supernatural powers to inexplicable phenomena, and later became god of those who use fire in their trade, blacksmiths, metalworkers and the like. According to myth his forge lay under Mount Etna in Sicily. He was represented as lame, and it would seem that we have here a clear case of the people shaping their gods in accordance with their own social patterns. In early communities the men who stayed at home to make swords for others were the physically handicapped, those who could not go out to fight or plough the soil themselves. In Homer Hephaistus is the butt of his fellow gods, stumbling around the banquet hall of Olympus. The tradition which makes the poet Homer blind may probably be explained in the same way. Poetry was a luxury in early society; only those who could not act themselves were permitted to sit idle and sing of the acts of others.

Hestia, goddess of the hearth, is a nebulous figure. Her name means 'hearth' and she is the spirit and embodiment of domesticity. *Ares*, god of war, is more vigorous but scarcely more interesting. The Greeks fought much but disliked fighting heartily. This dislike they vented upon the deity. He was supposed to live in Thrace, the cold, barbarous region to the north whose sea was a notorious hazard for sailors, and it is significant that far fewer stories are woven around him than around the other gods. In his country are located some of the murky incidents of Greek mythology:

> *And by the Dark Rocks at the meeting of two waters*
> *Lie the shores of Bosporos and Thracian Salmydessos.*

Here was a sight for the eyes
Of the city's neighbour, Ares —
The two sons of Phineus, blinded
By stepmother's fury, their sightless eyes
Appealing for vengeance, calling down a curse
*On her bloody hands and the shuttle turned dagger.*4

Apollo, one of the most important Greek gods, is also one of the greatest mysteries. For classical Greece he was the embodiment of harmony in all its aspects — in music and poetry; in social concourse, as god of law and order; in the human body, as god of health. He thus appears as the personification of the ideal Greek way of life. None the less, he seems to have been non-Greek in origin and to have come, in fact, from Asia Minor. Scholars have attempted to give him a purely Greek origin by deriving his name from Greek words: it has been derived from *apellai*, 'sheepfolds' or 'public meetings', thus making him originally god of herdsmen or god of the assembly; another theory derives the name from *apellon*, 'black poplar tree'; yet another derives it from the verb *apollunai*, 'destroy', and it is certainly as the destroyer that Apollo appears in Homer, where he shoots deadly plague into the Greek encampment to avenge his slighted priest.

Another main line of theory brings him in from the North. His worship was associated with the Hyperboreans, a mysterious people who dwelt, as their name indicates, 'beyond the North Wind'. But who these Hyperboreans were, or what connection they had with Apollo beyond sending annual gifts to his shrine, is open to question.

Without doubt the most probable theory is that which sees the god's origins in the East. Apollo was known in ancient times by the appellation of *Lykios*, or *Lykeios*, which seems to mean an inhabitant of Lycia, in Asia Minor (though here too there are arguments: some scholars would derive the name from *lukos*, 'wolf', and others from the root *luk* — 'light'). Certainly several of Apollo's more important shrines were found in Asia Minor, and whereas his festivals are comparatively rare in Greece, they are more frequent on the islands and in Asia Minor itself. In Greek mythology Apollo often appears as an intruder, driving out some earlier deity and taking over his shrine. What appeared to be a clinching piece of evidence appeared in 1936, when the name 'Apulanas, God of the Gates' was found on a Hittite altar in Anatolia, Asia Minor. The importance of this inscription is in the similarity of both name and function: the Greek Apollo was commonly known as God of Gates, and his altar, in the form of a conical pillar, appeared at the entrance of Greek houses. The reading itself has been questioned, however, and we are flung once more into controversy.

The origin of Apollo is thus full of difficulties, and the most difficult question of all is how a non-Greek god could become the embodiment of the Greek spirit. In classical times he stands out as the Averter of Evil, *apotropaios*, and God of Prophecy. His oracular shrine at Delphi was the most important prophetic centre in Greece; this will be treated at greater length below.

These twelve made up Homer's family of gods. Although membership of the list changes from time to time — Hestia, a dim figure, is elbowed out by more resplendent deities — the number tends to remain constant. Just as the Greeks pictured their gods in human shape, so they gave them status and character based on the values of their own society. Early Greece was feudal in structure. Warrior barons ruled autocratically over small settlements, and the man–god relationship reveals the same organizational pattern. In Homer, the gods are conceived as supernatural aristocrats. They have no duties to their worshippers, any more than a king has duties to his subjects; though, as it was politic for a king to give his people some measure of protection to ensure his own support in time of war, so the gods had an interest in keeping their worshippers from harm if they wished to receive the sacrifices they desired. It is a distant relationship, based on policy rather than devotion and on need rather than love. If the gods are nobles they must behave like nobles: the Homeric deities comport themselves in the manner of earthly barons, though on a grander scale, having all the virtues and the failings of an entrenched and hereditary aristocracy. They can offer protection, but at the same time can be capable of great cruelty. They can be friendly or callous as the mood takes them. They are susceptible to bribes or family influence. Homer shows the gods taking sides in the Trojan War: some gods had produced mortal children, and felt compelled to assist them. It is thus, for example, that Aphrodite, mother of Aeneas by a mortal father, rescues her son in the fifth book of the *Iliad*. The gods are jealous of each other, and far from respectful of each other's prerogatives. In *Iliad*, v. 889 ff., Zeus snaps at Ares, in a passage which well illustrates both the Olympian tendency to bickering and the low status of the God of War:

> *You who are changing ever, do not sit and whine*
> *Near me. Of all the gods who hold Olympus*
> *I hate you most, for your abiding love is quarrels,*
> *Wars, battles.*

The jockeying for position on Olympus is a celestial version of the prestige struggles in earthly courts.

Again, as nobles, the gods owe allegiance to no standards but their own. The morality of the Homeric gods is the morality the people observed in their own rulers. There is no shame, for example, in a god seducing mortal women, even though he is married to a goddess, just as Agamemnon feels no shame in acquiring concubines when he is married to Clytemnestra. There are numerous stories of Zeus making love to mortal women in disguise. At one point in the *Iliad* Zeus compares Hera favourably to his various inamoratas:

> *Not when I loved Ixion's wife, who bore me*
> *Peirithoos, the equal of the gods in counsel,*
> *Or the daughter of Akrisios, neat-footed Danae*
> *Who bore me Perseus, famous among all men,*
> *Or Phoinix' daughter, she who, so renowned,*
> *Bore to me Minos and the godlike Rhadamanthys,*
> *Or Semele, or Alcmena, she of Thebes,*
> *Who bore a son to me, the dauntless Heracles*
> *While Semele bore Dionysus, man's delight,*

Nor when I loved Demeter of the lovely hair
*Or glorious Leto. . . .*⁵

Hera pursued many of these illegitimate offspring with her vengeance. Tradition says that children of such unions, themselves semi-divine, founded families : many of the most important houses in Greece traced their descent back to the gods, with as much pride as a European may claim descent from the indiscretion of a Hapsburg or a Romanoff. By the double standard of this feudal society, however, women were expected to remain pure, and this too is reflected in the popular picture of the gods. Goddesses are either respectably married or remain virgin : Athena was known as *parthenos*, 'the virgin goddess'. There are, of course, exceptions to this : Aphrodite, as befits her character, is somewhat indifferent to the marriage vows, as in Homer's story of her affair with Ares, but on the whole the goddesses are treated with the respect accorded in the poems to a Hecuba and an Andromache.

As the commoner offered tithes to his baron, man paid taxes to the gods in the form of sacrifices, and like the barons, the gods were quick to take offence at infringement of property rights. The greatest offence a mortal could commit was *hybris* — the denial of divine authority, the failure to give the gods their due. *Hybris* is a word whose significance changes and expands, but initially it seems to mean simply a personal offence against the godhead. Prometheus stole the divine prerogative of fire and bestowed it on man. For this he was bound to a mountain peak in perpetual torment. Tantalus offended the gods by stealing their divine food, and was punished in the underworld by gnawing hunger and thirst. Ixion, the Cain of Greek mythology, was pardoned by Zeus for committing the first murder, and then had the bad grace to attempt the seduction of Hera. For this he was bound to an ever-revolving wheel. It is important to realize that these men were not punished because they had sinned — there is no moral judgement involved here — but because they had committed a personal offence against a deity. It is only later that the gods come to be regarded as embodying a system of morality.

E

In short, the first distinction between gods and men is purely temporal, a difference not in morality but in longevity. Men are mortal, *brotoi*, *thnētoi*, creatures of a day, while gods are the deathless ones, *ambrotoi*, *athanatoi*, who live for ever. In Homer the will of a great man is his law, and the will of the gods is theirs, whether they choose to apply it capriciously or with justice. This is, obviously, a system in which the moralist could find many flaws, and it was not long before such a critical examination took place.

NOTES TO CHAPTER THREE

1. Hesiod, *Works and Days*, 100.
2. Aeschylus, *Agamemnon*, 167.
3. *Hymn to Hermes*, 260.

4. Sophocles, *Antigone*, 966.
5. Homer, *Iliad*, XIV. 317.

Chapter Four

The Greeks and Their Gods: (2) Other Gods and Cults

THERE were other important gods who were not originally members of the Twelve. One such was a deity who had vital importance in Greek life and art, and whose worship can never be satisfactorily explained — the god Dionysus. His cult, particularly associated with women, involved drunkenness and wild orgies. Believers worked themselves into a state of frenzy in which they were able to perform apparently superhuman feats, similar to the dancing madness which struck Europe several times in later centuries and to the more modern manifestations of such orgiastic cults. Like Apollo, he was a foreign god, variously represented as coming from Phrygia in Asia Minor or from Thrace. In Phrygia Dionysus was known as Diounsis, and here too we find the name of a divine pair, Dios and Zemelo, who are probably the Asiatic versions of Dionysus' parents in the Greek tradition, Zeus and Semele. The Greeks, however, made Semele a mortal woman, living in Thebes, and visited by Zeus in mortal shape. The orgies and wild rites distinguishing the cult of Dionysus are familiar features of other Eastern cults but foreign to the harmony and order of the Greek tradition. Cybele, the Asiatic mother-goddess, was worshipped in such wild ceremonies, and later tradition mingled them with those of Dionysus. Thus we see him as a new and disturbing element.

He seems to have been a late-comer to the pantheon. Homer knows of his existence but gives him only a bare mention. The occurrence of his name in Linear B, however, has led to new speculation as to the date and origins of his cult in Greece. Dionysus must originally have been a fertility god. He manifests himself as a bull, emblematic of fertility, and an animal frequently associated with him is the goat. Though male, he has notable female characteristics. He is portrayed as pale, exotic, languorous. His femininity, however, is not softness; it is the perverse cruelty of the great cats with whom he is so often portrayed. A potentially savage god, many hideous stories are connected with him.

We have seen how goddesses originally responsible for all aspects of fertility became more specialized as religious thought developed — how Artemis, for example, narrowed her functions to become specifically responsible for young things and for childbirth. In the same way the functions of Dionysus are limited to make him god of wine. There is an obvious connection between drunkenness and the frenzy of the Dionysiac orgies, but the latter was more than mere intoxication. Naturally this wild cult was looked upon with disapproval, and myths preserve several stories of the hostility shown to Dionysus by both gods and men — notably by Hera, who treated him with the savagery she showed to all Zeus' illegitimate children. Mythology has transmuted the introduction of a new religion into stories of personal hostility. Lycurgus, in a story remembered by Homer, attacked Dionysus and his nurses and drove them into the sea, in punishment for which the god killed him, or drove him mad. Pentheus, King of Thebes, offered resistance to the cult, and Dionysus had him torn apart by his maddened worshippers, who in their frenzy mistook him for a wild beast. It is this story that Euripides took as the basis for his tragedy, *The Bacchae*. Note that in these stories it is always the god who wins and his persecutors who suffer. Historical fact bears out mythology: the worship of Dionysus did in fact infiltrate other, longer-established cults. The Greeks looked upon any form of madness or possession as a divine affliction. The possessed person was regarded with a mixture of reverence and dread. Nevertheless, the most important aspect of the Dionysian cult is in another of its manifestations. The songs and dances in which Dionysus was worshipped became the origins of drama, and Dionysus, as well as being God of Wine, came to be heralded as God of Tragedy. This development will be discussed in greater detail in connection with the theatre proper. Thus we find the new god, for one reason or other, assuming immense importance. He is the personification of the irrational, the occasional reckless fury disregarding all reason and restraint that every man has known at some time in his life. Despite objections that his worship encouraged immorality, his temple and theatre on the slopes of the Acropolis were among the most important buildings in Athens, and he was numbered ultimately among the Twelve Gods, ousting one or other of the previous members.

Other gods standing outside the Olympian group, though for different reasons, were the chthonic, or underworld, deities, the gods of the dead and of such dismal afterlife as the Greek religion provided. In Homer the dead are pictured as mere shadows of their living selves, insubstantial phantoms, weak and helpless, passing a grey and monotonous existence. In a famous passage in the *Odyssey* Odysseus conjures up shades of the illustrious dead, including Achilles, most famous of the Greek warriors to fall before Troy. Achilles sums up his state thus:

> *I'd rather live on earth, bound to another's service,*
> *Yes, to a needy man who scraped a meagre living,*
> *Than reign as king above the legions of the dead.*[1]

Far later, a poem of Anacreon embodies the same feeling of death as the end of all that is good and sweet:

> *Blanched are my brows now, and my crown is white,*
> *Gone grace of youth ; on dotard's teeth I bite,*
> *And but a little of sweet life is left.*
> *Fearing the dark to come I am bereft,*
> *For death is strange and deep, and sharp the way ;*
> *Once down, there's no return another day.*[2]

The dead were imagined as dwelling beneath the earth, and ruled by a king named Hades. Mythology made him one of the brothers of Zeus and spoke of an original tripartite division of the universe, with Zeus taking the heavens, Poseidon the sea and Hades the underworld. It has already been pointed out that in a stricter sense Hades is Zeus' opposite, the God of Darkness as

Zeus is the God of Light. Note that Hades is originally the name of the god and not of the place that he rules. This meaning came later, and the god was called by an alternative name, Pluto. This word, from *ploutos*, 'wealth', seems to stem from a confusion with fertility spirits, who also dwell beneath the earth and send up the soil's benison from below.

The Greeks recognized a number of local entrances to the underworld. These were sometimes places of particular danger, like Cape Tainaron, the southernmost point of Greece and a well-known navigational hazard. The 'gateway to death' in the metaphorical sense, it came to be so considered literally; it was through a cave here that the demigod Heracles was said to have emerged after one of his sorties into the Underworld. Another was the River Styx, in Arcadia, a gloomy river flowing between high banks and appropriate for the rôle the Greeks assigned to it. When a man died, he was led to the Styx by Hermes, in his function of *psychopompos*, 'conductor of dead souls', and ferried across by an old boatman, Charon, who survives to this day in Greek folklore as Charondas, the figure of death himself. Across the river lay the domains of Hades, guarded by a three-headed dog, Cerberus, of unpleasant habits:

> He has a cruel trick,   When men come visiting
> He wags his tail, and rubs his ears against them,
> But never lets them out ;   he keeps watch, and eats
> Whomever he catches departing through the gates.[3]

Within the courts of Hades sit the judges of the dead, among them Minos, former King of Crete; there may be found also the various picturesque sinners undergoing their punishments.

God could speak to man in various ways. He could do it by dreams. In Homer we see the dream as a divine messenger sent by Zeus to stand at the sleeper's bedside and counsel him:

> So spoke he ;   and the Dream, when he had heard, departed,
> And swiftly came to the fast ships of the Achaeans
> And went to Agamemnon, son of Atreus, finding him
> Slumbering in his hut and bathed in sleep ambrosial.

By his head he stood, in likeness of the son of Neleus,
*Nestor, whom of all elders Agamemnon honoured most.*4

Later ages were to reject this view. Heracleitus, the Ephesian
philosopher who flourished around 500 B.C., argued that in sleep
the channels of the senses were closed, thereby preventing the
mind from making contact with what lay outside itself, learning
and growing. He thereby rejects the popular view that in sleep
the mind was peculiarly sensitive to divine communion and
prophetic impulse. Herodotus, writing his *History* somewhat
later, includes in a story of Xerxes a surprisingly modern view of
dreams and their causes. He tells how the King, while debating
whether or not to invade Greece, was warned by a vision in the
night that he should not allow his advisers to dissuade him from
the war. When he related his experience one of his counsellors
remonstrated with him:

> These have no heavenly authority, my son. I am your senior by
> many years, and shall explain these things that come and go when
> men are sleeping. These shifting nocturnal apparitions are, for the
> most part, things that have been on our minds during the day.5

The gods could speak through omens, which manifested themselves in various ways — through natural phenomena, and the
behaviour of birds and animals — and through sacrifices, causing
results which could be interpreted by a skilled seer. Here, from
Sophocles' *Antigone*, is the dramatic account of such an observation:

> *As I took my place upon my ancient seat*
> *Of augury, where all the birds come flocking,*
> *I heard a noise I had never heard before,*
> *Their cries distorted in a scream of fury,*
> *And I knew that they were clawing, killing each other ;*
> *The whirring of wings told a tale too clear.*
> *I was frightened, and went at once to light the altar*
> *And offer sacrifice ; but from my offerings*
> *No flame sprang up. Fat melted on the thighs*
> *And oozed in slow drops down to quench the embers*
> *And smoked and spluttered ; and the gall was scattered*

> *Into the air. The streaming thighs were raw,*
> *Bare of the fat which once enfolded them.*
> *And so my rites had failed.*[6]

Thirdly, and most important, gods could speak through oracles. Places of oracular consultation were fairly frequent in Greek sanctuaries, but few attained more than local importance. At Dodona, in the mountains of Epirus, Zeus spoke through a talking oak tree, whose wood provided the prow for Jason's treasure-hunting ship, the *Argo*, and so gave the vessel power of speech. Another oracle of Zeus flourished at the oasis of Siwah in Egypt, near the boundary of Libya. These, however, were too remote for normal consultation. By far the most popular shrine was that of Apollo at Delphi.

Delphi stands inland, a few miles from the Corinthian Gulf, high and difficult of access among mountains of awesome beauty. It is a place where one might well imagine that gods might dwell. The name means 'womb'. Myth has it that Zeus, desiring to measure the world, set two eagles flying from opposite ends. Where they met, over Delphi, was the world's centre. Its religious importance caused it to be regarded as the world's spiritual centre, and once again metaphor was taken for actuality, as in the mediaeval maps of Christendom where Jerusalem is planted firmly in the middle. It has already been noted that Apollo was probably Asiatic in origin. The Greeks, in their own stories, naturalized him by explaining that he was the son of Zeus and the mortal Leto. Flying before Hera's wrath his mother had borne him and his sister, Artemis, on the tiny island of Delos, in some accounts created by Zeus especially for the occasion. Some would rationalize this as the picturesque account of a new island thrown up by volcanic eruption. The third-century poet Callimachus contributes a typical Alexandrian touch:

> *Starry and fragrant, the islands round about you*
> *Formed a ring, and you as in the dance took centre.*[7]

This was Apollo's most important Greek shrine for some time. The hymn attributed to Homer describes the celebrations here:

> *There the Ionians put on their long robes, and gather*
> *With their children about them, and their modest wives,*
> *And in your memory perform for your delight*
> *With boxing and with dancing and with song.*[8]

Delos was, of course, the island to achieve fame in later years as the home of the anti-Persian confederacy. It gained prosperity from Apollo's worship, for merchants traded here during the security of the religious festivals. Tradition next represents Apollo as journeying from Delos to Delphi, a colourful depiction of the Hellenization of his cult. Arriving at the site he killed a huge serpent that lived there (in more historical language, the new god replaced an existing fertility cult) and established his shrine. This is expressed genealogically, as the old gods handing over to the new:

> *First in my prayer I honour Earth*
> *Who first of gods gave oracles to men,*
> *And then to Themis, who second came*
> *To hold this seat of prophecy, her mother's,*
> *As legend tells ; and in the third succession,*
> *By Themis' free consent, with violence to none,*
> *Another earthchild, Titan-born,*
> *Came to inhabit it, and this was Phoebe,*
> *Who gave it as a birthgift to Apollo.*
> *So from her name he takes his name of Phoebus.*
> *He left the quarried waterland of Delos,*
> *Put in at Athens and her harboured shore,*
> *And so came here, to live upon Parnassus.*[9]

From this point Delphi's fame eclipses that of Delos; it was not until 426, when Delphi was barred to the Athenians by act of war, that the island was purified and its celebrations reinaugurated.

Pilgrims from all over Greece and beyond sought guidance from Delphi. Athenian and Spartan legislators brought laws for ratification. Kings and private citizens came with matters of state or personal problems. Apollo did not speak directly, but through his priestess, the Pythia, who went into a mediumistic trance and babbled incoherently. Her words were 'interpreted' by priests and the answer passed to the enquirer. The proceedings were similar to a spiritualist's seance, and as difficult to fathom. In other shrines the fraud is sometimes patent. At Corinth, for example, there may be seen a small and apparently innocuous altar, with a funnel-shaped orifice connected to it and concealed beneath it. A priest would crawl under the altar through a tunnel and call up replies to the impressed enquirer. The mechanics of Delphi were not so simple. It is probable that the priestess drugged herself, but of this we cannot be sure. There was obviously every opportunity for interference by the priests, for none could call them liars, and they could inject into their 'interpretations' any meaning that they considered appropriate. The oracle had a tradition of ambiguity, so that in many cases, whatever happened, it could be proved correct. A celebrated instance of this ambiguity is the answer given to King Croesus of Lydia, who was a distinguished patron of the oracle and consulted it when contemplating war on Persia. He was informed that if he attacked the Persians, a great empire would be destroyed. Thinking that his enemies were meant he made war, only to find that the empire destroyed was his own.

The Greeks were not credulous fools. The oracle was valuable to them and there was sense in their using it. Delphi attracted more visitors than any other shrine in Greece. While the cities kept themselves jealously apart, Delphi was open to all. Its priests, by judicious pumping of visitors, could acquire a wider knowledge of what was going on in the world than would be easily available elsewhere, and could use this knowledge to inform their answers. Analysis of the oracle's replies reveals traces of a consistent policy. Before the Persian Wars, for example, Delphi's advice to any city that enquired was that the Persians should not be resisted. There was self-interest in this. Being in an exposed position, the shrine — known from the number and magnificence of presents made to it as 'golden Delphi' — was afraid of being despoiled by an invading army. Apart from this, the priests were clearly offering logical deductions from information received. It seemed suicidal to resist a force of the size the Persians were known to be mustering. In war, however, illogic reigns, and Delphi was proved wrong. But this setback to her prestige was soon removed, and Delphi remained oracular arbiter of Greece well into Roman times. In A.D. 390 the Emperor Theodosius closed the shrine in the name of Christianity.

It has already been remarked that the conception of the gods as a superior race of nobles, acting more or less well according to their mood and susceptible to bribery or family influence, was one hardly calculated to satisfy the critical. Thus, as the years passed, men tended to ask 'What are the gods for?' and tried to equate the Olympian gods with a set of desirable moral standards. We find traces of this movement even in the Homeric poems themselves. Zeus in the *Iliad* is noble and proud, courageous but capricious; Zeus in the *Odyssey* is something more. He is no longer concerned purely with his own will; he recognizes his duty to protect suppliants; he is the god of hospitality, extending his protection over strangers and travellers. Thus we see Zeus becoming the personification of a moral code — that strangers should be treated well, and not injured; and that to injure a stranger and break the laws of hospitality was to offend Zeus himself. This is a great advance. The older Zeus could be offended only by a personal affront, if someone stole one of his possessions or made love to his wife. The new, more moral Zeus may be offended by someone transgressing against the code which he upholds. This change reveals itself in other ways. Murder and homicide now become crimes against the gods. If one man kills another it is their business. The archaic age — between Homer and classical times — saw the development of a concept of inherited guilt, an attempt to explain why the guilty may go free and the apparently virtuous may suffer, and why the gods seem blind to the wrongs done by mortals. According to this doctrine, a criminal may escape punishment himself but still pass the burden of his sin on to future generations.

> *Some say the gods disdain to mind*
> *Those who trample their feet on grace*
> *Of things forbidden them ;*

> *But this is blasphemy.*
> *For when there is surfeit in the house*
> *Beyond all right, and its folk are bloated*
> *With vicious pride, the father's sins*
> *Are visited upon the children's children.*[10]

Aeschylus in his plays and Herodotus in his *History* work out this theme. Aeschylus tells the story of the curse-laden House of Atreus, in which two generations pay for the crime committed by an ancestor. Herodotus traces the downfall of Croesus, King of Lydia, to the crime of an ancestor a hundred years back.

This tendency to correct the early myths sometimes manifests itself sharply. Herodotus' tentative excursions into comparative religion lead him to question some of the standard tales of the Greek deities. Xenophanes, poet and professional reciter, rebelled against man's tendency to make gods in his own image. Greek mythology and Greek art represented the gods as idealized human beings, supernatural powers in human form, possessing more than human beauty and strength. Xenophanes commented ironically on this. Ethiopians, he said, imagined their gods as black and snub-nosed, Thracians as blue-eyed and fair haired — that is, possessing the racial characteristics of the people who worshipped them. If beasts were able to draw pictures, they would envisage beast-gods, and depict them in their own likeness. Moreover, Homer and Hesiod were unjust to the gods; they had given them all manner of vices that in men are found objectionable. But Xenophanes' most original contribution is this: he admitted his private faith in a god not like men in appearance or in mind, but omniscient, omnipotent and unchanging. Thus we have a foreshadowing of monotheism in an age dominated by the Homeric pattern. Hecataeus, the geographer of Miletus, admitted that he found the myths funny. But these were still lonely voices. The majority of people still worshipped, in the old way, the gods of Olympus.

Moving further into the fifth century, we pass into a period of even more stringent rational and scientific enquiry. This change manifests itself in many ways. In feudal society the family had been the basic unit of social life, with the father dominating its members. This pattern is duplicated in the conception of the Homeric gods; father Zeus rules the heavenly family, just as the mortal father disciplines his children. The fifth century, however, saw the gradual emancipation of the individual from family responsibility. Thus the older notion of inherited blood-guilt tends to disappear. Free-thinking teachers — the so-called sophists, whose name meant 'men of wisdom' but who were too often concerned with teaching men merely what would gain them worldly advantage — encouraged open criticism of the established religion. Typical of this new spirit was Anaxagoras, the scientist, who shocked public opinion by declaring that the sun was not a god but a burning stone in the heavens. In the forefront of the movement was the dramatist Euripides, who used the stock themes of tragedy to criticize the old myths of the gods, analysing them mercilessly in terms of human behaviour. 'This is how we are told the gods behaved,' he argues. 'If human beings behaved in such a way, and showed such a consistent record of deceit, cruelty and immorality, should we not reject them out of hand ? Then how can we worship as superior beings gods who behave in the same way ?' The subject-matter of Euripides' plays more properly comes under the heading of the drama, and will be treated more fully there. It is sufficient to say at this point that, although criticism of the gods had been voiced before, and was being voiced more and more frequently in discussion, it had never been aired so publicly as at Euripides' hands, in the theatre, before audiences of 17,000 spectators, or with such deadly force and concentrated logic.

We must be careful at this point to distinguish between popular belief and the theories of the intellectuals. Men like Euripides were offering sensible, rational criticism of an institution they no longer found themselves able to believe in, but the popular mind, working more slowly, still clung to the beliefs and observances of former generations. At the end of the fifth century there is, in fact, a reaction of popular opinion against the intellectuals. Euripides, always unpopular, ended his life, involuntarily or by his own choice, in exile. Anaxagoras was put on trial, and so was Socrates, with familiar results. The books of Protagoras, a leading sophist, were burnt in the market-place. What was heresy in the fifth century, however, passed for orthodoxy in the fourth. As a working religion the Olympian gods declined. Their rituals survived, and the gods themselves continued to provide authors with a convenient literary mechanism within which to frame their writings. The Olympian deities became part of the poet's stock-in-trade, and gods and goddesses could still be appealed to, or represented, when there was no longer any belief in them.

In the course of this critical examination, some gods were treated more sympathetically than others. Those whose relevance to, and practical involvement in, the affairs of mankind could be convincingly demonstrated retained their prestige longer than the others. Apollo remained important, not only because of Delphi but for his concern with healing: here was one case where divinity could be shown to have practical value. Other healing cults also flourished, notably that of Apollo's son Asklepios, who appeared in Greek tradition sometimes as god, sometimes as hero, and who had offended against the gods by bringing men back to life. His shrine became firmly established at Epidauros, in the Argolid. Epidauros was the Greek Lourdes, attracting the sick from all over the country, who came to worship and be cured. Shrines, offices and dispensaries were built; there was a stadium, and, of particular importance, a theatre built in the fourth century B.C., one of the finest examples of classical theatre-building that we now possess.

We know something of healing-ritual from various sources. One important piece of evidence is from a comedy, *Ploutos* (*Wealth*) by Aristophanes. In this play the God of Wealth, traditionally represented as blind, has his sight restored in a healing shrine. A slave reports how this was accomplished:

> *Then we proceeded to the god's precinct,*
> *And when libations, loaves and offerings*

Were dedicated and consumed by fire
We bedded Ploutos down the usual way ;
There were lots of other patients there — you name it,
They had it. Then the acolyte snuffed out
The lanterns and instructed us to go to sleep.
'If anybody hears a noise', he warned us, 'keep
Your mouth shut.' So we all lay down in tidy rows. . . .
And after that I pulled the covers round my head
In fright ; there was the god in person, making
The rounds, examining his cases systematically. . . .
. . . The god then clucked his tongue
And out of the temple there came two snakes sliding.
Ooh, they were enormous !' [11]

The snakes lick Ploutos' eyes and he is cured. This account,
though fanciful, is related to actual healing practices. Epidauros
seems to have justified its reputation. Excavations have uncovered numerous testimonies to the healing power of the god.
The shrine remained important through Roman times, and had a
peculiar sanctity in Roman eyes. Many of the cures recorded seem
incredible, presenting the same difficulty as Lourdes and other
modern healing shrines. We cannot say how much is superstition, how much trickery, how much auto-suggestion and how
much healing by unknown means. Whatever the explanation, if
the gods were to be asked to perform some useful function in
society Asklepios certainly lived up to the demands made on him.

The Olympian religion failed because it did not equate worship
with moral responsibility. Under the Homeric scheme the
believer had no stimulus to behave well, nor was there much
hope of recompense in the afterlife for the virtuous man who had
suffered on earth. We hear mentions of the Elysian Fields, a
happy place reserved for the shades of the illustrious dead, but the
ordinary man could expect no posthumous rewards.

Thus, any ritual that offered the faintest hope of such reward
was assiduously cultivated, and a number of mystery cults,
promising various blessings to the true believer, grew up within
the context of the Olympian religion. By their nature they were
destined for longer survival than the Olympian gods themselves,

and indeed in some ways acted as precursors of Christianity. Most important was the cult that flourished at Eleusis, the so-called 'Eleusinian Mysteries'. This was based on the worship of that Demeter whom we have seen in Homeric religion as a survival of the prehistoric earth-mother, the corn-goddess, and her daughter Persephone. The Homeric Hymn to Demeter — called Homeric, though almost certainly not written by the author of the *Iliad* and the *Odyssey* — gives the main points of the story. Persephone wandered away from her mother to pick flowers. The earth opened, and Hades, god of the underworld, emerged from the lower regions and carried her away to live with him as his wife. Demeter, overcome with grief, put on the likeness of an old woman and wandered the earth in search of her. When she came to Eleusis, not far from Athens on the way to the Peloponnesus, she was given hospitality by King Keleos and his family. Here the Homeric Hymn brings out a significant point. When questioned by Keleos' daughters, Demeter tells them that she has come from Crete, and it is likely that we have here a half-forgotten tradition that the worship of Demeter had originated with the Cretan fertility goddess. Demeter was made nurse to the baby of the royal household, and in gratitude began to make the child immortal by burning away his mortality in the fire. The queen interrupted her while engaged in this process and not unnaturally jumped to the wrong conclusions. Demeter was compelled to reveal herself in self-protection, and although she could no longer carry out her design of making the child immortal continued to show favour to Eleusis in other ways:

> But I am that Demeter who has honour, who
> Is greatest grace and blessing, both to mortals
> And immortals. Build a temple to me, mighty,
> All you people, and an altar under it . . .
> And I, yes, even I, shall teach my rites to you
> So in the aftertime you may perform them reverently
> And lead me to look favourably upon you.[12]

While Demeter had been wandering about the country in search of her daughter she had neglected her duties as corn-goddess. The fields were barren and famine spread throughout the land. The other gods, observing the danger, tried to effect a reconciliation between her and Hades, and agreed that Persephone could return to her if she had eaten nothing during her stay in the underworld. Hades, however, had contrived that she should eat some pomegranate seeds; and so eventually a compromise was worked out whereby Persephone should spend one-third of the year as Hades' queen and the remaining months with her mother. Thus Persephone assumes a double rôle, and it is as Queen of the Dead that she customarily appears in mythology.

The nature-symbolism of this myth is obvious. It is a mythological account of the origins of the seasons: when Persephone is underground it is winter, and when she comes up to rejoin her mother spring and summer. At the conclusion of the Homeric Hymn Demeter is said to have given knowledge of agriculture to Triptolemos the Eleusinian, and charged him to impart this knowledge to mankind. The rites which the Hymn claims Demeter herself founded became the Eleusinian Mysteries, and brought the city great prestige. They grew into something much more, however, than a simple fertility myth. The theme of fertility and the theme of resurrection from the dead (for this is what happens to Persephone: she descends to the Underworld and rises again) combined to produce the belief that initiation into the Eleusinian Mysteries offered immortality for the human soul. This is how we find the Mysteries represented in classical writings. The Hymn to Demeter concludes with these words:

Blessed is he among mortal men who has looked upon these things ;
But the stranger to these rites, who has no part in them, must never
Have portion of such things when he is gone dead down to darkness.[13]

When Eleusis was annexed by Athens the rites came under Athenian control. As to what they were we have only the barest hints, and have to build up as clear a picture as we can from these. This was, after all, a mystery cult, and the initiates, sworn to secrecy, kept the mystery studiously. Public odium and penalty of law awaited those who were indiscreet. We are told that the

F

poet Aeschylus was on one occasion accused of having revealed some of the secrets of the Mysteries in a play, and only saved himself from physical danger by insisting that he himself was not an initiate, so that if he had transgressed it had been through ignorance. The general pattern seems to have been something like this. An essential preliminary rite was bathing in the sea, for purification, and all candidates for initiation had to do this. Then all left Athens for Eleusis in procession, along the coast road known as the Sacred Way. Twelve miles took them to Eleusis. The image of Dionysus, who had infiltrated into this rite as into others, was carried in procession accompanied by torchbearers, and there were frequent halts on the journey for acts of worship and celebrations of one sort or other.

At last the procession arrived in Eleusis itself, and the main part of the ceremony took place in the sacred buildings here. Eleusis has been carefully excavated, and the foundations of the most important buildings may still be seen; although factories have grown up near by, and a Christian church now overlooks the ruins, the site still retains much of its ancient dignity. It was approached through two magnificent gateways, gifts of rich benefactors; for Eleusis, like Delphi, grew prosperous on endowments, and was lavishly rebuilt at various periods. Inside on the right lies the Sanctuary of Pluto, a cave with a concealed entrance and small platform before it. It looks like a stage setting and may have been used as one; in any case it served as the symbolic entrance to the Underworld. Directly ahead are the ruins of the *telesterion*, a huge, rectangular, covered building that was the principal structure on the site. The foundations show a central courtyard surrounded by tiers of seats. It is conjectured that there was some arrangement for artificial lighting, or at least for shutting out the sunlight at will, an important part of the ritual that followed. This ritual seems to have involved a dramatic re-enactment of the Demeter–Persephone story, a rudimentary passion play, with priests acting the parts. We know the names of some of the officials of the shrine. One was the *hierophant*, 'displayer of holy things', whose duty seems to have been to hold up various cult-objects for the public gaze. The initiates gazed upon these and were allowed to handle others, seemingly under cover of darkness. But this is about all we know. Membership in the Mysteries was jealously prized, and remained an important honour well into Roman times.

Such survivals do not change the fact that by the fourth century the Olympian religion, for all practical purposes, had served its term. If the Hellenistic Age recognized any super-natural force working on human affairs at all, it was *tyche* — chance, fortune, luck, coincidence. Already towards the end of the fifth century this had been heralded as the decisive factor in men's lives. 'What has a man to fear,' cries Jocasta to Oedipus, 'when life is ruled by chance, and the future is unknowable?' Jocasta in the play is proved horribly wrong, but her sentiment is one that a growing number at this time would have shared. Thucydides in his *History* lays so much stress on chance as the dominant factor in affairs of war that he has been accused of writing false history and elevating this principle to the status of a deity. Although this is unjust to Thucydides, many others awarded *tyche* divine honours. An anonymous poet sings its praises:

> *Wing-shod, with many hands and faces,*
> *Chance, omnipotent intimate of mortals,*
> *How should your strength and virtue ever*
> *Be told? Whatever should shine on high,*
> *And proudly, let it come within your sight*
> *And down you tumble it straightway*
> *Dark in the dust and read it asunder;*
> *And whatsoever is mean and lowly*
> *Many a time you raise on wings,*
> *Lifting it high aloft, divinity.*[14]

It is a spiritually weakened, pessimistic age that speaks.

What purpose, then, did the Greek religion serve? The gods of Greece may seem inadequate to us, and we may argue that the Greeks themselves saw this inadequacy before much of their history had passed. However, we must try to see them compara-tively. Compared with the priest-ridden cruelty of the earlier

Asiatic and Egyptian religions they represent an immeasurable advance in thinking. They set ideals which men could strive to imitate. Even the Homeric gods, subservient to no moral law, personify individual virtues — courage, wisdom, strength, the heroic virtues of an age of chivalry which we shall see more clearly when we come to consider the Homeric poems themselves. The doctrine of avoiding *hybris*, that man should not take too much upon himself but give the gods their due, passed into one of the abiding tenets of Greek philosophy. The motto inscribed above the shrine of Apollo at Delphi — *mēden agān*, 'nothing in excess' — finds expression again and again throughout Greek literature. We shall find it in Herodotus, in the dramatists and in Plato, whose *Republic* comes to this conclusion: every element in the scheme of things should perform its appointed function to the best of its ability and attempt no more. The Greek religion perfectly exemplifies this point of view. 'Here are the gods, here are men. They have their part in the universal scheme of things, we have ours. Let us do our best.'

Observe too how this religion set the Greeks apart from their neighbours. The Greeks had passed the stage of worshipping vague, elemental deities, barely conceived forces of nature; they did not, like some of their neighbours, worship gods in bestial shape, or the sun, but cast their gods in human form, seeing in them the qualities they liked to see in themselves. There can be no doubt that this general unity of religion, modified though it was by regional discrepancies and variations, did much to counteract the national political disunity imposed by geographical factors. It is in its religion, not in its politics, that the national character is revealed; it is this factor that made the Greeks set themselves apart from other nations, the *barbaroi*, and see in themselves something finer and more desirable.

When man pictures his gods in human shape, and gives them human attributes and characteristics resembling his own, it is easy to make up stories about them. Around the gods and goddesses of Greece grew up a wealth of mythology. The stories accumulated and were productive. Though some have called Homer — misleadingly — the Greek Bible, it would be more accurate to compare the main body of Greek mythology to English folk cycles like the Arthurian legends or the story of Robin Hood. Moreover, people for a long time believed them. This will be discussed more thoroughly in the chapters on the historians and their methods, but it deserves mention here; for a long time, the statements of mythology were accepted as literal fact. Pheidippides, running from Marathon with news of the Greek victory, was said to have met the god Pan on his way; the Spartan law code was believed to have been authorized by Apollo. Fact and fiction were inextricably interwoven.

On this body of mythology writers could draw. Even works on secular themes drew on stories of heroes, and exploits of the gods, which everyone would know. The drama drew almost exclusively on mythology for its themes, and the same stories are told and retold in play form: the story of Agamemnon, the story of the cursed house of Oedipus, the tales of the Trojan War drawn from Homeric and post-Homeric sources. Art as well as literature drew on mythology for its subject-matter. Vase paintings showed mythological figures, episodes from the history of the gods, scenes from the heroic past. Sculpture represented the gods and goddesses in traditional attitudes and with traditional attributes — Zeus with his thunderbolt, Poseidon with his trident, Apollo with his lyre, Artemis with her bow, and so on down the list. Vase paintings continue this practice, and coinage, issued by individual cities, often bears the emblem of the city's presiding deity, as the coins of Athens bore the owl. Thus, in addition to so much else, the gods contributed what was virtually a heraldic system.

NOTES TO CHAPTER FOUR

1. Homer, *Odyssey*, XI. 489.
2. Loeb Classical Library, *Lyra Graeca*, vol. ii ; Anacreon 69.
3. Hesiod, *Theogony*, 770.
4. Homer, *Iliad*, II. 16.
5. Herodotus, *Histories*, VII. 16.2.

6. Sophocles, *Antigone*, 998.

7. Callimachus, *Hymn* IV (to Apollo), 300.

8. *Hymn to Apollo*, 147.

9. Aeschylus, *Eumenides*, 1.

10. Aeschylus, *Agamemnon*, 369.

11. Aristophanes, *Ploutos*, 659.

12. *Hymn to Demeter*, 268.

13. *Hymn to Demeter*, 480.

14. Loeb Classical Library, *Lyra Graeca*, vol. iii : anon. 129.

Chapter Five

Homer and the Poems

THE works of Homer are the earliest recorded Greek poetry, and the fountainhead of the European poetic tradition. They were not, of course, the first poems. The Greeks recognized that Homer had predecessors. Tradition identified one of these as Orpheus, represented him variously as the priest or as the rival of Dionysus and endowed him with magical powers of song. Torn apart by frenzied women, his head, still singing, floated to the island of Lesbos: thus did the Greeks represent the continuity of poetic tradition. Orpheus may have been a historical personage, or wholly mythical. Other names are even more dubious, Mousaios, Eumolpos, Philammon — were these ever living men, or merely allegorizations of the power of song? The *Iliad* and *Odyssey* themselves, however, refer to bodies of existing poetry on which the composer of the greater epics could draw. None of this remains; even the Greeks of the classical period possessed nothing earlier than the *Iliad*.

Who was Homer, and when did he live? These are not easy questions. The ancients were unanimous in believing in an individual and personal Homer, one man who had himself composed the poems in the form in which they came down to their readers. There were various traditions about his life. We have a number of so-called 'Lives of Homer', mostly late compilations and deduced from the poems themselves: the ancients firmly believed, and established as a principle of biographical writing, that a man's life could be deduced from his works, and that one had only to examine his literary products carefully enough to acquire detailed information about his life and character. Homer's father is said in some accounts to have been a god, in others a mortal, under various names; cities all over the Mediterranean are cited as his birthplace; the meaning of his name is given as 'blind' or 'hostage'; his date is anything between the Trojan War and 275 years afterwards. On one fact most of the accounts agree: he is said to have died on the island of Ios.

From these confusing and often contradictory accounts we may draw some general conclusions. Majority opinion places his home on the eastern side of the Aegean, and a better case can be made for Chios and Smyrna than for the other cities. It is hardly surprising that so many cities claimed to be the birthplace of so famous a man: each coveted the distinction. The same is true, though to a lesser degree, of Homer's Roman counterpart, Virgil, and has not been unknown in modern times: Nazi Germany claimed Shakespeare as her own, on the grounds that so illustrious a playwright could never have been a mere Englishman. In the so-called Homeric Hymn to Apollo, the poet speaks of himself as 'a blind man dwelling in rugged Chios'. This would be convincing, if we could only believe that this Hymn was really by the author of the *Iliad*, but modern scholarship is almost unanimous in rejecting it. None the less, although traditions about Homer's life vary in almost every detail, there was no ancient doubt that there had once existed a real, living Homer. Modern critics have been less sure, and this new questioning of old assumptions has thrown new lights on the status of poetry in the ancient world, on the techniques of early poetic composition, and on the value of the Homeric poems as historical records. It is with the main points of this discussion that the present chapter proposes to deal.

Of the works attributed to Homer, the greatest were the *Iliad* and *Odyssey*. We occasionally find other works identified as his — a lost epic cycle containing the Theban story and the sack of Troy, even in antiquity regarded as wrongly attributed to Homer, and, perhaps of greater interest, two comic pieces. One of these was *Margites*, named after its main character, a stupid youth who 'knew many things and knew them all awry'. He could only count up to five:

The gods had given him no skill in digging, ploughing,
Nor any art at all ; in each he was a failure.[1]

Plato and Aristotle unhesitatingly assigned this to Homer, though
modern scholars disagree. The other is the *Batrachomyomachia*,
The Battle of the Frogs and Mice. This is a fresh and delightful
parody of the heroic conventions of war, those same standards
that we find in the *Iliad* itself. It has been described as standing in
the same relationship to Homer as *Don Quixote* does to mediaeval
chivalry. A mouse, Crumbsnatcher, runs away from a cat, and
meets Puffjaw, King of the Frogs. The frog offers to take the
mouse across the pond on his back. When they are half-way
across:

Then lo, a watersnake appeared, that gave the twain
Great fear to see it, and reared up above the water.
When he beheld it Puffjaw plunged down, never thinking
Of his fellow, how he would leave him there to perish.
Down plunged he to the bottom and escaped dark death.[2]

So the mice declare war on the frogs, and, in true Homeric style,
the gods take sides. Athena refuses to intervene until the mice
pester her by eating holes in her clothes, and the frogs keep her
awake with their croaking. Eventually the conflict is decided by
a *deus ex machina* : the arrival of a swarm of crabs, and a thunder-
storm sent by Zeus, put an end to the war in a single day. This
is a clever poem, and fine parody. The frogs and mice arm, speak
and fight in the grand manner of the Homeric heroes, and the
glorious themes of the Trojan War become ridiculous when put
into the mouths of animals. However, the language of the poem
reveals itself to be far later than Homer. It is clear that we have
here the work of a later parodist, writing in the fifth or fourth
century, and not of the author of the *Iliad*.

By far the most important part of the Homeric apocrypha are
the so-called Homeric Hymns. Our collection consists of over
thirty pieces. Some have only a few lines, but the four major
hymns, to Demeter, Apollo, Hermes and Aphrodite, average some
five hundred lines apiece. That to Demeter has already been

discussed at some length in its religious connections, as has that to Apollo. The Hymn to Hermes tells the tale already quoted, of the theft of Apollo's cattle. This is a charming story, humorously told, and giving some slight indication of date. The lyre which Hermes presents to Apollo by way of appeasement is said to have seven strings, and the seven-stringed lyre, in place of the earlier four-stringed version, is traditionally attributed to the poet Terpander who was an old man in 676 B.C. If this has any value, the poem would belong at the earliest to the seventh century. The fourth of these major hymns, that to Aphrodite, is also the shortest, with a mere 293 lines; it tells of the union of the goddess with the mortal Anchises, from which sprang Aeneas, who was to be identified by later tradition as the founder of Rome.

These are strikingly beautiful poems written in the Homeric style, employing typical Homeric turns of phrase and often embodying direct quotations from the *Iliad* and the *Odyssey* worked into a new context. It is possible, however, to see several different hands at work, and it is almost certain that the poems were not by the author of the *Iliad* and the *Odyssey* but by conscious imitators of his style. Although antiquity attributed them to Homer, modern stylometric tests — analyses of word-usages and frequencies of particular constructions with a view to determining order of composition — have given a different impression; while revealing considerable uniformity in the major works, they suggest that the Hymns were composed at a later date.

It is easy to see how all these works could have been attributed to Homer. His fame was so great that he stood above all others as the father of epic poetry. He wrote in hexameters, and so any unidentified hexameter composition would come in time to be attributed to him. Modern scholarship is almost unanimous in rejecting these shorter, lighter works.

We are left, then, with the *Iliad* and the *Odyssey*, and we are at least fortunate in one thing: as far as we can tell, we possess these poems almost exactly as the ancients knew them. This is by no means always the case with ancient authors. Texts have been mutilated over the centuries, or corrupted by successive errors on the part of copyists. Given the conditions under which manuscripts had to be transmitted before the invention of printing, this is hardly surprising. Some authors have suffered more than others. The playwright Aeschylus, for example, tends to use an exotic vocabulary. Copyists, faced with unfamiliar words, assumed that they must be mistakes, and substituted others similar in spelling which made more immediate sense to them. Aristotle's treatise on poetic composition, his *Poetics*, was probably never given expanded literary form but existed only as lecture notes. Their compactness led to subsequent misinterpretation, and, it has been conjectured, to the inclusion of explanatory material that was not part of Aristotle's original design. One of the major labours of modern scholarship is to restore the text, by scrutiny and conjecture, to the form in which the original author left it. The very popularity of Homer, however, and the frequency with which his work was copied, have made the problem negligible in his case. The Oxford edition of the poems is based on a collation of 150 manuscripts, all of which are singularly free from corruption and scribe's errors. Although complete editions of Homer were expensive, they did exist in large numbers. Modern excavations have added quantities of papyri to the collection.

Now comes the greater problem. The ancient world saw the two great poems as the composition of one man, the work of one poet's hands. But were they? Modern scholarship is by no means so sure.

In classical scholarship, as in so many fields of learning, the nineteenth century brought a revolution in methods and approaches. Before this time, many traditional beliefs about ancient life and letters had been allowed to go unchallenged. They were accepted just as they had been handed down to us by the Romans. Then comes a new critical spirit. Scholars approach the old traditions in a mood of enquiry. They analyse, they question, they probe; they look for inconsistencies, and more often than not they find them. Often this higher criticism goes too far; the reaction against tradition tends to produce the view that all unsupported tradition must be false, an equally dangerous argument. In particular the German scholars of this period produced a wealth of detailed argumentation, sometimes with too little imagination behind it. But we are immensely indebted to this new critical approach; it produced much scholarship of great value, and paved the way towards a new understanding of the classics by revaluing established views in the light of merciless criticism. In 1795 Friedrich August Wolf published at Halle a treatise entitled *Prolegomena ad Homerum*, and it is with this that the problem of the composition of the *Iliad* and the *Odyssey* — the 'Homeric question' — really begins.

Wolf put forward the heretical view that the Homeric poems were not the work of one man at all, but of many, and that they only reached the form in which we have them by means of numerous additions and developments, the work of successive reciters. We know of a group called the *Homeridae*, literally 'sons of Homer', who were trained to recite the works, and regarded themselves as the true heirs of the Homeric tradition. We know as a matter of historical fact that an official text of Homer was prepared by Peisistratus, tyrant of Athens, in the sixth century B.C. Wolf argued that in the hands of the Homeridae and their like the texts of the poems were still fluid, and that it was only under Peisistratus that the various portions of what we now know as the *Iliad* and the *Odyssey* were brought together in anything like their present form. After this, minor alterations were made by arrangers until the text was finally established in the libraries of Alexandria.

Wolf did not entirely abandon the traditional idea of one dominant poet; indeed, he insisted that some one individual must have carried the thread of the story down some way, and even allowed that we might continue to give this poet the name of Homer. But this Homer, in Wolf's view, was the author of only a part of the *Iliad* and *Odyssey*, the rest being the work of other hands.

Two main arguments were brought forward in support of this view. First, it was argued that the art of writing was unknown in the time of Homer, or at least had not been brought into general use. When, in the *Iliad*, the Greek warriors draw lots to decide who is to fight Hector in single combat, each makes his own mark on the lot and throws it into the helmet; they shake and draw, and while each can recognize his own mark none can interpret the marks of the others. From this it is permissible to deduce that they possessed no common system of writing. In the Sixth Book occurs the famous story of Bellerophon, playing the part that Joseph suffered in the Old Testament. Bellerophon attracted the attention of his king's wife, who made advances to him. When he rejected her, she falsely accused him to her husband, Proitus, who dispatched him to Lycia with a letter. In the letter was a command that he should be put to death on his arrival. The point of this story is not merely that Bellerophon cannot read; rather, it is that the process of writing is invested with a dire, almost magical significance, and that the letter itself is regarded as an instrument of potential harm. The same attitude towards writing and letters continues well into the classical period. The majority of the Greeks were illiterate, and on various occasions we can detect the popular attitude towards this strange, almost runic art as having changed little since Homeric times. In much the same way the popular mind in the Renaissance long preserved a fear of the printed book, seeing it as an instrument of evil. Without writing, argued Wolf, it was impossible that poems as long as the *Iliad* and the *Odyssey* could have been transmitted from remote antiquity in anything like a coherent form.

The second argument was related. In an age without writing, when poetry could be enjoyed only by oral recitation — by hearing it spoken, not by reading it — such long, artistically constructed poems would have neither meaning nor object. Recitation demands short pieces such as can be produced at a single session. A long work of any kind implies a reader, one who can return to his book time after time until it is finished. Hence the artistic structure of the Homeric poems is something which tells against the antiquity of their present form.

These were Wolf's arguments, and at the time they carried great force. Other scholars followed in his footsteps, and, once the first breach in the idea of Homeric unity had been made, came forward with other arguments in his favour. They found many internal inconsistencies, loose ends and parts of stories that did not hang together. How, for example, may we account for the language of the poems? It is a composite language, showing a mixture of various elements, different dialects, different ages. The Homeric dialect, as we possess it, is not a language which could ever have been spoken at any one time or in any one place. How may we account for the fact that a warrior killed in Book Five of the *Iliad* is alive to mourn for his son in Book Thirteen? How is it that Odysseus, in the *Odyssey*, is represented as an archer of consummate skill — he boasts that only Philoctetes, who had a magic bow, surpassed him among the Greeks — while when the contest in archery is held in the *Iliad*, he does not even compete, though he has already participated in other events and distinguished himself in the wrestling match against Ajax? Thus scholars went to work to demolish the structure of the poems, attempting to separate them into their original elements and find the core on which the *Iliad* and *Odyssey* grew.

The new discoveries of archaeology also provided material for thought. Archaeology as an exact science only began in the nineteenth century. Before this, excavations had been conducted for profit, by treasure-seekers, or for intelligent amusement, by cultured dilettanti who had no more serious purpose than to bring back some vase or statue to decorate a nobleman's house. But the nineteenth century saw the appearance of the first great giants of archaeology — Heinrich Schliemann, the business man and self-taught scholar; his more scientific pupil Dörpfeld; Sir Arthur Evans, who spent his fortune on the Cnossos excavations rather than tolerate public interference with a private dream. These were men who saw archaeology as a precise tool to help in piecing together the past. Schliemann was an incredible man, who had risen to financial eminence from the humblest origins. In childhood his imagination had been fired by the Homeric poems, and he devoted his life to restoring the city of Troy. The necessary scholarship he acquired himself, learning languages with fantastic rapidity. He used Homer as his guide, in spite of the scorn of his contemporaries who insisted that a work of poetic imagination was hardly authentic history, dug for the lost city where Homer said it was, and found it, together with its predecessors and successors on the same site. He found more than the city. In Troy he discovered Bronze Age objects, artifacts answering closely to descriptions in Homer. His smuggling of these objects out of the site and the country did not endear him to the Turkish government, and made things difficult for those who wanted to excavate the area after him. After Troy Schliemann turned to Mycenae, and found other objects there. All these — for he was a romantic at heart — he tried to identify with specific descriptions in the poems, and labelled them as Nestor's cup, Helen's necklace, and so forth. The authenticity of these identifications, however, is irrelevant: the point is that these discoveries substantiated the unmistakable descriptions of Bronze Age techniques in Homer. Among these were the large, figure-8-shaped body-shield used by the warriors; the double throwing spear; the art of inlaying metal, implied in the description of Achilles' shield in Book Eighteen of the *Iliad*, which certainly went out with the Bronze Age; and the constant reference to the use of bronze in weapons. Now comes the crux of the matter for the Homeric scholar. In the *Iliad* and *Odyssey* as we possess them these Bronze Age techniques are mentioned side by side with later inventions — the smaller, round shield which replaced the large body-shield; the single thrusting spear, which replaced the old double throwing spear; the new military formation of the phalanx, where soldiers fought not as individuals but as members of a tight-packed unit. The poems, then, contain archaeological strata just like those of an excavation. We have descriptions of things which died out with the Bronze Age; we have others of things which superseded them; and these are all together, in the poem, without any evident sense of incongruity. Scholars seized eagerly upon these differences. Does this not prove, they

said, that the poems we now have are really collections of various
pieces composed over a long period and tacked together without
any regard for discrepancies ? Thus was the picture of composite
authorship fortified — a picture that has been well summed up
by Hilaire Belloc in his talk of 'those admirable poets, Homer'.

There are cycles in scholarship as in all things else, and after
this wave of higher criticism came the reaction. The scholars of
our own day look with more kindly eye on the unity of Homer.
Wolf's argument, that the poems in their present form could not
have existed without writing, no longer seems so strong as it did
when first formulated. The retaining power of human memory
is stronger than is generally believed; it is particularly strong
when there is no other means by which valuable material can be
preserved. There are proven modern instances of people learning
enormous quantities of verse by heart. Sir Maurice Bowra, in his
study of Homeric composition, refers to a forge-worker in Bir-
mingham, England, who knows the whole of Byron's poetical
works by heart; also to a Croatian bard at the end of the last
century who sang a total of 80,000 ten-syllabled lines, approximately double the number of words in the *Iliad* and *Odyssey* combined. If this can be done today, how much more possible
would it have been in antiquity! When there are no books, or
few books — and there was never any wide circulation of them,
even in classical times — learning by heart was the only way, if
there was something that the society or the individual wished to
preserve. We know that Xenophon, the fourth-century writer
and historian, had contemporaries who knew the whole of the
Iliad and *Odyssey* by heart; he refers to them in his *Symposium*.
We know that there were professional reciters, literary descendants of the Homeridae, whose business it was to learn and recite
Homer. One of them, Ion, appears in the dialogue by Plato to
which he gives his name, and inspires Socrates to discourse on
aesthetics. In a bookless society transmission must be oral, and
without the aid of writing a trained memory is essential. The
memories of the Greeks would have been better trained than ours
by necessity and habituation. If we need to know something, we

need only go to a library to consult a work of reference; if the Greeks needed to know something, more often than not they could only consult their own memories. Works, even works of great length, could be committed to memory provided that they were in memorable form; and we shall find, when we come to consider the structure of the Homeric poems themselves, that they are in just such a form, with many built-in aids to memorization and oral appreciation.

For us, growing literacy and the power of the eye have made extensive memorization redundant, just as the invention of the adding machine is slowly but surely destroying our ability to do mental arithmetic. One of the most important results of the Homeric controversy has been this illumination of the almost totally oral orientation of Greek society — the power to absorb information through the ear rather than through the eye, and to retain it in the mind rather than on the printed page. This is important to our understanding of many aspects of Greek civilization — of the importance of debate in government, for instance, or of the Athenian drama, written to be heard rather than watched or read and so following different rules. In such a society poetry itself has a practical importance that it no longer has in ours. Verse, as any actor knows, is easier to remember than prose. This accounts for the use of poetry in record-keeping and the preservation of lists — elements vital in the formation of Homer's own poetry, as we shall see — and for subjects we do not generally consider to be poetic material nowadays. A few years ago, the Welsh National Eisteddfod asked for prize poems on the subject of atomic energy. The Greeks would have been immediately sympathetic to such a use of verse. Early scientists were accustomed to expound their theories in this way; Solon, the Athenian statesman, wrote a poem explaining and defending his policies. The Romans were to continue the tradition. Lucretius wrote *On the Nature of the Universe* in verse, and Virgil composed his *Georgics*, a poetic manual of farming.

Nor do the archaeological objections to Homeric unity seem as serious as when they were first formulated. When it was still

G

a new science, archaeology, with its insistence on the material object and the concrete fact, carried perhaps a disproportionate amount of weight in argument. When all is said and done, the problems caused in the poems by the juxtaposition of different historical periods can easily be resolved. It is now generally agreed that the poems are the work of one final, creative hand, and that there is no reason why we should not give the artist the name of Homer. It is equally agreed, however, that he drew on a large body of traditional stories, handed down in verse form from one generation of reciters to another, and some much older than the rest. When the *Iliad* and *Odyssey* were cast in their final shape, many of the discrepancies and anachronisms would have passed unnoticed. Others may have been noticed, but proved impossible to remedy. It has been suggested, for instance, that to update a Bronze Age poem to the Iron Age is difficult because of the metrics involved. *Chalkos*, 'bronze', fits easily into hexameters, but substitute *sideros*, 'iron', and you must rewrite the whole line, or more.

And, in the last analysis, the best witnesses to the unity of the poems are the poems themselves. They are no mere ragbags of disconnected tales and incidents, put together haphazardly around a linking story. On the contrary, they are artistically unified and consciously contrived, so structured that each incident is relevant to the central theme. The poet of the *Iliad* announces his theme in his first lines: it is the wrath of Achilles, and the sufferings that it brought on the Greeks. This wrath and its consequences are paramount throughout. We may see the *Iliad* as divided into three main sections, tracing the progress of this wrath. First Achilles quarrels with Agamemnon over a girl, part of the booty. His prize is taken away from him, he feels himself — with justice — hard done by, and he refuses to fight. This quarrel has serious repercussions. The Greeks, deprived of their finest warrior, fare badly in the war and are driven back on their own encampment. An appeal is made to Achilles. Agamemnon offers apologies and reparation, but is rejected. This marks a turning point, the beginning of the second stage of the poem.

Up to this point Achilles' anger has been justified. It is no longer so. He continues to nurse his pride after just amends have been offered, and suffers moral degeneration. Still the Greek army suffers. Achilles' friend, Patroclus, goes out in Achilles' armour and is killed. Thus Achilles is punished. The third section shows him humbled by disaster, coming to his senses and making up the quarrel. Returning to the fight he kills the Trojan hero Hector with great brutality, but makes amends by his treatment of old King Priam when the latter, in one of the most moving passages of the poem, comes to beg back his son's body for burial. The moral is clear, and it is the familiar one: nothing in excess, do not carry a quarrel too far or persist unnecessarily in anger. Many would agree that the *Odyssey* was written later than the *Iliad*, though not how much later. It may still be the work of the same man. Although it is clearly based on two original stories — the adventures of Odysseus himself, and those of his son Telemachus — these too are interwoven in such a way as to reveal a conscious artistic purpose. Even if the *Iliad* and *Odyssey* are not from the same hand, they belong to the same tradition of reshaping old material, and employ the same techniques and devices.

It has already been remarked that both the *Iliad* and *Odyssey* contain evidence of a long tradition of pre-Homeric poetry. It is time now to consider what that evidence is, what it tells about the function of poetry in early times, and the hints it gives as to how the *Iliad* and *Odyssey* themselves were composed. What sorts of poem might Homer have found, and what sources were available to him when he came to assemble the old sagas and give them unified form ?

Firstly, there is a good deal of evidence for informal poetry, folk-song of several types. There are descriptions of marriage choruses, harvest songs and dirges — the latter exemplified by the deathsong of the Trojan women over Hector when his body is returned to Troy in the last book of the *Iliad*. All of these appear as popular, but by no means simple, verse-forms, handed down and elaborated upon for generations. The complex antiphonal dirge appears frequently in later Greek tragedy. Song has always been instinct with the Greek people. Michael Cacoyannis' film of Euripides' *Electra* memorably suggests this, when he realizes a tragic chorus in terms of folk-song. The chant begins with a handful of peasants and spreads along the ranks of workers in the fields until the whole hillside is vibrant with singing. It is this sort of musical spontaneity, in times of joy and sorrow alike, that we are discussing here.

There is equally strong evidence for more formal types of poetry, professionally composed and delivered. In the *Iliad*, when Achilles has quarrelled with Agamemnon and cut himself off from his fellow Greeks, he is represented as sitting sulking by his tent and amusing himself with the lyre; he sings of 'the glories of heroes'. This points to the existence of a pre-Homeric body of heroic poetry, songs of great men and valiant deeds, similar in content, and perhaps in form, to those which Homer himself composed. It is this sort of poetry that the professional reciters in the poems sing for their audiences. In Book One of the *Odyssey* the minstrel Phemius entertains the suitors who make merry in Odysseus' palace in the master's absence. Telemachus finds him singing of the Greeks' return from Troy, and the disasters that Athena made them suffer. Penelope suggests that, from his large repertoire, the bard might more tactfully select something which has a less personal application. Telemachus reproves her hypersensitivity, arguing that the bard is doing no more than his duty; it is always the latest song, he says, that audiences love the most. Later, in Book Eight of the *Odyssey*, Odysseus is receiving hospitality at the court of King Alcinous, and listening to the minstrel Demodocus. He too complains of the bard's choice of subject — Demodocus is singing, somewhat tactlessly, of the achievements and sufferings of the Greeks — and suggests that instead he sing of the making of the wooden horse. Demodocus does so, beginning his song with an invocation to the god — just as Homer's own *Iliad* begins with an invocation to the Muse — and unfolds the story of the fall of Troy in all its phases. Odysseus breaks down, and cannot listen to him without weeping.

From these accounts we can deduce a certain amount not only about the bard's status but also about the methods by which he worked. These bards are professionals, earning their living by their art. They do not simply recite their poems, but chant them to the lyre. This sense of the interplay of music and the spoken word is strong throughout Greek literature: rhythm is paramount, and the Greeks could hardly envisage poetry apart from music, any more than they could conceive of drama as apart from dance. The bards are admired, and hold a privileged position. In Alcinous' court Demodocus is led in by an equerry and seated in the centre of the company. Odysseus sends him as a compliment one of the finest cuts of meat. Although their status is respected, they rank below the chieftain; they may even on occasion be compelled, as Phemius is in Odysseus' palace, though as servants of the Muses they receive great honour and respect. As for their material, one characteristic is surely apparent — its topicality. Both Phemius and Demodocus sing of events that have happened comparatively recently. Thus we return to the principal function of verse in early society, to record and preserve. If an event is particularly memorable it has a song made about it, and those whose duty it is to remember the songs will hand them down to the next generation. In this way, the poem is the newspaper of early society, though a slow newspaper and one which takes a good while to circulate.

We may thus sum up Homer's poetic background as follows. There existed two main classes of poetry; simple traditional verses, sung at times of celebration or mourning, formed part of the common background of the people, and side by side with these there existed more organized poetry, recitations on set themes given by professional bards and singers who possessed a large stock of pieces and could select from them on request. We see the status of the bard in society as very like that of the minstrel or *scop* of the Middle Ages — a privileged performer who wandered from court to court with a topical repertoire to which he was constantly adding, and earning his keep by public recitations. Homer took these ballads and wove them together around his two great themes, but the Homeric poems still reveal many characteristics of the early recited lays. We may compare epic forms of other ages — the *Nibelungenlied* of Germany, the Icelandic sagas, the *Chanson de Roland* of France, the English *Beowulf* — all of which hark back to the function of poetry as a recording and preserving medium. What Homer did with his source material was what, in modern times, Wagner did with Teutonic mythology, welding a collection of disparate folk-tales into a connected saga expressive of the national character and purpose.

Once we accept this idea of poetic composition and the orally oriented society which produces it, we are able to suggest explanations of some of the features in the Homeric poems. These, it is evident, rely to a large extent on formulae and repeated expressions, devices which for one reason or other the poet found useful. It has been suggested that if we were to trace the use of such formulae back far enough, we should arrive at the courtly circumlocutions of royal documents and proclamations. Hypothetical reconstructions have been built up of the type of poetry that Mycenaean court society could have produced, and how its selected themes eventually produced the poetry of Homer. It must be emphasized, however, that such reconstructions remain hypothetical only. We can do little more than read our Homer and make inferences about what preceded him.

Certain striking characteristics present themselves. First, early poetry likes lists. We have already seen the importance of early poetry as an historical document. The kings, before whose thrones the poets sang, liked to hear their own city glorified, their family trees enumerated, and lists of allies and cities linked in a common cause. Poetic lists first formulated for record-keeping purposes — metrical versions, in fact, of the sort of material found in the Linear B tablets — assume an additional honorific value. The extent to which such poems were used as historical documents seems incredible to us now. When Schliemann attempted to use the *Iliad* in this way he was laughed at. In ancient times, however, mention in Homer was proof of a city's antiquity. Thus the poems could be used as evidence in terri-

torial disputes; thus, too, there was every temptation for inter-
polation if a particular city wished to add to its historical lustre.
The most important such list that we possess in the *Iliad* is long
enough to have earned itself a separate name, the so-called
Catalogue of Ships in Book Two. Some three hundred lines in
length, it enumerates the Greek cities represented at the mustering
of the fleet, with the commander and armaments of each. This
is clearly an early army record preserved over centuries, given
poetic form and used in its entirety in Homer. It also contains
one of the best attested interpolations in the poem. Even in
antiquity, widespread tradition asserted that Solon, the Athenian
lawgiver, had tampered with the text to support Athens' claim
on her rival, the island of Aegina. Verse 557 of the book tells
us that

> *Out of Salamis had Ajax brought twelve ships*

and the next line, said to be Solon's invention, continues

> *And placed them where the Athenian lines were drawn.*

Thus was Homer cited to prove the early dependency of Aegina
on Athens. An historical document has become a poem, and the
poem in turn is used as another historical document. The *Catalogue of Ships*, of course, is not merely a list thrust in without
reason, used because it remained in currency. Its historical origins
may be found in book-keeping, but its poetic purpose is to
contrast with the catalogue of Trojan allies found later in the
same book. The two together make an excellent formal opening
to the account of the hostilities, and display the magnitude of the
conflict.

Other such lists occur as genealogies. In Book Ten of the
Iliad Agamemnon instructs Menelaus to go through the camp:

> *But call out, wherever you go, and bid them waken,*
> *Naming each man by lineage and by his father's name,*
> *Giving each due honour.*[3]

In a country that knew no surnames the citing of the father's
name was essential, and when such pride was taken in tracing

ancestry back to the remote past, to mythical or even to divine figures, the listing of genealogies was a convenient form of honour. We may imagine how the touring bards sought favour and applause by enumerating the ancestors of the king their patron, and how these lists would have been handed down as a regular feature of this type of poetry. Examples of such gene-alogies in the *Iliad* are that of Agamemnon in Book Two, of Glaucus in Book Six, and of Aeneas' opponents in Book Twenty:

> *Then Aeneas slew two champions of the Danaans,*
> *The sons of Diocles, Crethon and Orsilochus.*
> *Their father's home was in Phere, a place*
> *Of standing ; he was rich in worldly goods, descended*
> *From the river Alpheios, whose wide waters flow*
> *Through Pylian country. He begat Orsilochus, to be*
> *Lord over many, and Orsilochus begat great-hearted*
> *Diocles, of whom twin boys were born,*
> *Crethon and Orsilochus, both knowledgeable fighters.*4

Elsewhere, the lists may take the form of tallies of men slain. Book Five has such a list of Hector's victims:

> *Now who was first to be slaughtered, and who last*
> *By Hector son of Priam and by brazen Ares ?*
> *Teuthras made in god's likeness, and Orestes*
> *Driver of horses ; Trechos, spearman from Aetolia ;*
> *Onomaus too, and Helenus the son of Oenops,*
> *And he of shining corselet, Oresbius, who lived*
> *In Hyle, careful of his property, and near*
> *Lake Cephisus.*5

This type also can be traced without difficulty to the patterns and conditions of pre-Homeric poetry. We would naturally expect that descendants of a hero would wish their ancestor commemo-rated by lists of the men he had killed or the cities he had con-quered. Are these lists history or fiction ? Do they ever repre-sent an actual historical event or process ? One school of thought argues that such lists of single combats are half-submerged memories of early wars and battles between whole peoples. Un-sophisticated people love to individualize, and it may well be

that a combat between two Homeric heroes represents some forgotten war of conquest. Whatever their historical foundation,
however, such lists have also their place in the poetic scheme. The
numbers of the dead increase the glory of the heroes, in fiction
as in fact, and thereby the stature of the work. Later Greek poets
borrowed Homer's technique. Aeschylus, in his *Persians*, represents the magnitude of the invading army in a list having the
authentic Homeric ring: the cumulative effect of these magnilo-
quent, exotic Persian names impresses us with the size and splendour of the host ranked against poor Greece.

From lists we may turn to repetitions. In both *Iliad* and
Odyssey the most obvious type of repetition is the use of stock
epithets. Athena is regularly 'owl-eyed', Hera 'ox-eyed' —
memories, perhaps, of primitive animal deities. Odysseus is
polymetis Odysseus, 'Odysseus of many wiles'. Dawn is 'rosy-
fingered', Achilles 'fleet of foot'. Sometimes the repetition has
so hardened into formula that its true meaning has been obscured
or forgotten. The common epithet of Hermes in Homer is
Argeiphontes, traditionally translated 'slayer of Argus' and referred
to the monstrous servant of Hera whom Hermes killed under
instruction from Zeus. This would seem to be one case, however,
where habitude has obscured etymology; it seems more likely
that the word means 'clear-voiced', and is used with reference to
Hermes' function as divine herald. In some cases, the epithet is
obscure because it appears in Homer but nowhere else, and we
have to guess at its meaning. This sort of repetition is characteristic not only of Homer but of most early epic. It is a problem
for translators, for such techniques are not part of our own poetic
tradition. Some translators preserve the repetitions, some omit
them, others try to find a different English word for each appearance of the epithet in Greek. Such measures as the last, however,
can only be taken at the risk of grave damage to the structure of
the work; they are not incidental ornaments but an integral part
of the oral-poetic tradition.

Not so frequent, but still obvious, are repetitions of whole
phrases, lines and even groups of lines: 'So they spoke such

words to each other'; 'Then he spoke, and all fell silent and still'; 'And then in answer spoke cunning Odysseus'; 'When rosy-fingered dawn had lit the sky.' Once again, this characteristic is shared with early epic from other cultures. In *Beowulf*, in the Old French *Chanson de Roland*, we find the same type of repetition as in the *Iliad*.

Why do they exist? We might suggest, first, that they spring from a tendency in both poet and audience to cling to the familiar and to delight in hearing the same words and phrases repeated. This is particularly true of the larger repetitions, those involving whole situations. In the *Odyssey*, for example, the episodes of Calypso and Circe follow a similar pattern. In both stories Odysseus is kept captive on an island by the charms of a woman, aided by magic. Homer, like Chaucer later on, does not hesitate to repeat his effects if they worked well the first time. This indeed is a general characteristic of Greek literature. Novelty is not sought after. Old tales may be told again, and what is worth hearing once is worth hearing twice, or any number of times. In the context of the long poem, of course, such repetitions of situation may have a more profound artistic purpose, but we must not minimize the basic delight of the story-teller in his art that first calls them into being.

We may also point to the special requirements of poetry memorized and recited, as distinct from poetry written to be read. Repetitions aid both the reciter and his audience — the former by providing a moment of relaxation, allowing the bard to utter the formula mechanically while thinking ahead to the section which is to follow, and the latter by pulling his attention back to the poem if his mind has wandered. In the course of a long recitation the tendency to relax the attention is inevitable. The repetitions strike the mind subliminally, recalling the hearer to the poem. Much of the recent work on Homer has been concerned with the process of formulaic composition, illuminating the ways in which formulae are employed and varied depending on their position and function in the poem and the line.

The *Iliad* and *Odyssey*, then, owe their genesis to man's desire
to record events in memorable verse, and their form to the exi-
gencies of an orally oriented society. The ancients believed in a
personal Homer and, with some reservations, there is no reason
why we should not. He is a Homer as summed up by Kipling in
a verse whose facetiousness conceals truth:

> *When 'Omer smote 'is bloomin' lyre,*
> *'E'd 'eard men sing by land an' sea ;*
> *An' what 'e thought 'e might require,*
> *'E went an' took — the same as me !* [6]

Old poems are worked into the context of the new, either by a
process of juxtaposing two stories, as in the *Odyssey*, or by that of
flashback and reminiscence used so frequently in the *Iliad*. The
stories that Nestor tells, for instance, must originally have been
separate short poems whose presence is justified here by putting
them into the mouth of a natural story-teller.

NOTES TO CHAPTER FIVE

1. Quoted in Aristotle, *Nico-
machean Ethics*, VI. 7. 1141.
2. *Batrachomyomachia*, 82.
3. Homer, *Iliad*, x. 67.
4. *Ibid.* v. 541.
5. *Ibid.* 703.
6. 'When 'Omer Smote.' (*Bar-
rack-Room Ballads* : Introduction.)

Chapter Six

The Homeric Characters and Their World

WE have already seen the importance of Homer in religion as collecting the diverse local traditions of gods and heroes and giving them both unified form and universal popularity. For this reason the Homeric poems are sometimes referred to as the Bible of the Greeks, a description that is fair enough providing we remember that, unlike the Bible, they impose no creed and lay down no rules. But Homer also bequeaths to his poetic successors a legacy of human characterizations. Even those figures who appear only briefly in the poems make their mark instantly and show themselves memorable. Thersites, the common soldier who rails at his overlords at the beginning of the *Iliad*, has only one appearance, but fixes himself in the mind as a representative of his class. The major characters are differentiated with sympathetic skill. Hector is not merely that bardic commonplace, the heroic warrior, but a man of feeling who is sensitive to the shame brought on his city by his brother's rape of Helen. Achilles is the hero who typifies the chivalric code of his time, placing his personal honour before all else. Ajax is the brute fighter whose virtue is his strength, sweating beneath his sevenfold shield. One of the most vivid descriptive passages in the *Iliad* occurs in Book Eleven, where Ajax, slowly retreating from the combat with his foes hanging about him, is compared to an ass driven out by boys and hounds, taking his time and going at his own pace.

The popularity of the poems would be sufficiently attested by the number of manuscripts we possess. But we hardly need these to make a point: Greek literature is full of Homer; quotations from him and allusions to him abound; later writers copy his style, borrow his characters, work over his subject matter, regard his writings as the background and foundation for their own. Xenophanes says that 'all have learned from Homer'. Aeschylus' tragedies were called 'slices of Homer's rich banquets'. Plato refers to Homer as 'one who has trained Greece'. The characters he depicts become refined or elaborated upon in later centuries, particularly in the drama. Odysseus in particular reappears constantly throughout ancient literature, recreated to respond to the demands of the period that uses him. In the *Iliad*, Odysseus is a warrior like his fellows, brave and resourceful. He distinguishes himself in combat against crowds of Trojans, he wrestles valiantly with Ajax. In addition to this, however, he possesses an ingenious mind that sets him apart from the others. His power of rhetoric is frequently noted. It is Odysseus who is entrusted with the delivery of Chryseis to her father; Odysseus who opens the debate on the possibility of returning to Greece; when the embassy goes to apologize to Achilles, Nestor gives them all instructions 'with many a glance at each, and most often to Odysseus, telling them how they should try to win Achilles over'. If any enterprise demands unusual mental agility, Odysseus is automatically chosen. He enters Troy on a spying expedition to steal the horses of the Thracian King Rhesus. On this occasion his companion is Diomedes, a man of like temper to himself. Diomedes is unfailingly resourceful: even when, in Book Six, he exchanges friendship-gifts with another warrior, Homer takes care to tell us that he makes over 900 per cent profit out of it.

In the *Odyssey*, though Odysseus retains his physical prowess, there is more emphasis on his mental accomplishments, and these are not always to his credit. Whenever he is in a predicament he can find some ruse to extricate himself, at whatever cost to others. So, in later literature, Odysseus becomes identified with the thinking man as distinct from the man of brute action, and the note of criticism becomes stronger. By the middle of the fifth century he has become the literary exemplar of the sophist, the man who is too clever, too resourceful, and recognizes no moral or social restraints on his own ingenuity; the man who can always lie his way out of a dilemma, and does not care who he offends in the process; the man who sees law and religion as human inventions answering a specific human need and thus able to be changed as the need changes. In Euripides' short play *The Cyclops*, based on the story in the *Odyssey*, we see Odysseus matched against the monstrous one-eyed giant, brain and sophistication against untutored muscle. In the play, although the Cyclops is a monster, the honours are not all with Odysseus; in the Cyclops there is more than a touch of the noble savage corrupted by his first contact with civilization; a comparison between Homer and Euripides is illuminating here. The Romans, who had a pronunciation problem with the name Odysseus, retitled him Ulixes, and made him the embodiment of knavery. In later classical tradition whatever nefarious deed is committed at Troy, whatever plot is hatched, Odysseus–Ulixes is lurking behind it.

Other Homeric characters develop in the same way. As Odysseus is distinguished by his cunning, Ajax is known by his strength. Later writers make him the prototype of the massive fighter, perfectly at home in combat but puzzled when any complicated demands are made on his powers of reasoning. Agamemnon, whose indecisiveness is already apparent in the *Iliad*, is seen in later literature as the prey of terrible dilemmas, or, in more caustic vein, as the ruler who cannot make up his mind. In many ways the ultimate repository of this developing literary tradition is Shakespeare's *Troilus and Cressida*, where we see the Homeric *dramatis personae* after the centuries have played with them. Ajax has become 'beef-witted Ajax', Odysseus is the scheming politician, Nestor, whose tendency to reminisce is already apparent in the *Iliad*, has become the insufferable bore.

What of the world in which these characters move ? In spite of the problems of dating the Homeric poems, and the fact that the poems themselves appear to draw on a range of periods for their material, certain clear features emerge which may be taken as representative of the Greek feudal age in general.

Geographically the Homeric world is a simple one. Greece appears to lie near the centre. The world itself is a flattened oval, around which flows the River Oceanus. Somewhere on the edge lie the Elysian Fields, where the shades of the glorious dead may roam. At the extreme East and West dwell the Aithiopians, 'favourites of the gods'. Homer knows the coast of Asia Minor and the Aegean Islands; he knows Phoenicia, the Nile and Egyptian Thebes. Outside this zone lie strange lands peopled with monsters. Some of Odysseus' travels may be plotted on a map; about parts of his voyage it is possible to hazard a conjecture; but for the most part the journey takes place in fairyland. Odysseus wanders to the land of the Cyclopes, the one-eyed giants; to the island of the Sun; to the island of Sirens and the land of Lotus-eaters; through the enchanted kingdoms of Calypso and Circe; and finally back to Ithaca. Sometimes an explanation suggests itself. The Straits of Messina, a natural seafaring hazard, have been put forward as the most probable explanation of Scylla and Charybdis. The monsters have been identified as octopuses or even seals. The one-eyed Cyclopes have been traced to prehistoric mammoth skulls: it is suggested that, finding these objects and unable to identify the large central hole where the trunk had been, primitive men postulated the existence of giants with a single, central eye. Here we see the simple man's view of the world around him. The farther away from home, the wilder the stories become. We shall find the same tendency later when we come to consider the work of the historian Herodotus, although geography and map-making were far more advanced in his day. The known world is a limited one, and beyond that lie marvels.

Turning to the social structure, we find that it is primarily aristocratic. The social tone is established early in the *Iliad*. In Book Two, the herald Eurybates assembles the Greek host for a debate:

> *And when he found a baron, a man of great note,*
> *He stepped beside him and addressed him with soft words. . . .*
> *But when he saw an ordinary man and found him shouting*
> *He drove him with his staff, speaking loud to him and angrily.*[1]

The only common soldier mentioned by name in the *Iliad* is Thersites, and his description is significant:

> *All the rest squatted in their places on the benches*
> *And only blabbermouth Thersites was still chattering* . . .
> *The ugliest man of all that came to Troy,*
> *Bandy, lame in one foot, round shoulders*
> *Hunched on his chest, and to top it off*
> *A head that was pointed, and a thin thatch.*[2]

It is in terms of the nobility, the great captains, that the action is worked out, and this bias is clearly dictated by the surroundings in which the original poems were given birth. The people in Homer are governed by kings, and it appears, in the description of Agamemnon's sceptre, that the monarchy was regarded as a time-honoured institution protected by Zeus and by divine law. In the *Iliad* each city is represented as having its own ruler. There is, of course, no tradition independent of Homer to help us reconstruct the picture of the monarchy at this period. We have to rely on the poems themselves, on a few myths, and on the scanty evidence of archaeology. Nilsson has attempted to fill out the picture by comparison with other early social systems, in particular that of the Viking peoples and of the early Teutonic monarchy, about which we know rather more. Here the kingship was hereditary within a certain family; the king was not necessarily succeeded by his eldest son but by that member of the family best suited for the position. This is a pattern that survives, in a roundabout way, in *Hamlet*, where the late king is succeeded not by his son but by his brother Claudius. It is nowhere suggested in the play that Claudius is a usurper; whatever troubles Hamlet, it is not that. Sometimes two brothers were made co-regents. The chief duty of the king was as war-leader. His power was comparatively small in peace, greater when the people went out to fight. The king was surrounded by a council of prominent men, and at his side was the army assembly, which possessed considerable rights. This is the oldest form of the popular assembly: the organization of the civilian state tends to pattern itself on the military structure, for it is military necessity that makes itself most strongly felt in early society.

This is the primitive Teutonic structure, and we find its main features duplicated in the *Iliad*. Agamemnon is king by hereditary right; he is the war-leader, and at his side are the council of elders and the army assembly. His power, within its clearly defined limits, is unshakeable. It is important to note that in Homer the king is not a lawgiver. What justice there is is administered by the assembly. For the closest approximation to a judge proper we must look, perhaps, to the description of the Shield of Achilles, in Book Eighteen. Here various scenes from everyday life are depicted, among them a trial by popular debate. Two men are disputing a case of homicide. The populace takes sides, cheering the contestants. The elders are present, there are heralds to keep order, and there is also what seems to be a wise man, or arbitrator-figure — someone, presumably, who knows the law, and gives his own influential opinion on the case. There is, however, no place for the king. There may be a parallel in Aeschylus' play, *The Eumenides*, where Orestes, after avenging his father's death by murdering his mother, is brought to trial before the council of Athenian elders. The goddess Athena herself acts as intermediary, to bring the case before the court. One may also notice, in the above description from the Shield of Achilles, the theatricalism which was to remain a part of Greek deliberative and forensic oratory — the sense of a speech as a performance, to be applauded on its own merits as well as on the merits of the case. We shall see many examples of the Greek susceptibility to emotional appeals, and of the way in which the orator is hardly distinguishable from the actor.

This trial by elders and popular acclaim must appear a very rough-and-ready method. It stands in marked contrast to the highly developed legal system of Crete which had gone before. There is a reminiscence of this in Book Eleven of the *Odyssey*. King Minos of Crete is portrayed as carrying a golden sceptre and seated on his throne, administering justice to the dead standing around him. We must also take into account the familiar myth

H

that Minos received his laws from Zeus himself, and the tradition that the Spartan legal system was modelled on the Cretan. But this is to wander from the matter in hand; at this point the administration of justice seems to have regressed, and to have become a matter for popular debate rather than for the individual lawgiver.

In matters of war, however, the king is all-powerful. The symbol of Agamemnon's power is his sceptre, and with this in his hand he appears before the army assembly. Nestor warns Achilles not to quarrel with the man who bears the sceptre, for the man to whom Zeus has given this glory is above all others. We may trace the development of this conception of monarchy into later Greek history. The Spartan kingship was very similar, except that there were two kings, not one, representing two original divisions or families. They were powerful in war but exercised only slight influence in peace, and their power was to some extent limited by the council of elders.

The Homeric monarchy is powerful but not the unlimited despotism of the contemporary East. The Homeric king is not a Pharaoh. In Homer the king consults the elders, and the army assembly, even in time of war. The Greeks considered the Oriental attitude despicable. In Aeschylus' *Agamemnon*, the king, returning from war and greeted, as he thinks, over-effusively by his wife, is made to say:

> My meed of praise
> Should come from other lips to honour me.
> As for the rest, do not pamper me
> Like a woman, or prostrate yourself before me
> As though I were some eastern potentate,
> Or bring down heaven's anger in my way
> With these rich tapestries.   It is the gods
> Whom we should honour with such ceremonies.[3]

The king in Homer consults the army assembly even in time of war — thus the various debates that are held in the *Iliad* — but he can override it. The assembly had considerable freedom of speech, but the king was not constitutionally bound to accept their decisions. This comes out strongly in the first book of the *Iliad*. Chryses comes before the assembly to ask, humbly and submissively, for his daughter to be returned to him. All the Greeks approve except Agamemnon, and his will triumphs: 'he roughly sent him away, and laid stern charge upon him.' The king, then, is not responsible.

But was there one king or many? The immediate impression from reading the *Iliad* is that Agamemnon is the only king, and that he is surrounded by his vassals, each commanding his own troops. But these vassals are sometimes called kings, and so, in the *Odyssey*, are all members of the nobility. Thus we may see Agamemnon as 'king of kings', though this title is in fact nowhere used of him. His power is pre-eminent, and he has the right and the means to call lesser rulers to follow him. It has already been pointed out that some of them, including the most famous, did this unwillingly. In the last book of the *Odyssey* there is a scene where the ghost of Agamemnon talks to the ghost of Amphimedon, Menelaus' son, in the underworld. Agamemnon recalls the visit to Ithaca to persuade Odysseus to join the expedition. This and similar stories indicate some sort of obligation on the smaller rulers to follow Mycenae's lead, and leave an impression of an era when the king who ruled that city commanded all the rest.

So much for the constitution. As war played so large a part in the lives of these people, it is fitting to enquire into the art of warfare as described by Homer. At first reading it seems a complicated and unsystematic business. There is no unified assault, no coherent plan of campaign. The Greeks base themselves on shore beside their ships, while the Trojans barricade themselves in their city; the ten years' campaign is confined to petty skirmishing and single combat between the champions of the opposing sides. The leading warriors appear to decide for themselves whether they will fight or not: the whole Greek position is jeopardized by Achilles' refusal to fight, and no one is able to do anything about it.

It is important to realize, however, that the whole age — or at

least Homer's conception of it — is dominated by a code of
chivalry, a pattern of what must and what must not be done,
resembling the knightly code of the Middle Ages. This is the
heroic age, and underlying the action of the *Iliad* is a conception
of knightly honour which lays down very strict rules, though
it is, fortunately, less complicated than the laws of mediaeval
chivalry. Its basis is personal honour. In Book One of the
Iliad, Achilles cannot bear to be insulted by Agamemnon, even
though the latter is his overlord. His personal reputation is of
more account than his loyalty to his colleagues. Here we move
again in the heroic world of *Beowulf* and the *Song of Roland*.
Roland will die rather than blow his horn and summon the needed
assistance. He prefers honourable death to safety, even safety in
victory.

The rape of Helen also becomes an issue of personal pride. It
is a slight to Menelaus, who cannot let her go without a struggle;
it is a challenge to Paris, who, once he has taken her, cannot
submit to her restoration without surrendering his personal
honour, even though his people beg him to. We have already
seen how this conception of personal honour is transferred to the
Homeric picture of the gods, and how it manifests itself in the
earlier stories of the Olympic deities. They are not concerned so
much with moral issues as with personal affronts, and will avenge
such slights with remarkable ferocity. When some mortal has
the arrogance to make love to his wife, the wrath of Zeus knows
no bounds; and as it is with Zeus and Hera, so it is with Menelaus
and Helen, and, in appropriate degrees, with the other Greeks and
Trojans. In Book Four of the *Iliad* Agamemnon goes on a tour
of inspection along the Greek front, and sees Odysseus and his
men hanging back. As their supreme commander he reproves
them angrily, but Odysseus replies with anger on his own part.
'Wait and see,' he cries; 'Now you are talking nonsense.' Agamemnon has to take his words back, and the warrior Sthenelus,
who is subsequently reproved in the same way, replies similarly.
Even the great king must respect his subordinate's honour.

This code, however, never becomes the empty poetic concept

of the mediaeval ballads. In Homer the hero's courage is tempered by a real fear of death. This is the true tragedy: respect paid to the dead body is of the utmost importance, another way in which the code of personal honour operates. The dead may bring all manner of suffering on their survivors if the expected offerings are not made to them, and the proper ceremonies not performed. It is a lonely code, however, and one which admits of few social responsibilities. Later writers were to examine the social conduct of his heroes, as they examined his gods, critically, and to compare the outworn chivalric ideal with more complex notions of responsibility and behaviour.

The social life of the Homeric people reveals a pleasing freshness and simplicity. Although the leaders are referred to as kings, one must not look for luxury and palatial splendour. Some of the rulers are rich — notably Menelaus — but most live on the same terms as their retainers, in much the same sort of house and engaged in the same activities. It is in war that the distinctions assert themselves; peace has a levelling effect. The Homeric house is a simple building with a central wooden column. Although it is the centre of entertainment, of singing and dancing, it has a plain floor of trodden earth. Palaces would be larger complexes of this basic structure. Odysseus' palace in the *Odyssey* is a good example. A single wall surrounds the whole: communication with the outside world is through the main gate only. Inside there are a number of adjacent buildings — accommodation for a king and queen and for a married son, since Odysseus built himself a house around the olive tree in the courtyard, and for his unmarried son, for Telemachus does not use his father's house. There must be room for Eurykleia and the fifty maidservants. The palace must have had an adequate number of store-rooms for oil, corn and wine, and at least in part an upper storey, since Penelope's bedroom is described as being upstairs.

This is the pattern of the Homeric palace, which we may discern from the *Odyssey* and take as fairly typical — nothing grand, but a complex of accommodations for several generations of the same family within a common enclosure.   There is clearly some correspondence between the palace of Odysseus and the Late Mycenaean palace brought to light by excavations at Tiryns.   Here the various rooms lead off a central great hall, the *megaron*.   It has a central hearth — used for religious rather than for culinary purposes, as has been made simply clear by the archaeological discoveries.   This *megaron* would have served as the council hall and the meeting place for the whole district when the need arose.

The Homeric palace is isolated.   Nestor's palace is built some distance from the sea, on an eminence rising above the plain.   This too reveals the aristocratic pattern of society.   Just as the people can be summoned to the great hall in time of urgency, so the palace can be defended from the people should they riot or rebel.   Within these houses we see a domestic life based firmly on the father's position as head of the family.   Children are subject to their parents and care for them dutifully in old age, just as Odysseus cares for his old father Laertes and sees that he continues to have honour and a roof over his head.   In these times children were important, not for sentimental but for very practical reasons.   If you had no children to look after you when you grew old and were unable to care for yourself, you were likely to starve.   The father–son relationship, like that between the king and his subject and the god and his worshipper, is based on mutual dependency.

The status of women in this society is high, certainly higher than in later Greece.   There is no trace of the orientalizing attitude which was to characterize later Athenian society, with the woman kept in strict seclusion.   She moves easily among men without interfering in men's affairs.   She concerns herself with the household; she directs her servants, spins, weaves and embroiders; she takes a prominent part in entertaining guests.   Princess Nausicaa is not above washing the linen with her household servants, and this shows how narrow the distinction between aristocrat and subject can be.   The aristocrat is set apart by birth and is expected to follow a certain code of behaviour, but his material existence differs little from that of his followers.   The woman is respected by the men, treated with honour and courtesy. This too is part of the heroic tradition. This is the age of the individual; it is the man who is important rather than the state. The submersion of the individual in the larger social complex is yet to come.

Another characteristic of this sort of society has already been noted — the code of hospitality. In the *Odyssey* it is Zeus who is the ultimate protector of the guest. We see travellers regally entertained, as Odysseus is in the palace of Alcinous and Telemachus in the palace of Menelaus. Even beggars are not turned away. Odysseus goes back to his own palace disguised as one, and the suitors' conduct towards him — one of them hits him with a footstool — is regarded as shameful in the eyes of right-thinking men. Another beggar, Irus, is already in residence, and the suitors arrange a boxing match between them. The mistress of the house is well disposed towards him, however, not merely because he brings news of her husband's return but because he is a stranger and a guest and so must be looked after. In fact this episode well illustrates the values and obligations of the code of hospitality: as in so many aspects of Homeric life, social observance leans on practical utility.

Physical prowess is important, and the art of survival. A man is measured by his strength and by his fighting qualities: note the importance of the archery contest in the *Odyssey*, when the suitors compete to see who can bend the great bow, and of the funeral games in the *Iliad*. It is a simple age, where you must fight for what you want, fight again to retain what you already have, and stand up for yourself, for there will be no one to do it for you.

NOTES TO CHAPTER SIX

1. Homer, *Iliad*, II. 188.   3. Aeschylus, *Agamemnon*, 916.
2. *Ibid.* 211.

Chapter Seven

State and Individual

WE have seen how both topography and temperament favoured the development of Greece as a collection of more or less isolated settlements, each growing up without reference to its neighbours and evolving its own way of life. In the fourth century, when Aristotle came to write his *Politics*, he had his pupils assemble constitutions for his study: there were one hundred and fifty-eight of them. As they evolved out of Mycenaean domination, states developed in different directions. Some, like Athens, took the long road to democracy — though even Athens, at the apogee of her power, did not regard her own constitution as ideal for everyone, and refrained from imposing democracy on states that she governed. Some, like Sparta, remained monarchical. Some chose oligarchy, government by a limited and privileged class. Some, like the great Sicilian city of Syracuse, saw long periods of tyranny. It is important to realize that the Greek word *tyrannos*, 'tyrant', does not necessarily have its modern pejorative associations. A tyrant in Greek political history is one who comes to sole power by other than legitimate means. Whether he is a good or bad ruler is irrelevant to the title. In Athens particularly, the period of the tyrants was a fruitful one: far from subverting the constitution, a tyrant could uphold and improve upon it.

Of all these cities and all these forms of government Athens and Sparta deserve special consideration, not only because they are important in their own right, but because the tension between them dictates a major part of Greek history. It is perhaps more convenient to consider Sparta first, for it represents an earlier stage of constitutional development. Certain states — Macedon was another — preserved archaic features in their constitutions and their way of life long after they had been abandoned elsewhere. Sparta is not typical of the Greek forms of political organization in their full development: it is a political fossil, a striking example of the way in which a constitution could be frozen in time, preserving features which had long since died out elsewhere. This was possible in a country like Greece, where strict segregation could be obtained without difficulty and, because of the geographical situation, outside influences could be rigidly controlled. Sparta, although atypical, has many features of considerable interest, and is an excellent illustration of the way in which an archaic constitution can be maintained, for a particular purpose, against all the laws of political development.

In its earliest history Sparta seems to have developed more or less like any other Greek city. It cultivated the arts and crafts. It had its poets, both local and visiting. Alcman, Terpander and Tyrtaeus wrote there, and made a rich contribution to the Greek lyric tradition. There was a fine local tradition of metalworking. At some point, this peaceful and culture-loving development was replaced by a new and stricter order by which Sparta was ever after to be characterized. The change is traditionally associated with Lycurgus, member of one of the ruling houses. The story runs as follows. Lycurgus was the son of the King of Sparta, Eunomus — a significant name, as we shall see. Eunomus, on his death, left the throne to Lycurgus' brother Polydectes. Polydectes in turn died, leaving his queen with child. The ambitious widow proposed to Lycurgus that she should kill her child and share the throne with him. Lycurgus pretended to agree, but when the boy was born cheated the mother's hopes by openly proclaiming him king and, as next of kin, acted as his guardian. To avoid suspicion of furthering his own ends he left Sparta, and is said to have visited Crete, the Greek colonies in Asia Minor and Egypt, even penetrating as far as India. When he returned he found Sparta in a state of disorder and thereupon remodelled the whole constitution, obtaining approval for his new laws from the oracle of Apollo at Delphi. He made his people swear an oath to keep the laws unaltered until his return, and then, in order that his constitution might endure unchanged for ever, left Sparta in voluntary exile. This seems to have been a popular trick among ancient lawgivers. Where he died is not related. Spartan tradition venerated King Lycurgus as the man who had laid down the severe constitution for which it was to be known throughout antiquity.

Such is the tradition. How much of it is true is one of the abiding problems of ancient history. Was there a real Lycurgus, or was he a myth ? We have already noted the ancient tendency to personalize history and to derive customs and institutions from individual lawgivers or wise men. It has been argued that Lycurgus the traditional lawgiver of Sparta is one more instance of the same phenomenon. There are indeed many suspicious features about him. First, he is described as the son of Eunomus, which name, compounded of two Greek words, means 'good law'. This hints that Lycurgus may not have been a man at all, but a mythic or allegorical figure — 'Lycurgus, the son of legality' — his traditional parentage expressing his function. Secondly, Lycurgus may have been a god. There was a cult of Lycurgus in later Sparta, and his name was worshipped : this may hark back to a first stage in which he was actually a deity, later becoming humanized and regarded as a historical figure. There are several gods, demigods or heroes named Lycurgus in other traditions, and the Greek root of his name, *luk-*, suggests a relationship with Zeus Lukaios, a local wolf-god. Again, he was traditionally represented as one-eyed, and this may mean that he is to be identified with the sun-god (the root *luk-* can mean either 'wolf', as in Greek *lukos* and the cognate Latin *lupus*, or 'light', as in Greek *lukabas*, 'the sun's course', or Latin *lux*, 'light'). The dispute about the derivation of the name is reminiscent of that over the name Apollo. Plutarch, who lived in the early Roman Empire and wrote many biographies of famous men of antiquity, begins his life of Lycurgus as follows :

There is so much uncertainty in the accounts which historians have left us of Lycurgus the lawgiver of Sparta that scarcely anything is asserted by one of them which is not contradicted or questioned by the rest. They hold quite different opinions as to the family that produced him, his travels and the manner of his death, but most of all in connection with his legislation and the constitution he created.[1]

In the face of this ancient confusion, modern perplexity is pardonable. The date of the reforms in particular is disputed. Ancient tradition argued for as early as the first half of the ninth century B.C., while modern opinion varies between that date and one far later, about 600. It is safer, perhaps, to allow Lycurgus — man, myth or god — to sink back into the mists of oblivion and concentrate on certain striking and indisputable features. First, there is no doubt that reforms were made, whoever made them. Second, it is a significant tradition that makes Lycurgus visit Crete. Here is a link, however faint, between the Cretan code, of acknowledged excellence, and the constitution of Sparta: so did the influence of Crete, even at this late date, perpetuate itself. The Spartan tradition offers one more example of the importance of this small island to the Greek world.

What were the reforms themselves? Perhaps it is too much to call them reforms. Rather, they seem to have been a codifying of the existing position, a precise defining of the relationship between the city of Sparta and her subject peoples. For this small state was in a position of perpetual danger. The citizens themselves were few in number — a group of families numbering not more than 25,000 persons — and they had to control a subject population, acquired in various local wars of conquest, nearly twenty times this size. The pure Spartans, the dominant class, were known as Spartiates; the subject peoples were divided into two groups — the provincials, who retained their personal freedom but were politically subordinate to the Spartiates and owed them allegiance, and, most important, the large slave population, the Helots. These were neighbouring tribes who had been conquered in earlier wars, and it was a constant problem to know how to hold them down. These Helots were state slaves. They were small farmers, each working an allotted portion of land, but they had to pay dues on this to their overlords. So, with a small ruling class and a large subject population, there was constant danger of revolt — revolt which did actually break out, and at one point put Sparta in the humiliating position of requesting aid from Athens. The purpose of the Lycurgan reforms — there seems no reason why the traditional name should not continue to be used — was to stabilize the organization of the ruling class in order to provide an added measure of security, and to establish precisely the relationship between Spartiates and Helots.

It has already been mentioned in connection with the Homeric monarchy that the Spartan constitution preserved several features of this. In the earlier system there were three main elements, the king, mainly a warleader, the council of elders, and the army assembly. These three divisions of authority are preserved in Sparta. There are some differences: in Sparta there is not one king but two, ruling conjointly — an awkward arrangement on occasion — and still, as in Homer, acting as generals in time of war. Then there was the council of elders, the *gerousia* — men over sixty, who with the two kings made a body of thirty in all. Real power, however, lay in the popular assembly, consisting of all adult Spartiates who possessed full civic rights and served in the army. This popular assembly answers to the army assembly in Homer, and the balance of power has shifted slightly from Homeric times. The assembly appointed an annual group of *ephors*, overseers, to ensure that their decisions were carried out. The popular assembly also elected the council of elders. Thus the Spartan constitution combined a hereditary double monarchy with a tightly knit assembly, providing an elaborate system of checks and balances. No one element could become too powerful, unless the system were extended too far: it was in time of war that the inherent defect of the constitution revealed itself, for when armies were abroad and it was no longer possible for one element to keep a close watch on the others, deviation was only too possible.

The real interest, however, for the modern student lies not so much in Sparta's constitution as in her social structure. Lycurgus' reforms reveal themselves as the first real attempt in history to introduce a system of state socialism. Under this new system the individual was entirely subordinate to the state. He had no property, no aims, no interests of his own; his whole life, from the earliest years onwards, was devoted to public service. Let us look for a moment at the career of a typical male Spartiate. The state is interested in him, and exercises its rights over him, from the moment of his birth. He is examined to see if he is fit. If so, he is kindly allowed to survive. If the baby is deformed in any way, or shows any sign of weakness, anything that hints he will not grow up to be a strong fighting man, he is calmly and without sentiment exposed on the neighbouring mountainside to die. Only the fit were wanted. An invalid or cripple was a burden on the state, and Sparta was too small to be able to carry passengers or rear those who could do the state no service in return. At the age of seven, the boy was removed from his family and entered one of the bands of boys who formed a state cadet corps. Here he began his military training, which was a strict one. The boy lived on plain food without any luxury or extravagance. He gathered reeds for his own bed from the banks of the river. His education consisted of marching and gymnastics, as one might expect; reading; and something which may sound surprising as the product of such an environment, music. This, however, was hardly a course in aesthetic appreciation. Music was an integral part of Greek life, providing a rhythmical basis for all sorts of activity. Even if we had nothing but Plato's later strictures on the musical art, it would be easy to see how the Greeks regarded music as vitally affecting human temperament and behaviour. We may therefore see the Spartan musical exercises as merely another kind of drill.

These boys lived a hard and testing life. They were given challenges and initiative tests to encourage cunning and self-reliance; they were engaged in constant competitions. Boys were urged to go out and steal food for themselves. If discovered they were severely punished — not for stealing, but for being found out. One of the most familiar Spartan stories is that of the boy and the fox — of how a boy, sent out to plunder, caught a fox and hid it beneath his tunic. He was stopped by one of his masters and stood there, with the fox gnawing on his body, all the while keeping a straight face and answering his master's questions. He died, but he had passed the test of endurance. There is something most primitive about these stories: they remind us of the endurance tests imposed by American Indian tribes on their young men; but the boy who passed the course successfully was destined to become the most efficient fighting machine the Greek world was to know for a long time. One of the most brutal rituals was the annual flogging of the boys at the altar of Artemis, whose shrine stood in Sparta, to see who could endure most strokes of the whip.

At the age of twenty the young man was enlisted in the regular army, and was now allowed to marry. The marriage ceremony, like the constitution, retained certain archaic elements: the groom had to pretend to carry off his bride by force, a relic from more primitive times when he actually did so. For some time he was kept separate from his wife and was allowed to see her only by stealth, a further test of his cunning and initiative; if he were caught visiting her he would be punished. The soldier joined a mess of fifteen members, with whom he trained and ate, taking his meals in the common hall. To these meals he was required to contribute a monthly share of barley, wine, cheese, figs and meat. It must be remembered that he had no property or income of his own: to give him the wherewithal to buy food, and to pay the subscription to his mess, he was allotted the income from one of the state farms worked by Helots. Thus he passed his life in training and in warfare, with the state supervising every movement and with no prospect of personal advancement beyond joining the council of elders when he reached the required age.

The woman's life was somewhat easier. Girls ran less risk of being left to die at birth — the physical requirements for women were not so high — but, from the age of seven onwards, they shared the same training as the boys. They too had to be hard and tough; they had to forgo even moderate comforts, and devote themselves to producing more warriors for the state. Sparta's aim was to turn its citizens into a super-efficient military machine, a permanent standing army in a state of constant military preparedness, able and ready to go out to fight at a minute's notice. Their whole training, their whole lives were devoted to this end. When we contrast this with the practice of other states, where armies were organized on more amateur lines and levied only for a particular purpose, we may see why Sparta was for so long the acknowledged military leader of Greece. Right up to the end of the Persian wars the other states looked to Sparta in time of crisis, and it was only when Athens revealed the importance of seapower as a dominating factor in the conflict that Spartan influence waned.

But this military superiority depended on an artificially constricted way of life. It could only be maintained because the Spartiates were free to devote every minute of their time to the state. They could afford to have no problems or interests of their own. The Spartan army could not have existed had it not been for the Helots, the serf population, who took care of the more mundane affairs. Thus the existence of Sparta depended on its ability to hold the Helots down, and every possible device was used to ensure that rebellion did not occur again. The Helots were forced to wear dogskin caps and cloaks of sheepskin, as badges of slavery; they were called by derogatory names; they were given no chance to assert themselves, to come forward as individuals or to think of themselves as anything other than serfs. Among them moved the secret police, the *krypteia*, ready to report any suspicious action. This caution was not confined to the Helots; any undesirable individual was liable to deportation, or worse.

Sparta had to limit herself in other ways also. State interests, as well as individual interests, had to be confined. We see Sparta taking little or no interest in outside affairs, except when these were forced on her notice. She did not share in the great schemes of colonization which occupied every other major state. Sparta founded only one colony, the prosperous port of Taras — the Roman Tarentum and Italian Taranto — in southern Italy. There is an amusing tradition connected with this founding — about

700 B.C. — offered almost by way of excuse for so untypical an activity. When the Spartan army was away at war their wives bore illegitimate children to the Helots, and to rid themselves of this embarrassing surplus population the Spartiates sent them off to found Taras. The city grew rich and prosperous, and became the most important Greek colony in Italy, but it was the only one that Sparta ever founded. Sparta simply was not interested in founding an empire. It had enough to do to suppress the Helots at home, without adding other subjects to its responsibilities. It is true that at times an imperialist party does manifest itself in Sparta; some kings and generals revealed a desire to extend their conquests and win, and so rival, some of the more luxurious cities. This is hardly surprising when one reflects that Sparta can have been no pleasant place to live in. Soldiers preferred the excitement of campaigns to the colourless monotony of home training, and must often have been tempted by the easier life and more comfortable conditions they observed elsewhere. The 'cult of personality' was so repressed at home that it flared up frequently abroad, when generals were removed from domestic discipline.

Military diligence stole time from the softer pursuits. Early Sparta was on an equal cultural footing with the other Greek states: it had its art and its poets. With the new emphasis on fighting readiness there was little place for culture. Later Spartan history shows a gradual artistic decline. It has sometimes been suggested that the arts were deliberately outlawed by 'Lycurgus' among the other reforms, as effeminate and unbecoming to a warrior city. Such a belief is exaggerated, and there is no evidence for any formal ban. It is far more likely that they died out of their own accord, through lack of time and enthusiasm. One of the most important factors here was the economic. Sparta clung resolutely to the old iron coinage when other cities had changed to other metals. This is yet another example of how Sparta could deliberately stop history at a fixed point. After this, there would be little financial inducement for visiting poets and musicians to come to Sparta as they had done in the past; foreign poets seem to disappear from the Spartan scene about 625 B.C.

They could find more generous patrons elsewhere, in Athens and the rich kingdoms of Sicily. Local art declines also, largely, no doubt, through lack of time; foreign imports, and their stimulus, cease. Here again economics plays a large part. Sparta was not rich enough to compete with more prosperous rivals. Athens had begun to control the markets of the Mediterranean and attract trade to herself. Merchants and artists could find a ready market for their wares in Athens, and had need of Sparta no longer. A comparison of Menelaus' palace in the *Odyssey* with the bleakness of the historical period will show how great the change was. This is not to say that the arts ceased to flourish altogether. The temple of Artemis, begun at a comparatively late date, remains one of the finest examples of Greek architecture. On the whole, however, art and literature were no longer important. Fighting was all that mattered.

Whatever we may think of the Spartan organization, there is no doubt that the city accomplished what it set out to do. It produced a magnificent breed of soldiers who fought bravely and with brilliance on many occasions. The most conspicuously heroic were the small band who held back the Persians at the pass of Thermopylae, until they were surrounded by the enemy and slaughtered. There is a famous remark by a Spartan soldier on this occasion, when told that the enemy would shoot so many arrows they would darken the sun: 'So much the better, we shall fight in the shade.' There is the equally famous epitaph over the Spartan dead: 'Go tell the Spartans, you who now pass by, that here obedient to her laws we lie.' Sparta created a tradition and a legend. Besides creating dependable soldiers she produced brilliant generals — somewhat surprising, in a state which frowned on individuality. Her people were, for Greeks, taciturn, though if the speeches of the Spartan envoys reported in Thucydides are any indication, they could turn as elegant an oration as anyone when the need arose.

Sparta was the chief Greek state to hold out against Philip of Macedon, and subsequently Alexander; Sparta resolutely maintained her independence, refusing to co-operate in the new unified

I

Greece, refusing to join Alexander's eastern campaigns. Many of her institutions remained unchanged well into Roman times, thus making it easier for us to study them and make inferences about her earlier past. Like Japan in modern history, Sparta, by segregating herself, was able to preserve her way of life in isolation. Whether the result was worth the cost must be another question; there were many eminent Greek thinkers who believed that it was.

It is interesting to consider not how different Sparta was from the other Greek states — the differences are sufficiently obvious — but in how many of its fundamental beliefs it was similar. The subordination of individual to state, though carried further in Sparta than anywhere else, was simply an exaggeration of a familiar Greek attitude. It was generally believed that a man's life could find full expression only through community service. The Greek word for 'private citizen' — that is, one preoccupied with his personal affairs — was *idiotes*: the English derivative suggests the Greek attitude. Citizens were regarded as children of their city, a doctrine often reinforced by local myth. The foundation stories of Thebes told how the population was descended from warriors who sprang from the soil, after Cadmus had sown there the teeth of the dragon he had slain. Athens similarly derived her people from an earth-born king. For these reasons civil war was regarded as the worst of conflicts, one in which brother turned his hand against brother, and for most Greeks banishment was a punishment equal in severity to death.

In the matter of slave-owning also Sparta merely possessed, in a greater degree, a characteristic common to most Greek states. It is important to remember, when we praise the Athenian democracy, that Athens too was a slave-owning state, and it is interesting to speculate on how far that city would have been able to pursue her cultural ideals had she been able to rely only on citizen manpower. Slavery was one of the ancient world's great evils: a slave's lot may have been better in Athens than in Sparta, but he was still a slave.

Athens too had kings in the early period of its history. Proud though it was of the democracy that developed later, the city looked back on these earlier monarchs with considerable affection. King Aigeus of Athens bequeathed his name to the adjacent sea. His son, the far more famous Theseus, was elevated to the rank of national hero. There seems to be no doubt that Theseus was an historical personage, and that the legends have some small basis in fact. Thucydides admits that he existed, and certain important developments in Athenian history are attributed to him — the unification of the surrounding district of Attica, and the bringing of Eleusis, with its famous rites, under Athenian control. Even the legends can be sifted for their historical value. The famous Minotaur story, in which Theseus, sent to Crete among the annual tribute of prisoners, kills the monster and escapes, surely represents, if it represents anything at all, the overthrowing by Athens of Cretan domination: it represents, colourfully and effectively, that moment in history when the emergent power was strong enough to stand on its own feet and defy the edicts of long-powerful Cnossos.

Other Theseus stories reveal the extent to which mythology could be used for political propaganda. It is obvious that several of these tales were developed solely to raise Theseus to the level of heroes of other cities, particularly Heracles, hero of Argos. In many ways the stories of Theseus and Heracles run parallel, the one being a deliberate imitation of the other. For example, one of the labours imposed on Heracles was to visit the Underworld and kidnap the three-headed watchdog Cerberus. If Heracles had done this, it was important for Athenian prestige that Theseus should make a similar visit. He is therefore represented as engaging, rather unwillingly, in an attempt to kidnap Perse-phone, Queen of the Dead. His visit, however, does not end so successfully. In one version of the story he is trapped in a magical chair and has to be released by Heracles himself, who pulls him loose by brute force but leaves a portion of him still clinging to the chair. It has been suggested that in this triumph of Heracles and humiliation of Theseus we see Argive propaganda proving itself superior to Athenian, the comparative success of the stories being represented by that of the heroes in them. It may be remarked here, parenthetically, that there are several such cases of the deliberate doctoring of myth and legend to foster national pride, at a comparatively late date in history. Myth was taken as expressing fact, just as the Homeric poems were accepted as historical documents. Some scholars have suggested that in the sordid tales woven around particular cities — notably the saga of Oedipus and his family in Thebes — we may see propaganda designed to arouse feeling against a city before an act of aggression. Certainly when Athens and Sparta are preparing to embark on the Peloponnesian War they drag up charges from each other's mythic history and hurl them back and forth with total seriousness.

To return to Athens: the early history of the city reveals the same pattern that we have found in Homer and later in Sparta, namely the tripartite division between king, popular assembly and council of elders. In Athens, however, the authority of the king is soon weakened by the creation of other officials who assume some of his duties. The monarch is assisted by the *polemarch* (literally, 'war-leader'), by the *archon*, a civic magistrate, and later by six junior archons. The word for king, *basileus*, is retained only as an honorific title for one of the archons who has authority over religious functions. This is the last vestige of monarchical power in Athens.

The elders make up what is known as the Council of the Aeropagus. This name means 'the hill of Ares'; it is the rocky prominence lying hard by the Acropolis, traditionally seized by the Amazons, a tribe of warrior women, when they invaded Attica in Theseus' time, and given the name of their patron deity. Here too it is believed that Saint Paul preached when he visited Athens. That he did not actually preach on the hill has not affected the popular tradition: a plate inscribed with part of his address is set into the rock, and the hill is regarded as one of the great points of confluence of pagan and Christian thought. Aeschylus, in his *Eumenides*, seeks mythic sanction for this most venerable of Athenian institutions by linking its foundation with the *cause célèbre* of Orestes, tried in Athens for the murder of his mother. The play has Athena, the city's patron goddess, establishing the council and charging it to guard the city for the future:

> *Here Respect shall have its seat*
> *Among my citizens, and by her side*
> *Fear of Wrongdoing, own sister to Respect.*
> *Day and night shall they preside among us,*
> *Provided only that my citizens are willing*
> *To keep their laws pure, and admit no influence*
> *Defiling. . . .*
> *And this the council I establish here,*
> *Compassionate and incorruptible,*
> *Yet swift to anger, ever vigilant*
> *Though others sleep, to ward our land from harm.*[2]

Criminal cases were tried here, with plaintiff and defendant poised on opposing summits and the elders gravely listening. All traces of buildings and carving in the rock have been worn away now; the Areopagus remains the favourite place from which to watch the sun set over the Attic mountains. In antiquity, however, the Council of the Areopagus continued in importance even when its criminal functions passed to other and more democratic courts; it came to hold a position not unlike that of the House of Lords in the present British constitution, a body with considerable prestige charged with important consultative powers and enjoying a rooted popular affection. It drew on men of experience who, though old, still had an important contribution to make. Isocrates, theorizing on politics in the fourth century, was to urge, too late, that the only hope for Athens' salvation was a return to the stricter constitutions of the past and a restoration of the authority of the Areopagus.

The popular assembly in Athens was known as the *ekklesia*, which by gradual restriction of meaning has given us the English *ecclesiastic*. This body met on the Pnyx, a hill lying opposite the Acropolis. A modern highway now runs between them, but on the hill itself the outline of the old meeting place, and the speaker's platform carved out of the rock, may still be seen. Where the assembly once met and debated, spectators may now sit to see the Parthenon and its adjacent monuments illuminated.

The political development of Athens is somewhat easier to chart than that of Sparta. There is no Athenian equivalent of Lycurgus, and though many important matters are obscure, the gradual transition from limited monarchy to democracy is fairly clear. First, the aristocracy is transformed into a timocracy, where position is regulated by income rather than by the accident of birth. This is a necessary consequence of the growing responsibilities of Athens and the need for a larger army. Citizens were distinguished on the basis of how much equipment they could provide, and the voting lists tended to be modelled on the army lists. The upper classes, known as *hippeis*, knights, were those wealthy enough to equip themselves with horses and full armour; these made up the cavalry, always the privileged arm of the service and the one with greatest snob appeal, in time of war. Next came the heavy-armed infantry — those who could afford armour but no horse — and finally the other ranks, the *thetes*, who could muster no special equipment at all but picked up what improvised weapons they had and entered the fight as best they could. Political privileges were at first confined to the upper classes. The *thetes*, excluded from possibility of office, were politically and economically oppressed. Many of them were forced heavily into debt, and compelled to pledge their persons in lieu of money. Solon, who was made archon in 594, was given special powers to remedy these abuses and restore order to this economic chaos. He writes movingly in his own poems of the desperate state of his country, and the steps he took for its improvement:

> This I perceive, and there is pain within my heart
> To see this land, the oldest of Ionia,
> Near to death.[3]

He suggests a reconciliation between rich and poor:

> And you who have satiety of worldly goods
> Quiet the heart that beats so strong within you

And set a measure on your high desires ; so neither
Shall we want, nor you lack what you have won.[4]

The reforms were ambitious. There was cancellation of debts
whose payment would mean bondage, and the practice of pledg-
ing one's person was declared illegal. Solon's most important
measures were economic. He forbade the export of corn, thus
making speculative cultivation—and with it, the greed for land—
unprofitable. Olive oil became the staple of the Athenian economy. Athenian coinage was revised to bring it into line with
that of other states, as was the system of weights and measures.
The *thetes* were admitted to the citizen body. In another poem
Solon celebrates his own achievement:

When Time weighs judgement I shall have there as my witness
The mother of the gods Olympian, most mighty,
The dark Earth, great in virtue ; for in time past I removed
The boundstones that covered her, that stood deep-rooted,
And gave her liberty that was a slave before.
'Many I recovered to their fatherland, to Athens
Founded by gods, who had been sold into slavery —
By law, or otherwise ; men who had gone to exile
Under the press of debt, and who no longer spoke
Good Attic, so wide and random were their wanderings.[5]

A subsequent period of tyranny did not affect the basis of these
reforms; from the time of Solon to the fifth century, the progress
of democracy is gradual but unmistakable, and the creation of
new administrative and juridical bodies puts more power into
the hands of the people.

In considering the form and function of the fifth-century
democracy it is important to remember the size of the city.
Aristotle, writing in the fourth century, suggested that the ideal
size for a city-state is one in which all citizens may hear the voice
of the crier at the same time — in other words, one where the
entire citizen population may assemble simultaneously and confer.
A. W. Gomme has calculated the citizen population of Attica as
172,000 in 431 B.C., the year of the outbreak of the Peloponnesian
War, 116,000 in 425 and 90,000 in 400, soon after the war ended.

The total population (including women, slaves and other non-voters) is estimated as 310,000 for 431 and 217,000 for 425. These figures have been questioned, but may be taken as approximately correct. They are certainly instructive. First, they show a city extremely small by modern standards. We see a state with a population approximately as large as that of present-day Coventry in England, or Worcester, Massachusetts. The present-day population of Athens is over 627,000; Piraeus alone, one of the harbours of ancient Athens and the principal seaport of modern Greece, numbers 184,000 inhabitants. In the small cities of antiquity the loss of even a few citizens was a major disaster. This is illustrated by one incident in the Peloponnesian War. In 425 Athens captured the Spartan outpost at Pylos, on the west coast of Messenia in the Peloponnese. Prisoners were taken — a handful, by the standards of modern warfare — but the Spartans were anxious to get them back, for they formed a significant proportion of the entire state.

Gomme's figures also suggest how much damage war could do to states so small. It will be seen that the entire population of Attica was approximately halved in the years of the Peloponnesian War. An event like the plague which struck Athens at the war's outset could assume cataclysmic proportions. Even today, when one stands in the heart of the ancient city, it is possible to have a vivid impression of this smallness. If you stand before the Propylaia, the monumental entrance to the Acropolis, you may see in a glance the main centres of Athenian government. To the right, beneath the Acropolis, lies the Agora, the city's administrative and mercantile centre. Here stood the record offices, the buildings which housed the various committees and administrative personnel, and the lawcourts. Barely a stone's throw away is the Areopagus. Just across the modern highway lies the Pnyx, seat of the assembly, and all is framed by the city walls, whose location can still be traced and which lie within easy eyesight of the Acropolis. This was a city small enough for anyone of importance to be easily known, small enough for government to flourish easily by means of popular debate.

The Athenian democracy under Pericles was regarded as a well-nigh perfect example of this type of constitution. Even those writers who dislike the idea of democracy in general speak well of the Athenian in particular. Here an anonymous commentator on the Athenian constitution grudgingly admits its merits:

> As for the constitution of the Athenians, I do not approve of their having chosen a constitution of this kind, because by so choosing they have decided to give the advantage to mediocrity at the expense of excellence. Those are my grounds of disapproval. But given that they have decided as they have, I shall demonstrate how ably they fortify this constitution and handle the other matters in which their fellow-Greeks consider them to have gone astray.
>
> First I shall say this: here is one case where it seems just for the mediocre, the poor and the mass of the population to be given preference over the wealthy and the nobility. It is the masses who keep the ships moving and provide the state with its strength. Steersmen, bosuns, bosun's mates, lookouts, ship's carpenters — these provide the city with its strength, much more than the heavy infantry, the well-born and the morally superior. This being the case, it seems only just that everyone be admitted to office, by the process of lot which now operates and by other elections, and that any citizen may speak who wishes to do so.[6]

The author's oligarchic bias could hardly be greater, but even he realizes that for Athens democracy is the logical form of government. Her strength depended on her seapower, and the ships depended on the men who propelled them: thus it was on the voice and feelings of the common man, the humble oarsman, that the security of Athens ultimately rested. The fleet was the democracy: would-be revolutionaries were soon to realize that by tampering with the fleet's affections they could most easily hope to change the constitution.

Aristotle in his *Politics* gives a lengthy definition of the perfect democracy. Its end is liberty, and one principle of this liberty is for all to rule and be ruled in turn. Democratic justice is the application of numerical rather than proportionate equality. It follows that the majority must be supreme. Every citizen must be equal, and therefore in a democracy the poor must have more power than the rich, for there are more of them. Appointment to office should be by lot. There should be no property qualification, or if there is one it should be as small as possible. No one should hold the same office twice, except for military office, and tenure should be brief. In trials, the judges should be the whole citizen body or their representatives. The assembly should be supreme over all causes. Services to the state should be paid for.

Thus Aristotle. Modern historians agree that his ideal democracy is modelled on the Athenian constitution in its heyday. What strikes a present-day reader as most curious is the use of the lot to decide administrative and executive appointments. Originally the use of the lot had a religious basis: the influence of chance in human affairs was attributed to divine intervention, as Homer's poems bear witness. By the time of Pericles, however, such religious associations had either vanished or been pushed to the background. None the less, although it was not used for every office, the lot was accepted as a fundamental of democracy. It was not so regarded by everybody. Xenophon tells us that Socrates thought the lot wrong and foolish, and Plato, after him, urges that only those trained to do so should govern. However, the use of the lot kept the democracy fluid and prevented the formation of a powerful and entrenched bureaucracy.

Ultimate power resided in the *ekklesia*. This was open to every citizen who had completed his eighteenth year. Women, of course, were ineligible. There were forty regular meetings a year. Voter apathy was a disease of the Athenian as of later democracies. Aristophanes sketches this vividly in the opening of his comedy *The Acharnians*, where an old countryman sits alone on the Pnyx and waits for the assembly to convene. He complains that the citizens are full of their private business, and evading the responsibilities of government: nobody wants to talk about peace, the burning issue of the time. 'How I hate the city', he mourns, 'and how I long for my own countryside!' To insist on every piece of business, however small, receiving the attention of the full *ekklesia* would have wasted time and energy, particularly with the growth of public business consequent on the acquisition of empire. A council of five hundred, the *boule*, whose membership changed regularly, was responsible for initiating motions and bringing them to the assembly. Its members were paid. The *ekklesia* could make motions and depute their execution to the *boule* with the assistance of specialist commissions in charge of dockyards, sacred buildings and so forth. There is some doubt as to how far the *boule* was empowered to act independently of the *ekklesia*. It does seem at least that *boule* meetings could be held *in camera*, and that the *boule* could occasionally conduct private interviews of citizens. None the less, for the most part the *ekklesia* was master.

Ten generals were elected annually by the assembly. They formed what was undoubtedly the most powerful body in the state after the *ekklesia* and *boule*. Pericles was elected general fifteen times, and in the fifth century almost every distinguished citizen was at some time or other a member of the board of generals. They had close contact with the *boule* and may have been *ex officio* members. In any case they seem to have had authority to make proposals before it. Finances were handled by the *boule* in co-operation with the appropriate officials, who were in every case appointed by lot and subject to rigorous examination of their accounts. Athenian financial administration was complicated by the collection of tribute and by the fact that much of the state budget was administered by a special body controlling funds deposited in the Parthenon. When it draws on these funds Athens is in fact borrowing from itself. Justice was administered by popular courts, the *heliaea*, consisting of jurors over thirty who, like the members of the *boule*, were paid. This practice of payment for jury duty was later to be abused: once again, Aristophanes is our best witness of the peccadilloes of his fellow citizens.

We see, then, a type of government in which every citizen had a voice if he only cared to use it. Age or youth were no apparent impediment. Xenophon tells of one Glaucon, who was attempting to become an orator and strive for leadership in the state: he was not yet twenty years old. In such a constitution, where every important decision was a result of public debate, rhetorical ability was essential. In a modern democracy the voting body elects its representatives, but these, once elected, are empowered to act as their consciences or their parties dictate, without reference to the voters who put them into office. Decisions are made at the top and handed down. In Athens they were made at the bottom and handed up to the appropriate officials for action. The man who sought power would have to learn how to speak and how to sway the crowd.

Thus we return to the idea of a culture where all important communications are made orally. It is a largely illiterate society, where the ear is more active than the eye; it is a society that operates by public debate and hearings in committee, so that rhetorical skill is of primary importance. The Athenian citizen would spend a large part of his life in meetings and committees. He would be constantly exposed to oratory. He would be habituated to imbibing information through the ear to an extent that is hardly possible today; to following an involved argument while at the same time appreciating elegance of phrase and diction; to comparing one speaker with another and adjudging the finer points of their performances, just as we now compare the merits of actors.

Rhetoric had always been a Greek necessity. In the fifth century it blossomed forth into both an art and a science. Impetus was given by the arrival of Gorgias of Leontini, in Sicily, on a diplomatic mission to Athens in 427. Gorgias' style was unusual and exciting. It stirred a new interest in the fundamentals of rhetoric. Demand for an education in this discipline increased, and teachers were readily found: it was a popular subject and one well suited to its time, when emphasis was on the practical and on striving towards accessible goals. The sophists, itinerant professors who flourished in the latter part of the fifth century, made rhetoric their most important subject. They were, after all, men who made a living by catering to public demand. They taught what was necessary for worldly success — and what more important to public advancement than the art of speaking?

Thus rhetoric came to be moulded into an exact discipline,

systematic and codified. Rules were formulated regarding the right use of words, the length and balance of sentences, the modes of delivery. Students were taught how to hold their bodies, how to stand, how to speak, how to play on the emotions of their hearers. Little of the fifth-century oratory survives. We catch the authentic flavour of Pericles, perhaps, when he is quoted in Thucydides' narrative. When Aristophanes parodies Cleon we have a glimpse of the demagogue's clichés and mannerisms, his shameless exhibitionism and also his real and frightening power. Antiphon and Andocides have left speeches that we may peruse. The words, however, are only half the speech. The ancient Greek expected a public speech to be a performance in a way that we do not. This is perhaps the principal difference between ancient and modern oratory: we tend to prize naturalness of delivery, and to suspect a speech that has an air of being too well polished, too rehearsed. The Greeks expected a speaker to rehearse like an actor, polishing not only his words but his gestures — for these, too, were codified, with recognized bodily movements to communicate specific emotions. Connections between stage and rostrum are strong, There are records of several actors who trained politicians, and of actors who turned politician themselves, like Aeschines, Demosthenes' opponent in the fourth century, or who were entrusted with diplomatic missions because of their skill in handling language and in moving their audiences. This says much, incidentally, about both the techniques and the prestige of the actor in antiquity. Modern performers who involve themselves in political activity tend to be regarded with suspicion, if not downright scorn.

The assembly was not, of course, the only outlet for oratory. There were also the lawcourts, a vital function of the democracy. Here the orator had to influence not one single judge, but a large jury; once again, the performing element predominates. Clients who felt themselves inadequate would have their speeches written for them by professionals.

The fourth century saw the art at its height. Demosthenes' career illustrates the training necessary. Born in 384, he had some early successes in the lawcourts and was emboldened to come forward as a speaker in the assembly. He learned his art from actors, and some of the devices he used to cure speech faults have become famous: he spoke with a mouth full of pebbles to cure his stammer, repeated verses while running uphill to acquire breath control and declaimed on the seashore, it is said, to accustom himself to the noise of the assembly. He first made his reputation in 355 with a series of speeches against Philip of Macedon, urging action to stop his increasing encroachments. Attacked by the pro-Macedonian party he defended himself in another great speech, *On the Crown*, in 330. One Ctesiphon had proposed that Demosthenes be awarded a golden crown for his signal achievements. His enemies showed their feeling for Demosthenes by attacking Ctesiphon's proposal as illegal. Demosthenes defended him, but Ctesiphon himself is of minor importance: over his head Demosthenes and Aeshines argued their respective policies. Demosthenes won, but to his cost; his city resisted Philip and was defeated. His last years are a sad story of political victimization and suspected peculation. He was forced to leave Athens, only to return in triumph on the Greek rising after Alexander's death. Defeated again, he took poison and died, leaving sixty orations behind him.

The danger of Athenian democracy was that the power of the spoken word sometimes drove out reason. By the nature of this democracy power was vested in the mob, and this mob was fickle in its attachments. Already at the end of the fifth century writers were beginning to show contempt for the populace. The temperamental versatility of the Athenians was their greatest danger: the history of the later war years demonstrates this clearly, as segments of the populace are urged first one way, then the other, and any continuity of diplomatic activity is rendered impossible. We may consider here the case of Alcibiades, one of the most brilliant men that Athens had ever produced, estranged from his city and forced into fighting for Sparta by the crass stupidity of the electorate. Isocrates, writing in the fourth century, praises the concept of democracy but not the democracy as then practised in his own city. He hankers for stricter discipline and for some limited forms of government — the forms of earlier days. This is no mere conventional sighing for the good old days, but a sad recognition that a mighty potential has been dissipated. He contrasts present with former incumbents in office:

> They regarded their charge over the commonwealth as an opportunity for public service, not for private profit ; nor did they go around from their first day in office looking for any perquisites their predecessors might have passed over, but rather for any pressing business they might have left unconcluded.[7]

He writes of the duties of the young, in a famous passage often mistakenly attributed to his near-namesake Socrates:

> And so the younger generation did not waste time in gambling houses or with the flute girls, or in the kind of company they spend their time in nowadays. No, they stayed within the lines laid down for them, admiring those who did it best and trying to imitate them. So studiously did they avoid the agora that even at the times when they were forced to cross it they did so with every appearance of modesty and discretion. For them contradicting their seniors was more reprehensible than sinning against your parents is nowadays.[8]

Complaining that modern youth has gone to the dogs is a familiar enough sport, but the passage which follows has nothing commonplace about it. From the same speech, it is one of the noblest descriptions of the ideal democracy ever written.

> But what contributed most to good government was this. We acknowledge two concepts of equality, one treating all the same, and the other giving every man his due. They did not fail to recognize which of these was the more serviceable. That good and bad should be rewarded equally they rejected as unfair. That every man should be rewarded or punished according to his deserts they found far preferable ; and it was on this theory that they governed their city, not filling offices from the whole citizen body by lot but selecting the best and ablest for each undertaking. They expected that the rest of the population would take on the character of those who were given charge of their affairs.[9]

What is most sad about Isocrates' work is not the lost glory that he celebrates, but his own lack of perception. Writing thus of the *polis*, the city-state, he did not realize that the days of this type of organization were numbered. Alexander and his armies were soon to deprive the states of their autonomy and much of their individuality, and propagate a Greek culture which would be wider spread than any known before, but immeasurably weaker.

NOTES TO CHAPTER SEVEN

1. Plutarch, *Life of Lycurgus,* 1.
2. Aeschylus, *Eumenides,* 690.
3. Loeb Classical Library, *Elegy and Iambus,* vol. i : Solon, fr. 28a.
4. *Ibid.* fr. 28b.
5. *Ibid.* fr. 36. 3.
6. Anon. *Constitution of Athens* (attributed to Xenophon), 1.
7. Isocrates, *Areopagiticus,* 144. 25.
8. *Ibid.* 149. 48.
9. *Ibid.* 143. 21.

Chapter Eight

The Greek Theatre
and its Plays

ON half a dozen week-ends each summer, the narrow, winding roads to Epidauros, former shrine of the healing god Askelepios in the Argolid, are unusually full of traffic. Coaches crammed with excursionists come from Athens, Corinth, Nauplion; hundreds of private cars jostle for space with the heavy buses. Some have made the two-hour journey by boat from Athens. Many have come earlier to stay in the cliff-hanging hotels by Nauplion's harbour, or to camp under the trees at Epidaurus itself. Around five on a Sunday evening all these thousands converge on the ancient site to await the opening of the theatre for the current performance. They are continuing, on a world-wide scale — for the annual Epidauros Festival attracts visitors from every country — a type of celebration which originated in Greece, and in which Athens was the prime mover. In classical times every important Greek town had its own theatre and its own drama. Athenian plays outshone the others, and it is fitting, now that Epidauros is internationally famous for drama rather than medicine, that the National Theatre Company, which has its permanent home in Athens, should come down to play here. It is fitting, too, that Greek drama be given an important place in a book such as this, for it is through its drama, both by direct contact and by influence, that the ancient world speaks most immediately to the modern.

It has been noted earlier that the Greeks, like other Mediterranean peoples, were naturally inclined to dramatic expression, and that both private discourse and public celebration — particularly religious celebration — tended to take what we should now call dramatic form. In fact Greece seems to have created what we now call drama. Although earlier civilizations had evolved quasi-dramatic activities, Greece first welded these various manifestations into a distinctive form and gave this form a singular importance in public life. Exactly how the drama originated is now impossible to say. A number of theories have been put forward. It has been suggested, for example, that drama arose from the attested practice of reciting the Homeric poems at important festivals. These poems, which contain much exciting action and, more important, direct speech, can easily be dramatized. Modern experiments have shown that the *Iliad* can be put on the stage with surprisingly little adaptation. We know from Plato that the professional Homeric reciter was to all intents and purposes an actor.

Another suggestion evolves Greek drama out of tomb-ritual: when a great man died, his life was re-enacted in his honour, as an act of mourning. It has also been suggested that this is why Greek tragedy avoids the display of death. When a tragic hero dies he normally does so offstage, and the event is merely reported. Could this be a memory of the early tomb-celebrations, when the moment of the king's death would not be shown, being already too fresh in the minds of the spectators? Another theory, which has enjoyed considerable popularity among anthropologists and religious historians, is that both tragedy and comedy arose from fertility celebrations at the change of the seasons, and that the first dramas were mimic combats between the Old and the New Year, Winter and Spring. That such rituals existed can hardly be doubted. They can be shown to have produced, in other times and cultures, offshoots as diverse as the St. George Mummers' Play and the seaside Punch and Judy Show. Did they in fact produce Greek tragedy and comedy as well, and is Sophocles heir to the same tradition as Mr. Punch?

It is impossible to say that any of these conjectures is wrong, or solely right. The evolution of any drama form is a complex process, and many things contribute. All these manifestations may have helped, as may the conscious experiments of individual artists. We are told, for example, of a type of lyric tragedy attempted by Arion, a sixth-century poet whose reputation is now obscured by legend; we are told of Thespis, another sixth-century performer, who is reputed to have taken plays around the Attic countryside on carts.

The traditional explanation has much to recommend it. The Greeks themselves believed that drama arose out of choral song and dance in honour of the gods, and specifically from the songs, *dithyrambs*, composed in honour of Dionysus, who was to become identified with the theatre and take on a new area of influence as its patron deity. According to the Greeks, drama proper began when one of the performers stepped out of the chorus and impersonated a rôle, rather than confining himself to strict narration as before.

The Greeks identified this first actor with Thespis, and he seems to have been a genuine historical personage. Whether he did in fact take the vital step attributed to him is more doubtful. As we have seen, the Greeks loved to personalize their history, seeing the past in terms of great men taking single, decisive actions, and faced with the task of explaining so complex a phenomenon as the evolution of drama would have come instinctively to this sort of explanation. If Thespis had not already existed he would have been invented. None the less the tradition has plausibility. It accounts for the enormous importance of the chorus in the early stages of Greek drama — *ho choros*, the chorus, was virtually synonymous wtih the play — and also for the distinctive double rôle that the chorus plays. It is at once narrator and participant, half in the action and half out of it. It can be involved in the play in character, or step outside the action and address the audience directly, offering a moral, a comment, an explanation. This facility of direct address saves the dramatist a good deal of time.

It is also perhaps worthy of note that both Thespis, traditional founder of tragedy, and Susarion, supposed inventor of comedy, came from the same Attic deme, Ikaria. It is tempting to think — though with no proof whatever — that there may have been here some Greek Oberammergau, with a local dramatic tradition independent of the dithyrambic choruses, and that when the tyrant Peisistratus made the drama an official part of Athenian worship in 534 B.C., all that he did was graft this type of performance on to the existing choral repertory. Certainly the result was displeasing to some. One critic remarked that this type of entertainment was 'nothing to do with Dionysus'.

Once officially received, tragedy grew rapidly in popular favour. Comedy had to wait a while to achieve respectability. Tragic drama developed as an alternating pattern of acted scenes and sung choruses. While there was still only one actor, his function would necessarily have been limited. He could soliloquize, or converse with the chorus, and that was all. Subsequent playwrights explored and enlarged the potentialities of the actor-chorus combination. Phrynichus, for whom the first date we have is 511, is said to have added women's rôles — not, it must be pointed out, actresses; all women's parts were played by men. Aeschylus (525/4–456) is credited with the introduction of the second actor and Sophocles (c. 496–406) with that of the third; in this he was copied by Aeschylus in his later plays. The number of actors probably never rose above three in tragedy. Why, it is not easy to explain. Probably the competitive element was important. In Athens the plays were offered at festival time and competed for a prize. Limiting the number of actors would force the dramatists to show their skill under limitations. The economic factor must also have entered into this. In the fifth century actors were paid by the state, and there are hints that money for drama was not always freely available. General aesthetic considerations and the influence of tradition — always stronger in a theatre with limited output, like the Greek — must also have been important. In the fourth century, when the increasingly spectacular nature of the drama might have brought about an increase in the number of actors, the theatre had become a largely commercial proposition and no manager would be inclined to pay more actors than he had to. In any case, the dramatist was limited only to three *actors*, not three *characters*. Each actor could take several rôles in the same play, a versatility made easier by the nature of Greek stage costume.

As the number of actors increased the importance of the chorus automatically declined. Once two actors were available they could converse with each other without reference to the chorus. When the third appeared it became possible to write scenes of considerable complexity, and the chorus subsided even further into the background. While the chorus is a vital part of early drama, by the end of the fifth century it has become little more than a stage crowd, and its songs little more than mood music. This decline in importance is paralleled and assisted by a diminution in size. Here again economic pressure may have been applied. The size of the earliest tragic chorus seems to have been fifty, a popular number for large mythological groups — there are fifty Argonauts, fifty daughters of Danaus — and related to the size of the dithyrambic chorus. At some point (tradition says in 458, after the production of Aeschylus' *Eumenides*) the number was reduced, probably to fifteen. It remained this size until the fourth century, when commercial considerations brought about a further reduction.

Tragedy seems at first to have ranged wide in its search for material. Some of the earlier plays were little more than spectacular pageants. Others drew on recent events, like Phrynichus' controversial *Capture of Miletus* (493) which found its inspiration in the abortive revolt of the Ionian colonies. The first Greek tragedy we possess, Aeschylus' *The Persians* (472), is of this nature. It tells, as through Persian eyes, the story of their great defeat at Salamis eight years previously. Aeschylus' play, however, is far more than the topically provocative work that Phrynichus' seems to have been. He uses the story of the Persian disaster to preach a sermon on the folly of human ambition and the dangers of taking more than one's due. King Xerxes, a character in the play, displays the depths to which men may fall when they aim higher than they should.

For the most part, however, tragedy confined itself to a fairly small range of traditional stories. The range was not so small as it now appears to us, for we possess only a tiny fraction of the total Greek dramatic output. A more serious loss perhaps has been that the only plays to survive complete are Athenian compositions. In the drama as in so much else we are obliged *faute de mieux* to view Greek history with an Athenian bias. Homer provided a good deal of material; so did the other poems, now lost, dealing with later events in the Trojan War and the return of the Greek warriors to their homeland. Originality in material was not sought for. The same plots and stories reappear, but differ in the meaning that the author extracts from them. Once again the Greek dramatist is able to practise economy. He can usually take it for granted that the audience is familiar with the outlines of his story, and need not explain the background or the identity of his characters. He was, of course, free to manipulate details as he wished. Comparison of Sophocles' *Antigone, Oedipus the King* and *Oedipus at Colonus* and Euripides' *The Phoenician Women*, all plays based on the same set of incidents in the doomed house of Thebes, will show how wide the possible range of variation could be. Comparison between the Greek and the English religious drama is also instructive. The Greeks had no sacred book, no set text to which they had to perform. The anonymous playwrights of the Middle Ages were limited by the Bible. Thus the Greek plays can develop in any direction the dramatist wishes, and be adapted to express any set of values he thinks important. The mediaeval plays, concerned with giving dramatic immediacy to holy writ, can only develop up to a certain point and so must be, in the long run, sterile.

THE THEATRE AND ITS APPARATUS

The theatre at Epidauros lies like a great bowl hollowed out from the hillside. It is enormous, with an official capacity of 14,500 people; more can be pressed in as the need arises. Seats rise steeply in tiers. They are not numbered individually but divided into *kerkides*, wedges, and rows, more expensive at the bottom, cheaper further up. The uppermost seats are within the range of almost every pocket. The lower seats also have cushions, which the modern spectator finds very necessary. He is less hardy than his ancient counterpart and built to different proportions, and for him the theatre is not comfortable. The seats almost wholly surround a circular dancing floor, flat and paved. This is the *orchestra*, surprisingly small, about sixty feet in diameter. Behind this, where there are no seats, was once a stage and a wall with doors through which the actors entered. The original structure has disappeared, but for modern use a different reconstruction is made for each new production. Behind this again is the magnificent background of the mountains. Nature vies with the actors for attention.

The Epidauros theatre was designed by the architect and sculptor Polycleitos in the fourth century B.C. We are fortunate in its preservation. Only a little restoration was necessary to fit the building for modern uses. It was the first Greek theatre to be constructed by a professional architect, and retains most of the features of the classical period. Earlier theatres, such as that in Athens, were put up more haphazardly. In most societies a permanent theatre is an afterthought; the first actors and playwrights have to display their art in buildings designed for other purposes and roughly adapted to a dramatic function. It is some time before plays are accorded the honour of a building specially designed to house them. This was as true in Greece as in other times and cultures. Probably the first theatres were threshing floors, paved areas in the village fields, used communally. Here the corn was beaten and winnowed. Many examples may still be seen in the Greek countryside. When the theatre became more important in community life, a space for the chorus to dance, based on the old threshing floor, could be set against a temple wall, and the audience could sit up the hillside to watch.

Thus the basic Greek theatre design arises naturally out of the resources available, and takes the shape so well represented at Epidauros. In many of the other theatres the fifth-century pattern has been lost, submerged under Hellenistic and Roman alterations, and the original circular orchestra has been reduced in size. Epidauros, for some reason, survived these changes;

though built in the fourth century it still shows the principal features of the fifth.

There is little reason to suppose that the Greeks indulged in scenic elaboration. There were no painted backdrops, no built sets which changed from play to play or scene to scene. This was the simplicity, not of ignorance, but of deliberate intention, as in Shakespeare's theatre, where the avoidance of realistic representation gave great flexibility and freedom of movement. If the Greeks had wanted elaborate scenery they could have had it; they certainly possessed sufficient mechanical ingenuity. But the circumstances of the theatre were against it. In so vast a building visual effect had to be subordinated to oral, and the poetry of the spoken word took pride of place. The Greek poets used language to create their scenery. All plays took place against the same unlocalized façade; this could be re-identified by the characters of each successive play, or even within the same play, for when the scene is initially blank it needs only the imagination to make it change. The Greeks called this façade the *skene*, a word which originally means 'hut' or 'booth' and presumably dates from the earliest theatrical times when the only scene building was a simple erection at the edge of the threshing floor. From it, through the Latin version *scaena*, we get our word 'scene'; from *orchestra*, the word for the dancing floor, we take both the word for a group of musicians — thus retaining the musical connotations of the original — and *orchestra stalls*, the seats nearest the spectacle and so the best in the house.

Mechanical contrivances were simple. The fifth-century theatre had a crane-like device for showing people or objects in flight. Its name, *mechane*, is itself significant in regard to the simplicity of the Greek theatre. It means what it looks as though it means, 'machine'; and apparently it was not necessary to specify 'flying machine', for this was about the only machine that there was. We hear also of a rolling platform — some think a type of revolving stage — working from within the *skene* and used to display tableaux. Note that both these devices were used for sudden dramatic appearances or revelations, performing a function that in the modern theatre has been taken over by curtains or lighting. The Greeks had none of these. Their theatre offered no curtain to conceal or reveal, and performances were given in the full light of day.

At Epidauros plays are now given at night, and modern stage lighting techniques are employed — one of the few important differences in this theatre between ancient and modern practice, and a concession to the changing patterns of living and working. Apart from this, although there is no striving for sterile archaeological exactitude, every effort is made to recapture the essence of the original performance. This is most obvious in the handling of the chorus. In modern revivals the chorus is often neglected. On the proscenium stage it is an embarrassment, but in the open theatre of the Greeks was a natural and vital part of the proceedings. The Greek playwrights employed a unique combination of song, dance and the spoken word whose secret is lost to us for ever. The original music has vanished, except for a fragment from Euripides' *Orestes*. Much of Euripides' choral music survived into the Byzantine era, where it was adapted for Christian liturgical uses. The early Christians, torn between their official condemnation of pagan art and their private recognition of its excellence, frequently made such compromises. But this too was swept away in one of the numerous liturgical purges that occupied the Orthodox church. There are tantalizing hints that passages still survive in Russia, but apart from this nothing is known. The modern Greek revivals go as far as they can in restoring this musical element to the performances, practising a remarkably effective combination of song and dance-rhythm which must come very close to what the ancients employed. There is one other major difference between the ancient performances and the modern revivals: the modern players wear no masks. In the fifth century the mask was regularly worn. Its use seems to have been contemporaneous with the earliest drama, and to have originated from religious necessity. An actor impersonating a god dons a mask for two reasons — to overawe the spectator, and to shield himself from any possible resentment on the part of the deity he is impersonating. Tradition credits actors of Thespis' time with various mask-substitutes, such as daubing the face with white paint or draping it with leaves. In the later theatre the mask had the practical advantage of exaggerating the features and helping to overcome the problems created by the theatre's size. Fifth-century masks were relatively simple. The grotesque and horrific distortions so often attributed to tragic masks and visible in illustrations stem from Roman revivals of the Greek plays in an era when such distortion was commonplace. Costumes, so far as we may judge, were non-realistic. Simple formal robes lent the actor dignity, and realistic touches, at least in the earlier years, were few. Characters were visually differentiated, for the most part, by the properties that they carried — the warrior with his double spear, the king with his sceptre, the herald with his wreath. Certain characters wore traditional and readily identifiable garb. Heracles, with his club and lionskin, was familiar to the audience and needed no announcement. So was Athena with her shield and helmet and the distinctive mantle, her *aegis*. The elementary nature of this costuming meant that actors could change easily from one rôle to another, by slipping on a new mask and making some simple alteration to the garments. In all its visual effects the theatre sought to liberate itself from the particular and, by merely suggesting costumes and locations, to liberate the audience's imagination and allow them to concentrate on the universal applicability of the myth.

THEATRE FESTIVALS

A modern performance at Epidauros is a single event, presented for its own sake and organized on a commercial basis. A fifth-century performance was part of a larger complex of events, publicly financed as an act of homage to the gods. At Athens, with which we must be chiefly concerned, dramatic performances were confined to three principal festivals each year, and of these by far the most important was the City Dionysia (or, 'festival in honour of Dionysus'). Although its composition changed over the years it came to embrace both tragedy and comedy, together with non-dramatic events such as public announcements, processions and dithyrambic choruses. In the later organization of the festival a typical day's programme would consist of three tragedies, a satyr play and a comedy. The tragic poet's responsibility was heavy. He had to offer not one but four plays. His three tragedies could either be composed around a single theme, thus forming a *trilogy* in which each play, though self-contained and capable of being performed independently, in effect formed one act of a greater whole. Alternatively, they could be three distinct plays, each with different theme and subject matter. Aeschylus seems to have preferred the former approach, his successors the latter. Only one complete trilogy survives, Aeschylus' *Oresteia* (*The Story of Orestes*) comprising *Agamemnon*, *The Libation Bearers* and *The Eumenides*. This was produced in 458, and tells the saga of successive generations of the royal house of Argos. (Aeschylus, for political and historical reasons, shifts Agamemnon's dominion from Argos to Mycenae.) The tragic poet's task was not finished there. He was also responsible for the satyr play, which was a short mythological burlesque, probably associated with the subject matter of the preceding tragedies. These slight plays served a double purpose, offering the audience necessary light relief and testing the dramatist's skill in a totally different medium: the writer of tragedy had to display his prowess in composing broad farce. Only one satyr play survives complete, *Cyclops*, by Euripides. It tells the familiar story of Odysseus' adventure with the cannibalistic Polyphemus, and has the traditional chorus of satyrs which gave the genre its name. It should be noted that there is no etymological connection between satyr and satire: a satyr play may well be satirical, but our word springs from other sources.

The comic writer's responsibility was lighter. He had to provide only one play. Thus, in the fifth century at least, the burden falls chiefly on the tragedian. We are dealing at this point with a fundamentally serious theatre, one which acts as a forum for the discussion of important issues. In the fourth century the view of the theatre as pure entertainment predominates, and we have escapist comedy as the most popular drama form.

All writers, tragic and comic, had to submit their scripts to the archons for preliminary approval. What guided the selection we do not know. At any rate the authorities seem to have been remarkably broadminded and there was considerable, if not total, freedom from censorship. Once his script was accepted the author was, in the technical phrase, 'awarded a chorus'. Actors in the later fifth century were state-paid, and the costuming and training of the chorus — a long, complicated and expensive business — was financed by a private individual of means who was allowed this way of paying his taxes in kind. The dramatist had no financial commitment in the performance nor could he expect any profit from it. Plays were given for the most part once only, in competition. Festival entries were judged by an elected panel, themselves presumably influenced by popular applause, and the winning playwright and, later, the best actor, were given awards. As in other branches of the arts the idea of the professional writer is slow to emerge in Greek society.

This organization of the drama into festivals, made possible by the willing co-operation of hundreds of private citizens, produced a type of people's theatre which later ages have tried unsuccessfully to emulate. There was, until the fourth century, no sizeable corps of professional actors. The man in the street was liable to have a participant's knowledge of the technicalities of theatre, having taken part in choruses himself. The shape of the theatre represents perfectly the drama's place in society. Just as the play evolves in the centre of the audience, so did the drama itself spring from total community participation. Just as the actor is always conscious of the audience's presence, and can address the spectators freely and directly, so is the dramatist aware of his value and his duties as a member of society. He does not hold himself aloof and take undue pride in the mysteries of his art. When Aeschylus died, his tomb recorded the battles he had fought in but said not one word about his plays. He shared his public's life and they shared his. The Greek audience was highly knowledgeable about plays, and followed the drama as avidly, and with as keen a memory, as modern spectators pursue cricket or baseball. The poets, although they did not write for a living, wrote to win, and a sure way of pleasing the audience was to dwell lovingly on Athens' glorious past. The patriotic element in Athenian drama is strong, and there are many appeals to local deities or national heroes calculated to stimulate the audience into applause. It is a drama which is very conscious of its place and time, as well as of its duties.

THE WRITERS AND THEIR AIMS

Greek drama, like Greek literature generally, was expected to work for its living. The arts were never considered merely as diversions, but as performing some practical function in the state. When a fifth-century sculptor carved a statue he was interested not only in his work's aesthetic qualities but in the uses to which that work would be put — to adorn the temple of a deity, to serve as votive offering in a shrine, to stand high in a public place. When the painter decorated a vase he was concerned with making a household object beautiful, not with creating something to be set apart on a shelf and admired. Art for art's sake, like the idea of artistic professionalism, is slow to develop. Of all literature, in both the Greek and Roman worlds, it is the love-poem that receives the least serious consideration, because its purpose was professedly private and not public. In the Greek state, drama, which is literature at its most public, was a teaching instrument. The playwright was *didaskalos*, teacher, in two senses: he taught his choruses, acting as his own producer-director, and taught his public through his chosen medium. In his comedy *The Frogs*, staged in 405 B.C., Aristophanes shows a debate between the two tragedians Aeschylus and Euripides. Both were dead when the play appeared, and Aristophanes represents them as arguing in Hades and typifying opposed schools of playwriting. Although they differ on almost everything else, they agree on the fundamental purpose of their art. It is 'cleverness, and good advice, and making better citizens'. This didactic function of drama is shared most obviously by history. We shall see later how both Herodotus and Thucydides make similar pronouncements about their own writing. When Plato comes to discuss the function of drama in the Ideal State, he treats it primarily as an educational medium, and this view justifies many of his harsh comments. It is not until Aristotle and his *Poetics* that the drama is discussed as something of value in its own right, apart from its public utility.

This is not to say that Greek drama should be treated as a sermon or the Greek theatre viewed as a church. Nor does it mean that the play was drearily 'educational'. The association of Greek drama with religious ritual has often misled modern readers into thinking of plays in this way, but nothing could be further from the truth. It means simply that the drama did not work in a void. It was 'engaged'; it was indissolubly bound up with the questions of the age; it saw its function as illuminating contemporary problems through the use of popular mythology. Aeschylus seems to have been the first to elevate tragedy to this stature. His earliest play to survive, *The Persians*, has already been briefly noted. The Athenians regarded him as a second founder of their theatre, and in a grander sense than Thespis. He was the first dramatist whose plays were officially preserved, and besides *The Persians* six have survived for us to read. By far the most important are the three plays making up the *Oresteia* trilogy. Here Aeschylus takes as his starting point a primitive family feud. A curse is laid on the royal house to which Agamemnon belongs because of crimes committed in the past. Agamemnon, returning victorious from the Trojan War, is murdered by his resentful wife Clytemnestra. In the second play she, in turn, is murdered by her son Orestes, bound to avenge his father. In the third, super-natural forces align themselves in the conflict. The Furies, em-bodiments of the most primitive code of blood-guilt and revenge, declare that Orestes is a murderer and must be punished, while Athena and Apollo, Olympian gods and representing a superior order of justice, argue extenuating circumstances and urge that the concept of the blood feud should be replaced by the civilizing force of law. Thus a barbaric folk-tale is elaborated into an allegory of developing civilization. We have already seen how Aeschylus was one of the writers who sought to repair the omissions of the Homeric religion and equate the Olympian gods with some sort of moral order. The *Oresteia* is a fine example of this, for in it we see the gods developing and refining their own natures. Apollo, for instance, is shown in the first play as a typical Homeric deity, concerned only with his own selfish ends and vindictively forcing mortals to his will. By the end of the trilogy he has become the Apollo that later Greeks loved to reflect upon, the embodiment of harmony, order and the civilized virtues. Not unexpectedly, the story is bound up with praise of Athens. The issue is decided there; Athena shows herself just and merciful and the various sacred places of the city are mentioned with honour. She wins over the Eumenides, the black Furies, and transforms them into beneficent spirits who will make their home in Athens for all time to come:

> Such are my actions, ever provident
> For these my citizens. I have won over
> Great and jealous deities to dwell among you.
> All of man's estate is given
> Into their keeping
> And he who never felt the weight of them
> Shall be smitten in his life, and know not how or why ;
> For crimes inherited from past generations
> Drag him before their judgement seat,
> And cry he never so loud, Destruction
> Will never answer him, but lay him low
> In the bent of her anger.
> CHORUS. And I pray there may never come upon
> Your trees a wind destroying — such
> The blessing I pronounce — or sunburst
> Out of time and season, blasting buds
> Of grown things. May they never wither
> Nor their fruitfulness fail. May Pan

Grant the flocks at the appointed time
Increase, making them bring forth twofold,
And may the fruit of earth, the buried lode,
Be manifest, a rich endowment of the gods
And treasure for the finding.[1]

In another work, *Prometheus Bound* (which some critics think not Aeschylean but a later imitation of his style) Aeschylus seems to pursue the same ideas, though here the argument is less clear because two parts of the trilogy have been lost. A probable reconstruction would show Zeus himself, the very king of gods, changing for the better, just as Apollo changes in the *Oresteia*. We are shown the rebel Prometheus, who stole the god's prerogative of fire and bestowed it on man, in conflict with the tyrannical godhead. The play we have is probably the second in sequence and tells the story from Prometheus' point of view, leading us to sympathize with his sufferings at Zeus' hands. The first play, if we had it, would no doubt tell Zeus' side of the story. By the end of the trilogy it seems that both softened and that Zeus became aware of the moral responsibilities of the governor towards the governed, just as Prometheus recognized his own deficiencies.

Aeschylus treated cosmic themes and clothed them in appropriate language. The trilogy form encourages magnitude. He is not interested in the detailed delineation of individual characters, though here and there he will introduce a shrewdly observed vignette such as Orestes' old nurse, a completely human character, in *The Libation Bearers*. But such personages are the exception. In Aeschylus it is the arguments that are important and not the people; the characters themselves are either the embodiments or the victims of mighty forces, the clash between which provides the substance of the play. Later audiences found his dramas unwieldy, his language ponderous and his choruses, vitally important, difficult to stage. The changing tastes and interests of the mid-fifth century created a new kind of drama which, though continuing traditional patterns, laid greater stress on the psychology of the individual.

The earliest: prehistoric houses, Cnossos

Minoan elegance: South House, Cnossos

Minoan pomp: Grand Staircase, Cnossos

Mycenaean austerity: fortress wall, clumsy doorway

Athens, Acropolis and Agora: fortified hill, peaceful plain

Delos: tavern in commercial sector

The drama of debate: Athens, the Pnyx. Tourists' chairs wait where the Assembly argued

Village threshing-floor.   The Greek theatre may have begun here . . .

. . . or here, from dan
spectacles in this c
at Cno.

Theatre in full flower.   The author in the orchestra at Delphi

Theatre for initiates: hall at Eleusis, home of the Persephone passion play

The plays of Sophocles embody these new trends. He is said to have entered his first dramatic contest in 468 and to have beaten the old master Aeschylus, who promptly left the country in a fit of pique. This story is usually dismissed as apocryphal, but there may be truth in it. Sophocles' language is limpidly clear by contrast with Aeschylus' involved imagery; his characters, being closer to the level of ordinary humanity, encourage empathy. It may well have been that the popular audience found this approach to playwriting more to its taste. In any case, Sophocles went on to enjoy immense esteem, holding several important public offices besides his literary activities. Of the seven plays which have survived, *Oedipus the King*, whether or not it deserves its reputation of being the best Greek tragedy ever written, has won a permanent place in the theatre repertoires of the world. As with the *Oresteia*, a barbaric tale is made the vehicle for a drama of immeasurably wider import. The story of Oedipus is first noted in Homer: it seems there to concern a hereditary curse, and Aeschylus, who treated it in a trilogy now two-thirds lost, seems to have developed it along the same lines as the Orestes story. Sophocles sees it differently. He takes the story of the curse on Oedipus — that he will kill his father and marry his own mother — and uses it merely as his framework. The focus of the play is on Oedipus himself, who is on stage for nearly all the action, and on how he reacts to the ghastly circumstances in which he is placed. It is a drama in which oracles and curses play a part, but it is not a play *about* a curse, any more than *Macbeth* is a play about witches. It is a play about a man who believes in the power of human reason to solve all riddles; who applies this reason to the problem of his own identity; and who finds, in the end, that he has solved nothing, but only uncovered his personal disaster. Here Sophocles responds to the feeling of his own time, just as Aeschylus had done to his. Just as the earlier poet had been exercised by contemporary criticisms of religion, so Sophocles is disturbed by the tendency of his own generation to devalue the supernatural and make human intelligence the sole controlling force in human affairs. Oedipus is a man who applies

L

his powers of reason to a situation, and ends by devastating himself. Towards the end of the play, when he has blinded himself, he laments the senses that led him into error:

> *Do not tell me I am wrong.   What I have done*
> *Is best as it is.   Give me no more advice.*
> *If I had sight, I know not with what eyes*
> *I would have looked upon my father, when*
> *I walked among the dead, or my sad mother,*
> *For sins so great cannot be paid by hanging.*
> *Or do you think the sight of children born*
> *As mine were born could give me any joy ?*
> *No, never to these eyes of mine again,*
> *Nor the proud walls of our city, nor the holy*
> *Statues of the gods ;   these I, ten times accursed,*
> *I, who was noblest of the sons of Thebes*
> *Have set behind me by my own command*
> *That all cast out the sinner, the man revealed*
> *By heaven as unclean, as Laius' son.*
> *And tainted thus for all the world to see*
> *How could I look my people in the face ?*
> *I could not.   If I could have stopped my ears,*
> *My fount of hearing, I would not have rested*
> *Till I had made a prison of this body,*
> *Barred against sight and sound.   Happy the mind*
> *That can so live, beyond the reach of suffering.*[1]

Other plays treat the same problem, and less sympathetically. In *Philoctetes* (409) a clear contrast is drawn between the old way of life, with its insistence on fundamental decencies of behaviour and the observance of a traditional moral code, and the new cynical doctrine that expediency rules, and that the end can always justify the means. But, whatever the subject, Sophocles is concerned with people. The focus of drama has shifted from the gods and the issues they embody to the individuals who are caught up in those issues. It is easier to identify with Sophocles' characters, for they have corporal substance : they are men caught in circumstances over which they have no control, trying to understand the laws by which the world works and grappling manfully with the problems that confront them. Although the mythical apparatus remains, later fifth-century tragedy begins to turn towards the secular.

Euripides (c. 485–406) was the last of the three great Athenian tragedians and Sophocles' almost exact contemporary. A convenient, and quite typical, Greek tradition links the three great men with the same momentous event in Athenian history. Aeschylus is said to have fought at Salamis, Sophocles to have led the chorus celebrating the victory, and Euripides to have been born as the battle was fought. Like Sophocles, Euripides was a product of the sophistic age; unlike him, he tended to take the sophists' part. Sophocles stands midway between the old and new, Euripides is for the *avant-garde*. Although he is aware of the dangers of sophistry when carried to extremes, and in several plays makes sophistic characters his villains, he acts as the sophists' most effective propagandist in the most public setting that Athens provided. He exploits the new scepticism, and castigates the simple trust with which his public accepts the stories of the past; he sets forth the sophists' doctrine of the lack of absolute standards, arguing that morality and law are man-made, that our ideas of right and wrong are for the most part based upon expediency; he uses the techniques of rhetoric that had always been present in Greek drama and with which the sophists were particularly concerned, and so turns the stage into a lawcourt in which burning questions are argued and the audience turned into a jury.

His first play to survive, *Alcestis* (438) is technically not a tragedy at all, but a work offered in the festival in place of the traditional satyr-play, the light relief. This gives the play its tone, and supplies the key to much of Euripides' later work. He takes a traditional mythological story, of a wife who saves her husband from death by going to the underworld in his place only to be rescued in turn by the hero Heracles who wrestles with Death for possession of her. Euripides treats this story quite frankly as a fairy tale. The nobility and self-sacrifice of the heroine, slightly parodied, are set against a background of

grasping self-interest. Admetus, the husband, weeps piously for
Alcestis' demise, disregarding the fact that her death is his fault.
He and his father have a long discussion in which the salient fact
to emerge is that they are interested in themselves alone: duty to
kindred is pushed to one side.

Euripides' method is avowedly critical. He retains the traditional subject matter of Greek tragedy while exposing it to merciless analysis. His purpose is to shock the audience into re-exam-
ination of standards and values heretofore complacently accepted;
this, in his opinion, is the function of drama. It attains its status
as an educational medium by forcing the audience to use their
minds.

Aeschylus and Sophocles had struck new values out of the old
stories, but had accepted it as fitting that the stories should exist.
Euripides considers it ridiculous that many of the stories should
exist at all, or be permitted to influence the popular mind as they
have. Aeschylus and Sophocles had entered into controversy
but attempted to find a solution. Aeschylus' trilogy form provides a perfect vehicle for this: the three plays make statement,
counterstatement and resolution. In Sophocles this dialectic is
compressed into one play: two points of view are presented and
an answer suggested at the end. In Euripides two points of view
are presented and that is all. The audience is left to argue out its
own solution.

These attacks won him enemies. He enters controversy with
abandon. His satirical treatments of old stories of necessity
involve the gods themselves, and cast doubt on the wisdom of
having gods who behave as these have been accustomed to do.
In *Medea* (431) he takes another well-known tale, strips the hero
Jason of his romantic pretensions and reveals him as a sordid
adventurer. As in *Alcestis*, it is self-interest that motivates the
characters' actions. His *The Trojan Women* was written in 415,
just after the revolt of the island of Samos from Athenian domination and its suppression by the Athenian fleet. Euripides chooses
this moment to appeal to the conscience of his audience. He
writes about the suffering of the conquered — ostensibly in the

Trojan War, but in reality at any place and in any age.

The street named after Euripides in modern Athens is one of the principal shopping centres of the city. It is lined with small businesses, bursting with busy trade. This would surely have delighted Euripides, who throughout his work reveals a desire to bring tragedy down to the level of popular understanding and talk to the common man in a language he can comprehend. Thus his plays are more often focused on domestic matters, things within the ordinary comprehension. His characters are more fully rounded, drawn from all ranks of society and bearing a closer resemblance to real life. He made certain innovations in costume and acting techniques, designed to impress an audience with the fact that they were watching a real event, taking place in a strictly localized spot at a fixed point in time. These changes naturally led him away from the accepted idea of tragedy. A writer concerned to show human beings in all their aspects — not merely, as Sophocles did, selected facets of their characters — must soon find himself working from tragedy to tragicomedy, for little of human behaviour is purely tragic. Several of his plays emerge as romantic melodrama or even high comedy. It is significant that Menander, greatest comic poet of the Hellenistic age, cited Euripides as his favourite author.

COMEDY

Little has been said so far about the third major genre of Greek drama. It deserves separate discussion, not so much for any differences of method — in its outward theatrical expression comedy is much closer to tragedy than appears at first sight — as for the different hold it had on the affections of the Athenian public, and for its place in the theatre's historical development. We are limited in our judgements by the small amount of material available for study: in tragedy we have at least a small selection of masterpieces, but in comedy one author only, Aristophanes, is represented from the fifth century, with one complete and several near-complete plays of Menander from the fourth. Thus any judgement about Old Comedy, as the fifth-century plays are rather arbitrarily called, must necessarily be judgements about Aristophanes.

Comedy was late in attaining respectability. It seems to have developed in much the same way as tragedy, with an alternation between acted scenes and choral song. In comedy, however, there were fewer formal restrictions and the pattern was much more free. The chorus (numbering twenty-four in comedy) may take a major rôle in some sections of the play and be silent except for casual comment in others. The three-actor restriction does not apply: several scenes in Aristophanes call for four. Perhaps the most important difference is that the comic poet is free to seek his material where he will, and is not bound to a few standard stories. As a result, comedies tend to be longer than tragedies. The comic writer, developing original material, must devote more time to exposition.

As in tragedy the element of debate is strong. Most of the Aristophanic plays contain a set argument (agon) which is the kernel of the play, such as the Aeschylus–Euripides debate in The Frogs. There are also long passages of direct address to the audience, usually at least one substantial speech in each play in which the chorus, in or out of character, discuss some matter of topical importance or express the playwright's personal opinions. The comedies regularly end with a scene of lively song-and-dance, sometimes with a marriage, and with a processional exit. Some scholars have argued that these features are legacies from pre-dramatic fertility rites, but it is probably theatrical expediency rather than any religious sense which dictates the shape of the plays.

Apart from these recurrent features the plots proceed as they please. They normally move on the level of high fantasy. Examination of the lists of characters reveals much about the nature of Old Comedy. Some of the characters are fictional, having their origins in the author's imagination. These are usually the protagonists — shrewd old country fellows in whom the plays abound, with sharp eyes and mordant tongue, over-

coming all obstacles by their unblushing rascality. Sometimes
there are ingenious heroines, like Lysistrata in the play of that
name who organizes a sex strike to stop the soldiers' war, or
Praxagora who leads the women into office and establishes a
communist state. In a masculine-oriented society the spectacle
of independent womanhood would have been automatically
funny in a way that it no longer is in ours. Then there are
characters from mythology, usually presented in burlesque form.
Heracles is a favourite: in his comic aspect he appears as a fool
and a glutton. Prometheus has a brief scene, and the gods themselves, Dionysus, Hermes, Poseidon, are represented on the
Aristophanic stage. Where Euripides was censured for satirizing
the gods in earnest, Aristophanes can portray major deities in
absurd situations and escape condemnation: comedy, by definition not serious, had the freedom to comment without offence
that the musical theatre enjoys today. Finally there are characters
drawn from real life, poets, philosophers, politicians and scholars,
all living people caricatured on the stage under their real names.
Euripides is portrayed in three of Aristophanes' plays; the philosopher Socrates, the politician Cleon, the mathematician Meton,
the generals Lamachus, Nicias and Demosthenes were all caricatured without fear of direct reprisal, for the ancient world knew
no laws of libel and slander. The plots are such as one might
expect with such a heterogeneous group of characters. Fantasy
mingles with up-to-date political commentary, knockabout farce
with literary parody. The resulting mixture has no real parallel
in later theatre. The Gilbert and Sullivan operettas, perhaps, come
closest: they blend social, political and literary satire, fantasy,
delectable music and the caricaturing of fashionable personalities
in much the same way. They are hampered, however, by legal
restrictions and a system of conventional propriety that Aristophanes never knew. Gilbert cannot employ the sexual outspokenness which is so characteristic of Aristophanes, and so
frequently the embarrassment of his translators. Nor can any
modern playwright be so free in his attacks upon living notables.
In Athens a production of Aristophanes' *The Birds* was recently

mounted in which the ancient topicalities were replaced by modern, and references inserted to contemporary politics and the Orthodox Church, just as Aristophanes satirizes the fifth-century democracy and the ritual of sacrifice. The production was immediately suppressed by the Greek government. Such is the difference between the old freedom and the new.

Like tragedy, the Aristophanic comedies served a purpose beyond entertainment. Seizing avidly on anything of note within the city, distorting, exaggerating and heaping it with ridicule, they acted as a levelling device. The more attention a man attracted, for good reasons or for bad, the more likely he was to be noticed in the comedies. Often there is serious commentary beneath the fooling, although it is dangerous to identify Aristophanes with any particular school of thought or any one political party. All was grist to his mill. Anyone who got himself talked about was potential comic material, and in a city as small as Athens, where every man knew his neighbour, such personalities abounded.

There is hardly any aspect of Athenian life that Aristophanes does not touch. In his earliest play to survive, *The Acharnians*, he presents a jovially idiosyncratic view of the Peloponnesian War. The protagonist, a shrewd old Attic countryman, tires of war and negotiates a private peace. Setting up a free market he enjoys the blessings of prosperity. At the other end of the stage a general bleeds while he drinks and makes love: the play ends in a surrealistic imbroglio whose meaning is all too clear. Other comedies explore the war situation and point the same moral. Often Aristophanes' attitude to war is as scathing as that of Euripides, but, as in religious matters, he escaped the criticism that lashed the tragedian. When the tragedian speaks he is taken to mean it seriously, but Aristophanes is permitted to flaunt his heterodoxy under comedy's licence.

Turning from external to internal affairs Aristophanes exercises his wit on that most solemn of Athenian institutions and one most fundamental to the democratic ideal, the lawcourts. In *The Wasps* there is a chorus of jurors, wasps ever ready to sting and harass the defendant; the central character is an old man so obsessed with the process of litigation that he has to be forcibly persuaded into reason. This hit the Athenians where it hurt — the law was their favourite vice — but they still seemed to enjoy smarting. *The Clouds* (423) is less fair but no less funny. Its subject is philosophy, and it purports to satirize the contemporary fashion for sophistry in the person of Socrates. This comic Socrates is grotesquely different from the figure that we know from Plato and other disciples. He is rather a compendium of several well-known and sometimes contradictory philosophical attitudes, labelled Socrates and given a physical likeness to the master. There is something of the experimental scientist in him, and something of the mystic, much of the rhetorician and a great deal of the charlatan. This is no Socrates, but that well-known farce figure, the Comic Professor, a character put together out of scraps of popular knowledge. It is a sobering thought that many Athenians, those who were not potential Platos, would actually have thought of Socrates in this way.

As the Peloponnesian War progressed Aristophanes' subject matter becomes less particular. It is possible to see the process of censorship, overt or implicit, operating here. The frank criticism contained in the earlier plays could be tolerated only by a state that felt itself secure. By the same token the outspokenness of Gilbert and Sullivan, who satirize many of Great Britain's most cherished institutions — the courts of law, the parliamentary system, the monarchy, the universities, the army — was only possible in an empire which was at the apogee of its power and believed that power to be unshakeable. As the events of war become less favourable to Athens, the comedies shift to the more general, or at least to those particularities less likely to give offence. *The Birds* is a more general satire on political utopias and imperial ambition in general: it contains far less topicality than the earlier plays, a fact which is probably responsible for its popularity in present-day revivals. *Lysistrata*, the least typical of Aristophanes' works, has achieved the wrong sort of fame by reason of its subject matter. Here the Peloponnesian War serves as the pretext for the examination of another and more enduring conflict, the war between the sexes. Although the immediate setting is topical, the theme is eternal; once again, there is a marked absence of pertinent political comment. This lack is doubly significant, for this was the year of incipient revolution, one of the most exciting periods in Athenian politics since the expulsion of the tyrants, when the democracy was almost subverted by the oligarchical factions inside and outside the city. Of this Aristophanes says not one word: the implication must be that he was afraid to speak. In other plays the subject matter is literary, for this can give no offence; it is always safe to lampoon Euripides. Thus comedy loses its earlier pungency and turns mild.

Aristophanes' last play, *Ploutos*, or *Wealth*, is assigned to the transitional genre of Middle Comedy. Devoid of personalities, it is a simple allegory about the blind God of Wealth who has his sight restored, and thereafter distributes his blessings only to the deserving. This leads to the disorganization of society. *Wealth* is a play sad at heart, marking both the end of a career and the end of an era. It is tired and uninventive, a patchwork of incidents and characters remembered from earlier, more brilliant plays. Its obsession with money is painfully applicable to Athens, financially exhausted after the Peloponnesian War, and struggling to afford her independence. The characters in *Wealth* are no longer intended to represent specific living individuals. They are types, they represent various classes of society, and they usher in a new sort of comedy.

There were other reasons besides censorship why comedy should change its shape. With the turn of the century the theatre began to adopt a more commercial approach. Although the regular dramatic festivals were still given, and continued to attract cosmopolitan audiences through Roman times, it was now admitted that play-acting might be a full-time activity. Touring companies took plays throughout Greece, performing wherever they could find an audience. They went to the Greek colonies in Sicily and Southern Italy, thus taking Greek drama within the

Roman orbit; they went East in the train of Alexander's armies. Often they found a stone theatre ready for their use. If not they played on fit-up stages, simple platforms supported on trestles of which illustrations still remain on vases discovered in Italy. These troupers had an enormous influence, making their mark on early Roman comedy on the one side, early Indian drama on the other. Obviously the Aristophanic type of comedy could not survive in such circumstances. It was too personal and too limited. The plays are eternal in their themes but topical in their detail. They were preserved more for their academic value than for their theatrical popularity. Outside Athens, much of their humour would have been lost. We are in a better position to appreciate Aristophanes' comedies than the Greeks who lived ten years after his time. Two thousand years lend a certain piquancy, but yesterday's joke is merely dull.

The type of comedy that emerges — New Comedy — is therefore one that can be played at any time, in any place, so long as the audience understands Greek. Its situations are no longer limited to Athens or to any one city in particular, but universally comprehensible. In practical terms, this means that the play must concentrate on domestic situations and family relationships, things which are the same the world over. Characters, although their names may change from play to play, represent the same restricted range of types. In one form or another these continue to appear in popular comedy through the centuries — the angry father, the foolish old man, the prostitute, the foolish slave, the cunning slave, the young lovers, the boastful soldier. They are easily recognizable from the masks appropriate to each character, and the humour demands no special knowledge on the part of the audience.

Until recently we knew these plays only through Roman imitations. None of the Greek New Comedies had survived complete. Our knowledge of this dark period has now been illuminated by several substantial discoveries, culminating in the appearance, in 1959, of a complete play by Menander, whom the ancients recognized as the greatest writer of his time. Found on a papyrus in Egypt and transferred to the library of Martin Bodmer, the Swiss scholar and bibliophile, it was first edited and translated into French and performed in Switzerland; an American version rapidly followed, and a number of translators have subsequently been attracted to the work. It is called in Greek *Dyskolos* and in English *The Bad-Tempered Man*, *The Grouch*, *The Misanthrope* — the last a mistake, for to translate the title thus suggests an analogy with Molière's comedy which is far from evident. The plot is more or less what we would expect. A curmudgeonly old farmer lives in self-imposed seclusion in the Attic countryside. He has alienated himself from friends and neighbours, having only his daughter and an old servant to keep him company. A young Athenian sees the girl and falls in love with her. Love at first sight is mandatory in New Comedy. Much humour comes from his attempts to prove his worth to the girl's father, and the softness of city living is contrasted with the painful rigours of the countryside. Then the old man falls down a well. While awaiting release he suffers a change of heart, and begins the reform that leads to a happy conclusion.

During the fourth century the shape of the theatres changed to suit the new style of play. The chorus vanished, and so their dancing-place, the orchestra, was no longer needed. It was cut down in size or filled with extra seating. Actors now dominated the theatre where the poet had been triumphant before, and their area, the stage and the *skene*, became more important. Most of the theatres still to be seen in Greece and its former colonies suffered this sort of change — Epidauros is a notable exception — and were modified even further by Roman hands. The Theatre of Dionysus in Athens, the one theatre in which every historian of the drama must be interested, has become an archaeological palimpsest, showing work of all periods from the mid-fifth century to the age of Nero.

The modern idea of comedy takes Menander as its starting-point. When Ben Jonson turns to classical sources for his inspiration, it is ultimately Menander and his contemporaries on whom he is relying. There has been an almost complete break between modern comedy and the Aristophanic ideal. Of all classical dramatists he is the least frequently produced and the most difficult for a popular audience to assimilate — not so much because of the topicality of his humour, but for the all-inclusive nature of his comedy, which is foreign to our comprehension. We lack the temperamental versatility which made it possible for the Greeks to shift so rapidly from one mood to another, to appreciate venomous political satire one moment and slapstick the next. Aristophanic comedy, with its breathtaking flights of fancy, inspired irrelevancy, rapid *volte-face* and changes of pace, accurately reflects the land and city that gave it birth. New Comedy is slower, safer and more cosmopolitan.

Although the literary influence of Greek drama has been enormous, it has had less renown in the history of the living theatre. Fourth-century scholars made selections from fifth-century plays and circulated them as school-books. Only Euripides has any substantial history of performance. In the Middle Ages knowledge of Greek plays and theatres virtually disappeared, and even in the Renaissance there was long hostility to Greek studies. Most playwrights, like Ben Jonson, were more familiar with Roman imitations than with Greek originals. Serious interest in the revival of Greek drama did not begin until the latter part of the nineteenth century. University performances of the Greek texts led to renewed enthusiasm and the production of actable translations. Some five or six Greek plays have now won an established place in the theatrical repertoire, and university performances often allow us the privilege of seeing less familiar works. In Greece the revivals are taken, as is appropriate, with great seriousness. As well as the annual festival at Epidauros, plays are regularly given in the Roman theatre at Athens; ancient tragedy and comedy are also performed throughout the year by smaller groups, notably by the Peiraeus Theatre, which has had overwhelming success on its tours of Great Britain and the United States presenting ancient tragedy in modern Greek. Some attempts have been made to film Greek tragedy, with varying degrees of success: one of the most notable has been

Michael Cacoyannis' version of Euripides' *Electra*, deriving visual power from the authentic harshness of Mycenae and the surrounding countryside.

NOTES TO CHAPTER EIGHT

1. Aeschylus, *Eumenides*, 927.   2. Sophocles, *Oedipus the King*, 1369.

Chapter Nine

The Greeks and Their Past

'HISTORY' is itself a Greek word: it derives from *historie* or *historia*, which in modern Greek means an idle tale or excuse, but for the ancients meant a tracking down, an enquiry. This is what the earliest Greek history was, an enquiry into human and natural causes of events, into strange places, peoples and customs, an enquiry into the many facets of the rapidly expanding world. The Greeks, this strange race of invaders who swept down from central Europe and established themselves in opposition to the already powerful civilizations of the Near East, for a long time had no history in our sense of the word. As has been already plentifully stressed, they were never a unified nation: the Greeks were a people of scattered communities, each developing individually behind a barrier of mountains, each preserving its own traditions, making its own laws, establishing its own constitution without reference to its neighbour. They were content to act, and possessed neither the desire, the need nor the ability to establish elaborate records of their activity. Community traditions were handed down orally. The first approximation to history was the epic poem, which purported to recount historical incidents and interwove them inextricably with mythology. Homer was consulted over territorial disputes; poetic genealogies, tracing human families back through the mists of antiquity to divine ancestors, were accepted as historically valid. For the average Greek of the archaic period history was myth, myth was history.

But the developing Greek mind fostered a new spirit of criticism, and this we associate chiefly with the important Greek colonies of Asia Minor, the cities of the region known as Ionia. These cities stood in a peculiar position. They were founded by

Greeks, occupied by Greeks and maintained Greek principles and customs, but were in foreign territory, cut off from their own kind by the sea. They thus fell under the influence of whichever Eastern ruler happened to be predominant, first the humane philhellenic King of Lydia and later under the harsher despotism of Persia. Theirs was a dangerous position but a stimulating one. They were able to compare the traditions of their people with the different traditions of the Near East. They had access to the vast fields for intellectual exploration offered by the Lydian and Persian empires. They were freed by their geographical situation from that narrowness and parochialism which was the mainland Greeks' worst fault and most dangerous enemy.

Thus we see in Ionia, and particularly in the flourishing merchant city of Miletus, a growing spirit of dissatisfaction with the accepted myths, a spirit of rationalization and scientific enquiry. Miletus produced the first geographers, the first philosophers, the first historians, although, to begin with, these fields of enquiry were hardly distinguished from each other: they were only various aspects of the enquiring Greek mind probing the problems of man's origin, his surroundings and his destiny. We have Xenophanes branding the heroic myths as fictions; we have Thales of Miletus speculating on the origin of matter; we have attempts to equate the gods, in Homer obeying no law but their own, with moral principle. We have theories on the nature of sin, the doctrine of inherited guilt, an attempt to define the way in which man may show himself offensive to the gods.

For our purposes the most important name of this period is that of Hecataeus, a citizen of Miletus. He compiled an account of the history and traditions of various families under the title 'Genealogies', and expresses typical Ionian dissatisfaction with accepted stories: 'What I write here is the account which I consider to be true. The stories of the Greeks are numerous and, in my opinion, ridiculous.' Another of his works, 'Journey Round the World', was largely geographical, but also contained descriptions of countries and places, ethnography and ancient history.

At this point in time the various strands of Greek thought begin to separate. Examination of the myths and their religious and human content is left to the poets, playwrights and philosophers. Hecataeus' successors, Charon of Lampsacus and Dionysius of Miletus, were more concerned with history proper — the latter with Oriental material, the former with Greece as well. They wrote histories of Persia up to and including the Persian invasion of Greece. The treatment of history from the Persian point of view is, at this time, standard. The history of the Greek cities was so diverse and complicated as to offer no convenient starting-point. Herodotus partially follows this tradition. When he begins his investigation of the Greek cities, it is through the eyes of Croesus, who sends around Greece to compare the character of the various states. The more stable and unified tradition of Asia Minor offered the historian more scope. We may add to these early names that of Scylax of Caria, employed by Darius to survey the course of the River Indus, who wrote an account of his exploration as well as a work of contemporary history. Note how closely geography and history are still connected, although the other disciplines are beginning to establish their individuality. Increasing knowledge of the world and widening frontiers gave the historian more material to work on; improved facilities for travel offered the stimulation of new scenes and peoples. A later literary critic, Dionysius of Halicarnassus, says that the aim of these early historians was simply to compile and publish traditions and records without adding or subtracting anything. They came to be known as *logographoi*, record-compilers. The spirit of enquiry in the historical field was as yet confined to discarding divine machinery and collecting material: there is as yet no critical historical sense.

A vital figure in these formative years was Hellanicus, of the island of Lesbos. He seems to have been the first to have grappled seriously with the important problem of chronology. Archaic Greece possessed little in the way of chronological data. Priests might compile lists of local events for the temple records. Some natural phenomenon, such as an eclipse, might be used as a basis

M

for dating. For the most part, however, the Greeks remembered not years but rulers, and it was often impossible to date the rulers accurately at all. There is no date-basis in early Greek history. The practice of historians in the Christian era of dating events from the Nativity is unhistorical and illogical, but at least it works. In strictly historical terms Christ was born either some years B.C. or some years A.D., depending on which calculation you accept. Nor is there any year 0 in this system, the series moving from 1 B.C. to A.D. 1 without a break. These things are unimportant, however; it does not matter how arbitrary the system is, as long as everyone accepts it and adheres to it. Roman historians found their own starting-point in the year that their city was traditionally founded, and when a mutually satisfactory date — 753 B.C. — had been agreed upon, could chronicle subsequent events by counting *ab urbe condita*, 'from the founding of the city'. French Revolutionary historians, for a brief period, sought a new starting-point in the overthrow of the monarchy. But Greece had nothing so convenient. Some writers attempted to work from the traditional date of the Trojan War, but this was by no means a universal practice. Some dated events by reference to the Olympic Games, established in 776 B.C. and held quadrennially thereafter: it was thus possible to date events in Olympiads. Individual cities had their own lists of records: Athens, for example, erected a list of its archons carved in stone, fragments of which still survive. But there was no system which was applicable to the country as a whole and by which the histories of various cities could be correlated. It was thus more convenient to continue and systematize the practice begun by earlier historians and date Greek events by relation to Eastern. The dynastic rigidity of the Eastern monarchies lent itself to accurate record-keeping. Just as modern archaeologists date Cretan history by reference to Egypt, so ancient writers attempted to establish a Greek chronology by reference to simultaneous events in Asia Minor, and in this development Hellanicus seems to have been an important figure.

Such then was the intellectual climate of the period, and the stage to which the writing of history had progressed, when Herodotus made his appearance. He is the first real historian in the modern sense of the word, and ancient and modern scholars alike have regarded him as the father of history.

Herodotus was born at Halicarnassus, in Caria, part of Asia Minor, reputedly in 484 B.C. The accuracy of this date is dubious. Common ancient practice was to date a man's birth, when the actual year was unknown, forty years before the most important event of his life. In Herodotus' case this was thought to be his participation in the founding of Thurii, a panhellenic colony in South Italy, in 443. Herodotus wrote in a colloquial blend of the Ionic dialects of his native country. His subject is the relations between Greeks and the oriental powers from the accession of Croesus to the capture of Sestos in 478, with frequent digressions. The present division of the work into nine books, each one bearing the name of one of the Muses, was not due to Herodotus himself, but introduced centuries later when the text was edited in the libraries of Alexandria.

Herodotus has two sources, eye-witness and hearsay. The extent of his own travels and observations has been disputed, but from the general tone of his work and the way in which he refers to his subjects it has been held reasonable to assume that he made three principal journeys, perhaps as a merchant, collecting material and recording his impressions — one to the region of Pontus, the coast of the Black Sea and the North; one from the island of Samos to Sardis, capital of the Persian Empire; and one to Egypt, to which he devotes a disproportionate amount of space: he was obviously fascinated by the country, its history and its inhabitants.

Herodotus' methods have been questioned. When did the idea of writing history first come into his mind? Did he begin as an observer and enquirer and only afterwards envisage his project of a grand history, or did he begin with the final shape of the work in mind, only to leave it unfinished? For one thing seems clear, the work is not complete. It seems, from various internal cross-references that are not taken up, that Herodotus had to leave it before it was in its final shape, and also that he planned and perhaps actually wrote a more extensive account of the ancient East than has been preserved for us. However, we must take the work as we find it and ask what it is worth as history; what does it tell us of the scientific historical mind ? The answer is, sadly, rather less than one would expect. Herodotus is a critic only in the sense that Hecataeus was a critic. He distrusts the old myths and tends to suspect superhuman and miraculous occurrences which contradict ordinary human experience, but is never dogmatic on the subject. He will often give the traditional explanation of an occurrence and then offer his own, but usually lets the two accounts stand side by side without implying that one is more valid than the other. This is also his general principle in the case of differing historical traditions: he will give the existing accounts one after the other and then give his own, but he does not indicate that his own is to take precedence over the others. In Book Seven he states, 'I hold it my duty to relate what I was told, but not to believe it all myself', and this impartiality, offering his material to the reader unedited while reserving his own judgement, reveals itself early in the work. In Book One he discusses the various stories of mythological rapes from which the hostility between Greeks and Persians may be derived. Noting that the Persian and Phoenician accounts differ, he continues: 'These then are the stories that the Persians and Phoenicians tell. I am not going to say that things happened one way or the other.' The same impartiality reveals itself in descriptions of technical processes. In Book Two, which deals at length with Egypt, Herodotus is discussing the construction of the pyramids, and how the stones for their upper stories are hoisted up the stepped sides:

> When the stone reaches the first tier it is placed in a second derrick which is standing there, and from this it is drawn up by yet another derrick on to the second tier. There are as many derricks as there are tiers of steps. Alternatively there is only one derrick, and that easily portable, which they carry from tier to tier to haul up the stone. Both stories were told me, so I shall simply pass them on.[1]

Sometimes a process of selection is indicated. In discussing the rise of Cyrus in Book One, he writes:

> I shall be guided then in what I write by some of the Persians who have no desire to magnify the history of Cyrus but merely to relate the facts as they happened. There are three variant accounts, however, that I could relate if I wanted to.[2]

Such a process, however, is the exception rather than the rule. For the most part we are given the accounts of others and of Herodotus himself side by side. Later discoveries have sometimes proved him right, sometimes the others. A theory of the sources of the Nile, for example, which he offers as only one explanation among several and dismisses as implausible, has turned out to be the correct one; on the other hand, his derivation of the Etruscans, the non-Italic race of Northern Italy, from a migrant Asian tribe, is now accepted by most ethnologists as substantially correct.

He himself was content to keep an open mind. His own criterion was more simple and more fallible: he gave greater credence to things that he had seen himself, or to what he had learned from first-hand report, than to second-hand or traditional accounts. 'I know this', he says often, 'for I was there myself.' But this criterion puts him at the mercy of every native guide who will invent an interesting tale for a gullible tourist, and much of his Egyptian book is vitiated by this readiness to accept as historical truth anything that has been told him on the spot. He is proud of his investigations and attempts to trace things to the most knowledgeable source. Sometimes he is petulant over the incredulity of the untravelled. Here he discusses Babylonian farming:

> As for millet and sesame, I shall give no record of the heights to which these plants grow. This is not from ignorance, but because I am well aware that even what I have said about corn is disbelieved by those who have never visited Babylonia.[3]

In Book Two he stresses his painstaking care:

> I heard other things at Memphis also when I talked with the priests of Hephaistus. I visited Thebes and Heliopolis for this very

purpose, because I wanted to know if the stories there would agree with those I heard at Memphis. The people of Heliopolis are said, of all the Egyptians, to be the most skilled in history.[4]

In some matters Herodotus can easily be faulted. As a military historian he is sadly lacking. When he purports to give an account of the Persian invasion of Greece, his grasp of strategy is negligible. His account of Xerxes' army, and its fantastic size, has already been mentioned: this is not reasonable history but historical romance, a grossly exaggerated description of oriental might and luxury. He is ignorant of the basic problems of logistics — the necessity for supplying a large army, the failure to foresee which was largely responsible for Xerxes' failure, seems to elude him as it eluded Xerxes. When he describes the battle of Plataea it is extremely difficult to reconstruct the action from his account or to see where the various incidents of the battle are supposed to have taken place.

If Herodotus' work is not a critical history, what then is it? Let us listen to the author himself in the first paragraph of his first book:

> The history of Herodotus of Halicarnassus is here set forth, in order that time may not obliterate the achievements of the past from human memory, and that the redoubtable accomplishments of Greeks and Persians, particularly the causes of the war between them, should not lack renown.

Herodotus' purpose, then, is avowedly didactic: he wishes to record the glories of past ages and of his own, so that men may remember them and, it is implied, take example from them. Are we so far in spirit here from the opening of the *Iliad* with its invocation to the Muse and its trumpeting forth of its heroic theme? Homer sang of the great deeds of the Trojan Wars, Herodotus tells of those of his own time. In Herodotus as in Homer there is a discernible artistic pattern, a deliberate contrasting of the Greek and the Oriental spirit, which is the underlying theme of the History. Once we see the work as an artistic unity rather than as a critical history, much that was puzzling falls into place. The main theme, the contrast between Greek and Oriental, comes into prominence in certain set dialogues. There is one between Solon, the wise lawgiver of Athens, and Croesus, the rich oriental king. This is not history but a moral tale couched in quasi-historical form. Croesus asks Solon who is the happiest man in the world, obviously expecting the answer 'Croesus'. Solon, somewhat untactfully, quotes examples of obscure men who may be said to have been perfectly happy. The moral is that riches do not automatically produce happiness; wealth is nothing without a good life. A later dialogue between Xerxes and Demarchus makes substantially the same contrast, Greek quality as opposed to Persian quantity. There is also an episode in which Persian conspirators, plotting to overthrow the established regime, discuss what form of government they shall put in its place, and debate the relative values of different constitutions:

Otanes recommended that the conduct of affairs be entrusted to the whole body of Persian citizens.

'If it is a question of making one of our number king,' he said, 'I am against it. There is no joy or advantage to be got from this. . . . What sense or system is there in monarchy, when the ruler can do as he likes and is not accountable to anyone ? . . . Government by popular acclaim has, first, the virtue of its excellent name — equality in the sight of the law — and second, it does not act as a monarch acts. Public offices are distributed by lot, officials must render an account of themselves, and every decision must be brought out in public.'5

Against this Megabyzus, another noble, argues that 'nothing is more stupid or more prone to violence than a useless mob'. He seeks an oligarchy, a group of select citizens who will rule in concert. Darius upholds the virtues of monarchy, and it is Darius, of course, who wins. It is inconceivable that such a discussion could ever have taken place, or that any Persian noble, used to centuries of monarchy, would have argued so forcefully for the Greek democratic system. None the less, the story makes its point, and brings into sharp focus the contrasting ways of life which form the great issue of Herodotus' work.

Herodotus' resemblance to Homer was noted in ancient times. Dionysius of Halicarnassus comments on the stylistic similarities. There was an ancient tradition that Herodotus recited parts of his work in Athens, and was well paid for doing so: we may see here another likeness to the old bards who read their heroic tales in public and enlivened them with amusing digressions and entertaining stories. Herodotus is never afraid to digress. He has a good theme and one worth listening to. He enlivens it with an amusing story where the narrative suggests it, and an occasional moral reflection. The themes we see running through Herodotus' work are not properly those of history, but rather those of Greek tragedy. There are many resemblances here, including at least one example of direct borrowing, on one side or the other. Herodotus tells of the inherited blood-guilt which brings about the downfall of Croesus; of the foolish presumption flying in the face of destiny and moral law which ends in ruin for Xerxes and triumph for the virtuous Athenians. Modern work on Herodotus has thus tended to take two directions. On the one hand, historians have scrutinized the value of his statements, using him as a source for history rather than as history itself. His accounts and anecdotes have been checked where possible against other sources — later writers, epigraphical evidence, the findings of archaeology. On the other hand, scholars have been concerned with the structural qualities of Herodotus' work, finding in it the same balanced form as in Greek tragedy and suggesting that the author may often sacrifice logic and historical accuracy to the making of a point by deliberate juxtaposition and contrast. In any event, Herodotus satisfies the primary requirement of Greek literature, that it be functional: it educates by the display of worthy examples. For the beginning of true scientific history we must wait for a man already writing as Herodotus drew near the end of his life, Thucydides of Athens.

We have more information about Thucydides than about Herodotus, although not all of it can be considered authentic. Several 'Lives of Thucydides' were written; he is said to have been born in 471 — a suspicious date, forty years before the outbreak of the Peloponnesian War — and to have studied with Anaxagoras the philosopher and Antiphon the rhetorician, two of the most perceptive and most critical minds of his time. He had influential political connections and inherited an estate in Thrace, with a rich gold-mine. His father's name was Olorus, and we know of a Thracian prince of that name. It was probably these Thracian connections which led to his assignment to that area during the war, an assignment which was to lose Athens a general and give the world a historian. Made general in 424 and given the command in Thrace, he lost the battle of Amphipolis to the Spartans and was banished. The Greeks, always liable to rapid changes of mood, did not deal kindly with failures. In 404 he was allowed to return to Athens, and we may judge that he died before his *Histories* were completed: the last book shows signs of lack of revision and polishing. We may note here one important fact about these ancient historians: that throughout the Greek and Roman worlds they were hardly ever professionals but men of affairs, who took to writing only as a side-line; men of means, who did not need to depend on writing for a living — and indeed there would be small living for men of letters in an age when books were few and expensive and could be counted on to reach only a small and select public. In history as in the other branches of literature and scholarship the idea of the professional is slow to evolve. Thucydides was a rising man of action who had to face the problem of a broken career. We may surmise that had he been more successful as a general — and his failure was hardly his fault, for he faced brilliant opposition — he might have had no time to write his account of the war he was involved in.

By force of circumstances Thucydides had valuable qualifications for a historian, particularly for a historian of his own time. His training gave him the necessary military experience. When he discusses the conduct of a battle he knows what he is talking about. His political connections gave him the facilities for obtaining authentic information. His twenty years of banishment gave him the power as a neutral, a non-belligerent, to acquire an impartial view and study the war objectively through the eyes of both sides.

'I lived through the whole war', he tells us, 'being old enough to see what was going on and following it closely so as to obtain accurate information. It was my fortune to spend twenty years in banishment after the Amphipolis command, and as I saw the action from both sides, not least from the Spartan, because of my banishment, I was able to observe things more easily at my leisure.' 6

He had little restriction on his sources of information. For a historian in those times, this was infinitely valuable. A historian of contemporary affairs needs access to much unpublished material. In our own time this need is mostly filled by broadcasts, interviews and the ephemera of the newspapers. Thucydides had none of this; much of his material could only come from first-hand accounts, from people who had actually taken part in the fighting he describes. Thus his years of exile, ruinous to his career in Athens, furthered his work as a historian. It is possible to suggest in some places the sources from which his information came. The siege of Plataea, for example, is described in such a way as to make it certain that he drew his information from the Plataeans themselves. The fighting at Pylos and Sphacteria is described from both the Spartan and the Athenian points of view, revealing knowledge that he could only have had from consulting both sides. It has been reasonably argued, indeed, that Alcibiades himself was one of Thucydides' main sources — Alcibiades both loved and feared by the Athenians, who himself walked a tight-rope between the two sides, joining first one and then the other, and so would have had unrivalled opportunities for a balanced view of the war.

Thucydides could of course use some published material, in the shape of treaties, decrees and public proclamations. Sometimes the formula of the original document seems visible under Thucydides' prose. Such is the language of the financial provisions made in 431, early in the war, after the first Spartan invasion of Attic soil:

They also resolved that of the money deposited on the Acropolis one thousand talents should be set apart as a reserve fund, and not be spent ; the war could be financed with what was left. If anyone should suggest or put a motion that this money go for any other purpose — except in the case of enemy attack by sea and the necessity for defence — he should be sentenced to death.[7]

So, in the events of 425, the terms of the truce after the Spartan defeat at Pylos seem to be taken straight from the relevant document.

In discussing how ancient historians handled their material we must remember that, for the ancients, mere history was not enough. A historical treatise had also to be a work of art, with literary as well as historical principles governing its final form. Although Thucydides had to survey various accounts and decide which to embody in his work, the principles of literary composition dictated that he should present his final conclusions without indicating divergencies. This is one great difference between Herodotus and Thucydides; where the former will set down a number of accounts, sometimes indicating his own preference but more often not, the latter, generally speaking, is chary of mentioning the reports that he personally doubted. There are a few instances where he does this, but not many. Thus the *Histories* of Thucydides represent one man's reasoned conclusions on the events of his time. We do not see his mind working, nor can we assess for ourselves the evidence on which he bases his conclusions. This is a fact of considerable disappointment to modern historians. However, in those cases where it has been possible to check his narrative from other evidence, he has been proved to be extremely accurate. In the eighth book — the one which was left unfinished — it is possible to study his methods, at least to a certain extent. This book is rather a collection of material than a reasoned summary. The narrative is continuous but contains certain contradictions, in fact as well as tendency, and there are several things that would probably not have appeared had the work been brought to completion. For example, three treaties of alliance between Sparta and Persia are set out in detail. Two of these were transitory and had no real historical importance. It is unlikely that we should have seen them in the finished version.

The most striking feature of Thucydides' history is the use he makes of speeches. He was not the first to do this; here Herodotus had preceded him. His employment of them, however, is unusual. They are not reported speeches — not verbatim accounts of debates in assembly or of political negotiations — but for the most part, speeches composed by Thucydides himself and put into the mouths of historical characters. He has this to say of them:

> As for the speeches made by various individuals either prior to or during the hostilities, it has been difficult to recall verbatim what was said, either in the examples that I heard personally or where reports were brought to me from various other sources. Therefore the speeches have been given in the language which I surmised the various speakers would have seen most fit to use in the context of the current situation, while adhering as closely as possible to the general sense of what was actually said.[8]

This is, so far as we may judge, exactly true. Some speeches Thucydides must have heard. The funeral speech of Pericles is one example. But this is hardly differentiated from other speeches which Thucydides could not have heard, although it is tempting at times to surmise that the authentic Periclean turn of phrase comes through. Occasionally we have an echo of what the original words must have been — when the Spartans, for example, begin an oration by announcing, typically, that they are not accustomed to making long speeches — but for the most part the style is Thucydides' own. There has been much argument on this subject, and some critics have professed to be able to distinguish genuine Periclean phrases from Thucydides' own; others have suggested that Thucydides used a plain, simple style when he was merely reporting, and a more elaborate turn of phrase when he was trying to convey his own conclusions through the medium of the speech. These are purely subjective arguments, and one can discuss, endlessly and profitlessly, how much of a given speech is the speaker's own and how much the historian's. Any discussion of style is complicated from the outset by the fact that Thucydides' own style has certain peculiarities, deriving perhaps from his northern associations. Described with undue harshness by one critic as 'at best good Thracian', it departs in several respects from stylistic orthodoxy.

To return to the speeches, however, they are much more than mere impressions of what the speakers actually said. Thucydides was undoubtedly influenced by the dramatic techniques of his time, and uses set speeches as a dramatist does, to sum up a point of view or to present vividly and concisely what would demand much more space if treated as pure narrative. Here again we may see the concern with the writing of history as a manifestation of literary art, and the far-reaching effect of rhetoric. Thucydides' work represents the concern with presenting an argument, and the convincing marshalling of facts, that occupied the orators of his day. Like the dramatists he employs techniques with which his public would be familiar from their daily experience. When he discusses his own work it is, clearly, with oral preconceptions:

> The lack of the fabulous in my work may well give it an appearance less pleasing to the ear . . . it has been composed not as a theme to catch the hearer's attention for a moment, but as a possession for all time.[9]

The speeches, then, are used as a dramatic heightening of the narrative, serving both to vary the author's style and to put special emphasis on points worthy of special attention. This is particularly obvious in the so-called 'Melian dialogue', a discussion between the representatives of Athens and the rebel state of Melos on the subject of whether the latter should be destroyed. No doubt there were speeches made on this occasion, but Thucydides can hardly have heard them, and it is unlikely, given the emotions aroused by the situation, that they were set out with such conciseness, force and deadly logic as appears there. Thucydides has employed debate form to present as strongly as possible the philosophy that force must triumph, and that 'justice' is the advantage of the stronger.

Let us now turn to Thucydides' methods as a historian. One of the first things to strike us in comparing him with Herodotus is his principle of exclusion. Thucydides is writing a history, and he takes care that it remains a history. He does not wander off into geographical excursions, except where they are strictly relevant. He does not speculate on anthropology, on the history of religion, or any of the other sidelines which intrigued the discursive Herodotus. Nor does he include gossip — except, again, where it is strictly relevant and produces political repercussions, as in the case of the exile of Alcibiades, which must be seen, as Thucydides realized, in the context of public opinion. Secondly, we must notice his new standard of truth, the accurate reproduction of facts. He sets a standard here by which he finds Herodotus and the Ionians wanting, condemning them as entertainers. Here is Thucydides on his own methods:

> In reporting the hard facts of the war I felt an obligation to avoid casual information and guesswork, and to examine minutely every incident, whether I had been personally involved or was working at second-hand. Gathering this information entailed some labour, as those involved in the various actions differed in their reports of them according to the extent of their memory or their partisanship.[10]

In his preface, an excursion into early Greek history, he also reveals a keen sense of historical criticism. After Herodotus, this is a transformation. Among other things he is critical of poetic authority. For example, he accepts Homer as an authority for his own period but not for the Trojan War, distinguishing the age of the writer from the age about which he writes. He points to the culture of backward parts of Greece as an example of what former ages must have been:

> On the mainland also marauding was commonplace. Even today there are many parts of Greece where life follows the old pattern — among the Ozolian Locrians, the Aitolians, the Acarnanians and the mainland adjacent. The mainlanders' habit of going armed is a

legacy from the marauding life of earlier days. Indeed, all Greece went armed at one time : homes were unprotected and there was no safe travelling between one place and another. They carried weapons as a matter of course in their common daily occupations, just like barbarians. The survival of these customs in some parts of Greece is proof that they once prevailed in the country as a whole.[11]

He will even employ archaeological proof. He describes the reconsecration of the island of Delos in the early years of the war, and the discovery there of graves of an earlier, pre-Hellenic population. We are far from the world of Herodotus. Thucydides recognized the necessity for method and for rational criticism, using all the methods at his disposal to come near the truth.

We can say little about Thucydides' personal religious beliefs. It is likely that he would have been influenced by the increasing agnosticism of the later fifth century, as he was influenced in his critical method by the sophists. The gods still exist for him, although not in the personal form in which they appear in Herodotus. For Thucydides, it is an infallible sign of decay in society if awe of the divine is broken down. In his description of the great plague at Athens he paints a vivid picture of the undisciplined and panic-stricken populace 'deterred neither by fear of the divine nor by laws of men'. In Herodotus supernatural control manifested itself in the shape of a destiny controlling human affairs, and exacting appropriate, though late, punishment for sins committed in previous generations. In Thucydides the only supernatural element is *tyche*, chance, which manifests itself in the accidents of war and in human mismanagement — in the Athenian distrust of Themistocles and Pericles, in their suspicions of Alcibiades which led to his exile and contributed to their own downfall. An extreme view would have it that in his insistence on the operation of chance or coincidence in human affairs, Thucydides is simply substituting his preferred deity for others, and is not a true historian but a mythographer.

Thucydides is not a moralist. His concern is with things as they are, not as they might be or as they should be. He is a political historian — the first political historian. Thus he remains firmly detached from conceptions of right or wrong, showing no moral approval or disapproval. This is particularly obvious in the 'Melian dialogue' referred to earlier, which may be briefly summarized as follows: [12]

ATHENIANS. We shall not claim that we hold our power justly. Let us not pretend. The powerful get what they can, the weak surrender what they must.

MELIANS. But you have an interest in being lenient, in case you ever find yourselves in the position we are in now. Do as you would be done by.

ATHENIANS. We are not afraid of that. But if we exert our superiority over you it will be to the advantage of both of us. You would gain by giving in, for if you did not you would inflict horrible suffering on yourselves. If we allowed you to remain neutral we should lose face in the eyes of our subjects.

MELIANS. Has justice no place in this?

ATHENIANS. Justice is the advantage of the stronger. What you are concerned with is self-preservation. Will you come quietly, or will you be subdued by force?

Thucydides does not award praise or blame. He has satisfied himself that conventional notions of justice and right must yield before military strength, and so puts this callous doctrine into the mouths of those who are currently superior, the Athenians. As one modern critic has observed, Thucydides preserves the same moral detachment as Machiavelli; the difference is that where Thucydides simply observes facts, Machiavelli lays down maxims and prescribes methods.

What then is Thucydides' view of the function of history? Herodotus had it plain; he intended his work to entertain and to inspire, to preserve the record of the illustrious past and offer examples for future emulation. Thucydides makes his own statement. He seeks to impart 'an exact knowledge of events which have already taken place and which, in all human probability, are going to repeat themselves more or less exactly at some point in the future'.[13] We return to the idea of history as a science with a practical purpose. Although Herodotus and

Thucydides differ in their views of what history should be, they agree on what it has to do — to educate.

We may now touch briefly on trends in Greek historiography after the fifth century, and deal in particular with one writer who does not rank with those preceding but is none the less an interesting author who does a great deal to illuminate his times. This writer is Xenophon. Subsequent scholars inflated his reputation in their desire to revive the glories of Athens; this led them to attribute to any writer, if Athenian, an importance that his works did not necessarily deserve. His chief value to the modern classical scholar is as an introduction to the reading of the Greek language. Xenophon's Greek, like Caesar's Latin, is relatively simple and involves a small vocabulary. It is perhaps unfortunate that those who begin their Latin with the *Gallic Wars*, their Greek with the *Anabasis*, and then go no further, are left with the belief that the ancients wrote only about military matters.

The date of Xenophon's birth is unknown, but may probably be placed about 444 B.C. He appears to have lived to an age of over ninety. He is said to have been a pupil of Socrates at an early age, and the philosopher saved his life at the battle of Delium in 424. Xenophon was later to write an affectionate memoir of his old teacher in four books, the purpose of which was to defend Socrates' memory against the charge of irreligion and corruption of youth. Xenophon attacks not only the charges brought against Socrates at his trial but also the misleading views of him — many sponsored by the cult of his followers — that grew up after his death. This is an affectionate and sincere defence, containing many illuminating sidelights on Socrates the man even if it does not go very deeply into Socrates the philosopher. Xenophon wrote other works; his *Hellenica*, seven books, takes up the history of the Greek states where Thucydides left off. But Xenophon is no Thucydides, just as in writing of Socrates he was no Plato. He had some excellent qualifications for the work. Although an Athenian by birth and training he had cosmopolitan experience, living in other states — Sparta, Elis, Corinth — and knowing Persia from personal experience.

N

As a historian, however, he has certain faults. His work lacks continuity, it is difficult to follow, and is often extremely dull. He has an ardent admiration for Sparta, and especially for its king Agesilaus, with whom he served on Persian campaigns, which introduces a certain bias into his work. He shows a partisan spirit which finds nothing wrong in Sparta, minimizes her defeats and glorifies her successes.

His other works include a treatise on household economy and a detailed manual of cavalry training. From the list of writings alone a picture of the man begins to emerge: a well-educated young man of moderate talent with some skill in writing and enough natural adaptability to interest himself in many subjects, although in none of them deeply.

Xenophon also wrote the *Anabasis*, 'The March Up Country', a work of living history in the form of an account of the Persian campaign in which he was most concerned. This is a story that lies outside the main current of Greek history; it had little or nothing to do with what went on in mainland Greece; and yet it is an interesting and exciting tale, which reveals many things worth knowing about the Greek character.

After the close of the Peloponnesian War young Greeks who wanted military adventure found their thoughts turning more and more to the East. Mainland Greece was more or less quiescent. There would be no major upheaval until the arrival of Alexander. This being the case, Greek youths who wanted a soldier's life tended to enrol themselves in some foreign army as mercenaries, serving abroad in campaigns in which they had no personal interest. Greek insularity begins to break down. Men were becoming more interested in the East, in Persia and beyond, and this interest is reflected in the art and literature of the period. Orientalizing stories and artistic motifs begin to creep in, and this tendency is to be given a great new impetus by Alexander's Eastern conquests. Xenophon's *Anabasis* is an account of just such a campaign in which he himself took part, as a Greek fighting for Persian pay. The *Anabasis* is the story of the expedition which Cyrus the Younger led against his brother Artaxerxes II, King of

Persia, in the hope of gaining the throne for himself. Since the abortive Persian attempt to conquer Greece, internal politics had become more and more disorganized. Lacking a strong hand to control them, the satraps — powerful local governors — plotted against each other and worked for their own advantage. The history of the Peloponnesian War contains several examples of this, with satraps taking sides, plotting, conspiring, negotiating with Athenians and Spartans alternately and seeking for the most gain. In 401 this internal dissension finally came to a head. Cyrus, in his wartime negotiations, had come to learn the quality of Greek troops, and when he planned his *coup d'état* it was to them that he turned for support. The end of the Peloponnesian War had released from military service thousands of men who had neither the skill nor the desire to earn a peaceful living, and Cyrus was able to enlist a whole force of Greek soldiers in his service. Xenophon himself enlisted on the encouragement of a friend, one of Cyrus' Greek generals, and was destined to play a leading part in the events that he described. We have here an eyewitness account of a minor campaign.

The army formed at Sardis and set out to march through Lydia on the pretext of invading the small province of Pisidia. So large a force could not fail to awaken the suspicions of the authorities, and King Artaxerxes, forewarned, began his counter-preparations. Many of the soldiers had not been told that they were to be used in a rebellion, and before they had gone far the Greeks saw through the shallow pretence and refused to continue their march. Their commanders overpersuaded them, pointing out the dangers of returning without the goodwill of their employer. The army thought it as well to go on and take the consequences. So the march continued, somewhat discontentedly, through the southern part of Asia Minor. They followed the course of the River Euphrates into Babylonia, and here Artaxerxes met them with a large force at Cynaxa. The Greeks fought bravely and drove the enemy before them, but Cyrus, while pursuing Artaxerxes, was himself struck down and killed. 'Such', says Xenophon, 'was the manner of Cyrus' death. Of all who lived since the time of the elder Cyrus, he was the most kingly and the most deserving of rule. All who claim to have known him intimately acknowledge this to be so.' There follows a long description of Cyrus' upbringing and virtues which Xenophon was later to expand into a full work, a monograph entitled 'The Education of Cyrus'.

Cyrus' camp was plundered, but the mercenaries were still victorious and drove the enemy off. A paradoxical situation ensued. The Greeks had won the battle, but Cyrus was dead. There was no point in going on. A Greek force of some 10,000 men was stranded in a foreign country, far from sea and friends, without hope of assistance. Their despondency was increased by the treachery of the Persian commanders. The Greek generals, invited to a discussion under terms of truce, were promptly arrested and executed. Xenophon paints a vivid picture of the Greek camp that night:

> Brooding and despondent, few tasted food that evening. Few troubled to light a fire, and many did not even come into camp at all that night but took their rest wherever each man happened to be. Sadness and longing for country, parents, wives, children kept them from sleeping ; never did they think to set eyes on them again. In such condition each one tried to find rest.[14]

Here Xenophon comes into his own. Speaking of himself in the first person, he recounts how, inspired by a dream, he persuaded the troops to accept his leadership. Reorganizing the weary and despondent force, he began the long march for home. The absolute veracity of this description has been questioned, and some critics have argued that Xenophon represents himself as contributing more to the leadership of the expedition than he actually did. We have, after all, no other evidence against which to check his story. The story must be substantially accurate, however, and is a triumphant account of the power of human survival. The remainder of the *Anabasis* describes how this hopelessly outnumbered force made its way through the centre of a hostile country to reach the northern coast of Asia Minor and the Greek colonies on the sea. They were beset by enemies from all sides, suffering from lack of food and caught in the rigours of the Persian winter. Xenophon describes this in a passage which might easily be mistaken for an account of Napoleon's retreat from Moscow:

> Detachments of enemy soldiers kept close behind them, carrying off the baggage animals as their strength gave out and fighting each other for them. Soldiers too were droppng out, some with snow-blindness, some with their toes rotted away with frostbite. If you kept something black in front of your eyes, you had an eyeshield against the snow ; it helped your feet if you kept moving and never stopped for rest, and took off your shoes at night. If the men slept with their shoes on the straps always sank into the flesh and the shoes froze on the feet. After their old ones had worn out they were wearing brogues made of freshly flayed oxhides.[15]

So they were hunted through the country. It was fantastic that they should manage to survive against such odds, but survive they did, and at last reached the coast near the Greek colony of Trapezus. Here occurred the scene already described in this book, when the soldiers, avid for their first sight of the sea after so long, ran down to the beach crying their joy. Their journey was not yet finished. They had still to make their way along the coast amid continuing hostility and faced with cities unwilling to offer food and hospitality to the Great King's enemies, but the worst of their dangers were passed and they could now travel by sea. Many, like Xenophon himself, returned to Greece. Others stayed in Asia Minor, to enter on new campaigns under other masters.

The *Anabasis* is by no means a great work of literature, and the events it relates are a byway of Greek history. None the less it epitomizes certain important characteristics of Greek life and thought. First, it is a tribute to the amazing resilience of the Greek fighting man, his power to overcome obstacles, his adaptability to circumstances — an adaptability inculcated by his struggles against his own uncompromising environment. Secondly, it shows the extent to which the Greek and Persian positions had been reversed. Instead of Persia interfering with Greek affairs,

Greece could now interfere with Persian. The long-established Persian empire was crumbling, torn with internal dissension and waiting for Alexander's conquests. The balance of power was shifting westwards. Thirdly, the *Anabasis*, together with most of Xenophon's other writings, reflects the increasing practice of hero-worship. A man is now honoured not as the representative of his state but for his personal character and his personal achievements. Xenophon idolized Cyrus, both in this work and his later monograph; he also idolized Agesilaus, the Spartan king under whom he later served. This new attitude is typical of fourth-century thought. Interest turns from the institution to the man. We find this in all walks of life. In the theatre, interest is centred not on the plays, or even on playwrights, but on star actors. Artists shift from the idealization of man in general to the depiction of individual men in particular. Individual politicians become more important than the institutions they supposedly serve. The full danger of this shift of interest was not to be revealed until the time of Alexander, when the popular idolization of a successful leader prepared the ground for his attempts at self-deification. We cannot blame Alexander too much for taking a step so suited to the mood of his time. But it is a change that can only come about with a corresponding loss of dignity on the part of the idolizers.

Finally, Xenophon's work is important in showing the developing concept of historiography. From the Ionian writers onward the focus has gradually narrowed. First comes the universal history — accounts of all times and all peoples, with every sort of archaeological, anthropological, geographical and theological trimming added. Next come accounts of one particular period; finally, accounts of one particular campaign, biographies and individual memoirs. Interest in individual personalities had been awakened by sophistic teaching, and the biography emerged as a new branch of literature. This tendency was encouraged by other factors — by the movement towards stronger individual characterization in the later drama, for example, and by the growth of personality-cults around the memory of the martyred

Socrates. His eccentric and forceful personality, over and above his teachings, had made a great impression on his disciples. Most of them were writers and composed pen-portraits of their master. Plato's work contains several incidental examples of such portraiture, and Xenophon's own memoir is a striking example. This new art reached its high point in Plutarch's *Lives*, a series of short biographies of great men. To mention Plutarch here is to make a colossal leap in time, for Plutarch lived in the Roman world of the first century A.D., under the Emperor Claudius; but it is justifiable to allude to him at this point, for he represents the culmination of the Greco–Roman biographical tradition. He wrote in Greek, and his *Lives* are of considerable importance to English literature. They are for the most part written in pairs — a Greek coupled with an approximately similar Roman. Plutarch had read widely in sources no longer available to us, and his *Lives*, though often of dubious historical value, remain one of our main repositories of ancient tradition. With the Renaissance and its revival of interest in ancient learning the *Lives* were translated into English by North, and so used by Shakespeare as source material for his plays about the classical world.

To return to the fourth century B.C. and the development of history proper, Thucydides had other imitators and successors besides Xenophon. Cratippus continued where Thucydides had left off, but his work survives only in fragments and seems dull and unexciting. A Sicilian historian, Philistus of Syracuse, related the story of Sicily from the beginnings to his own time, and also composed the histories of two Syracusan tyrants, Dionysius father and son. Here again we must note the emphasis on personalities. Philistus took these warrior rulers as his models and wrote history as they made it. This was one of the few books that Alexander took with him on his travels.

A new movement was now making itself felt in Greece, the concept of the unity of the Greek people. In the days of Philip and Alexander the historian Ephorus wrote a work in twenty-nine books in which he recognized a unity of culture offering hope of a real Hellenic nation. Thus he produced what might be called almost a national history — a history of Greece, not of the whole world; non-Hellenic peoples only came in if they were involved in Greek history. This great advance in conception is balanced by a weakness of execution. History begins to be florid and demonstrative, to show off. In Ephorus' work there are several incongruous elements. Narrative passages are interrupted by moral platitudes, and the rhetorical element, so successful in Thucydides, becomes obtrusive here. History, like the other arts at this time, had begun to work for effect, and to work too hard. Truth and sense are sacrificed to sensation and display. It is sad that the idea of Greek unity should not have been exploited until there was no longer any historian worthy of exploiting it.

The exploits of Alexander increased this theatrical and romanticizing tendency still further. Soldiers returning from the East brought back strange stories with them, and these found their way into the histories of the time. There were some sober and dispassionate reports in the shape of memoirs written by Alexander's generals, foreshadowing in style and approach the Latin commentaries of Caesar on his own campaigns. But these were not popular. History and geography were the light reading of the educated public, and later historians sought to satisfy the same need of entertainment which had formerly been met by the compositions of the poets. Historians helped to fill the place of today's novelists.

The new knowledge of strange lands won by the conquests of Alexander stimulated the appetite for marvels. History could now appear as romance. Cleitarchus, an orator and teacher of Colophon, won popular success with his fantastic descriptions of the gorgeous East. This work, hardly deserving to be called history, became the standard book on the subject, and seems to have exerted a great influence on the traditional history of Alexander — a romantic, highly coloured tradition which found its way into mediaeval literature and modern Greek folklore. It was not until four hundred years later that Arrian composed a

genuine history of Alexander's conquests, basing his work on the
sober accounts of Alexander's aides and rejecting the more
popular tales.

NOTES TO CHAPTER NINE

1. Herodotus, *Histories*, II. 125.   9. *Ibid.* 22. 4.

2. *Ibid.* I. 95.   10. *Ibid.* 21. 2.

3. *Ibid.* 193.   11. *Ibid.* 5. 2.

4. *Ibid.* II. 3.   12. *Ibid.* V. 85.

5. *Ibid.* III. 80.   13. *Ibid.* I. 22. 4.

6. Thucydides, *History*, V. 26. 5.   14. Xenophon, *Anabasis*, III. 1.

7. *Ibid.* II. 24. 1.   15. *Ibid.* IV. 12.

8. *Ibid.* I. 22.

Chapter Ten

The Greek Philosophers

THE beginnings of Western philosophy, as of so many other things, are to be found in Greece, and philosophy at its inception has much in common with other studies. Philosophy, like history, is at the beginning a term of wide application. There was no demarcation between it and theology on the one hand, or natural science on the other. Nor were there, at the beginning, any professional philosophers, any more than there were professional historians or professional playwrights. Like so much else, the study of philosophy began with the Greek colonists on the mainland of Asia Minor, in the region known as Ionia. Just as the historians started by questioning the mythical explanations of their past, so the philosopher-scientists sought rational explanations for the state of the world around them. For background they had the mythical cosmologies, attributed to such vague figures as Orpheus and Musaeus and gaining lustre from their poetic employment. There was also the scientific heritage of Egypt and Babylonia, collected material arising from protracted scientific observations — though the extent to which the Ionians ordered and employed these data has been questioned. Their first enquiries were enormous ones, simple in their very enormity: What is the world? What is it made of? Where did it come from?

The answers found were largely dictated by the personalities and experience of the enquirers. These were scientists, concerned principally with practical skills — astronomers, land-surveyors, geographers. Thales, the father-figure of Greek philosophy, was the first to predict an eclipse of the sun (astronomical hindsight has shown the date to be 585 B.C.) and discovered the constellation of Ursa Minor, the Little Bear. He was interested in other

things also, like the question of the rise and fall of the Nile. His
so-called pupil. Anaximander, was credited with the first sundial
and the first map, besides several important astronomical discoveries. These early philosophers share a general interest in
what the Greeks called *ta meteōra*, celestial phenomena; they tried
to find explanations of heavenly bodies in terms of observable
phenomena such as the weather. Thales' preoccupation with the
stars became proverbial. A famous story about him tells how,
while walking along with his gaze fixed on the heavens, he
tumbled into a wall which lay unnoticed at his feet. The story is
later used to demonstrate the inability of philosophers to concern
themselves with things of material importance. The early philosophers had another thing in common: they were concerned
to find one basic substance from which all the world arose, although their opinions differed on what this substance might be.

Thales held that the prime substance was water, or moisture.
This was a common-sense theory drawn from his observation of
nature. Water is the principle of life. Water can take solid,
liquid or gaseous form as ice, water or steam. Thales argued
therefore that the earth was created out of water and floated upon
water. Anaximander had different and less concrete ideas. His
theory was that the basic substance was what he called 'the
infinite', a substance eternal and indestructible and containing
two pairs of opposites, hot and cold and wet and dry. The world
was formed from the interaction of these opposites. In Anaximander's cosmology the original neutralization of the opposites
was disturbed when a portion of the 'infinite' or 'unlimited'
separated from the main, dividing into a ring of hot embracing a
ring of cold as bark round a tree. The cold consisted of a ring
of air surrounding the earth. At first the earth was all wet, but
afterwards, by the drying up of the moisture, it had gradually
been dried. Thus the land and sea were formed. Anaximander
saw this as a continuing process, and held that in time all would
be dry. Meanwhile, the outer layer of hot itself disintegrated
into three rings. Each ring was a band of fire enclosed in air.
Thus we cannot see them in their entirety, but only through

occasional apertures in the surrounding air. These glimpses of fire we have come to call the heavenly bodies. Earth itself is cylindrical in shape, and holds its place by what Anaximander chose to call 'Necessity'.

Anaximander's biology was strangely prophetic of more recent concepts of evolution. According to him, life began in the wet element, the sea. First came fish, who later climbed out on to the drier part and established themselves there. There was not one world alone which endured for all time, but an infinite succession of worlds, coming into being by a process akin to the rising and dissipation of the clouds. Yet another prime substance was chosen by a third early philosopher, Anaximenes. He selected air as his substrate, and argued that it changed by a process of rarefaction and condensation. Air when rarefied became fire, and when condensed first wind, then water, then earth and finally stones. Earth was flat and rode on the air below it; eclipses were caused by bodies passing behind 'high portions' of earth.

So far we have a philosophy based on the observation of natural phenomena, with natural deductions, given the limitations of geographical and scientific knowledge, from study of weather and of heavenly bodies. But there is still a clinging to some aspects of the older and more traditional mythological cosmogonies. When Thales stated that 'all things are full of gods' he was speaking the language of animism. Nor were the early philosophers capable of imagining an immaterial prime substance; and, whatever the material, it was imagined as being held together by some force which was again borrowed from mythology or religion, a sort of 'justice' or divine necessity.

Political pressures in the Aegean world were responsible for frequent emigrations, and one of the most famous of these emigrants was Pythagoras, who went to Croton, in southern Italy, about 530 B.C. There he formed a brotherhood which was wrapped in secrecy. Later tradition had it that Pythagoras left no writings, and confined his teachings to a select circle; thus any statement about him must be made with caution, as we have little to go on but unreliable, and sometimes distinctly unsympathetic, testimony. His school seems to have been partly scientific and partly religious. It took mythic sanction from the Orphic story of a divine child, Dionysus or Zagreus, who was eaten by the Titans, primitive inhabitants of earth. Zeus in his wrath blasted the Titans with a thunderbolt and from their ashes created the new race of men. Thus the first men drew in their natures on both the eaters and the eaten, and all men since that time contain in themselves a little divinity and a great deal of carnality. The mortal body is the tomb in which the spiritual element is imprisoned. Greek makes a convenient play on words here: the body, *sōma*, is the tomb, *sēma*, in which the spiritual element is buried. It is doomed to this imprisonment, and to a series of reincarnations in a succession of mortal bodies, until it can purify itself and return to the divine world whence it came. The Titanic element must be eradicated by asceticism. The intellect has power to know the eternal and unchanging truth, and it is this that makes the soul divine. By perceiving the element of truth as it appears in nature the soul may educate and purify itself. What is this truth in nature? It is the element of form, order, proportion, harmony, limit in the universe, opposed to the chaos which is inherently bad. Truth was represented above all by the harmony and order of the heavenly bodies, by music and by mathematics, all three being, for Pythagoras, closely related. By contemplating these the soul is purified and returns to its former state. Hence the importance of mathematical studies is paramount.

It is hazardous to attempt a reconstruction of Pythagorean teaching, but the main points seem to be clear. Most important was the theory of opposites which Pythagoras seems to have considered as basic, with order in its various manifestations being opposed to different sorts of chaos (among other pairs of opposites, man was representative of the former and woman of the latter!) and, closely linked to this, the opposition of the soul to the body. Plato was to involve much of this in his own work: there we see again the doctrine of reincarnation in various forms, and the enormous importance attributed to mathematics. Pythagoras divorced philosophy from the study of the purely material, laying the foundations of both science and philosophy as intellectual disciplines and establishing the lines along which both were going to proceed.

Pythagoras saw the world as a battleground of opposites, and took sides between them: form and order were good, chaos was bad. In this he was challenged by Heracleitus, a philosopher of Ephesus, in Asia Minor, who argued that both opposites were equally natural and necessary. For him, the world was in a perpetual state of change and conflict. Change was the fundamental law of being, and the only possible harmony was the harmony of opposing tensions. 'Everything is in a state of flux,' he declared, and again, 'You cannot step into the same river twice.' (One of his followers was to elaborate on this, and argue that you could not even step into the same river once; by the time the second foot went in, the composition of the water had changed.) Yet even for Heracleitus, there is a governing principle. He calls this *logos*, a word which for the Greek had many meanings. It could mean speech, word, argument, debate; in later Greco-Roman slang it meant lies, and in the New Testament the Word of God. For Heracleitus it seems to have meant the law of measure which affects the harmony of opposing tensions. 'The sun will refuse to overstep his measure,' says Heracleitus; 'If he does not, the Furies, attendants of Right, will track him down.' Notice the constant recourse to mythology, even at this stage, for nomenclature and descriptive detail. The mythic apparatus, though officially discarded, is still much in use. The *logos* was the principle of life and intelligence to men, though they had the choice of accepting or rejecting it. This is Heracleitus' great contribution, and one in which he is followed by his successors — a perception of the living world as one in which things come to birth and die and pass into each other, but which is still governed by an overriding law.

Parmenides of Elea, who worked around 475 B.C., drew attention to the problems caused by this notion of perpetual change. How could it be reconciled with the idea of a single prime

substance ? The earlier philosophers had assumed that nothing
could come out of nothing, and that the world was derived from
a single everlasting principle. Parmenides asked how, if the
prime substance was eternal, it could ever divide itself and change.
He therefore postulated a prime substance which remained unchanged and immovable, and a visible world, the world apparent
to our sense-perceptions, which is illusion. It appears to change,
but does not; there is a gulf between reality and appearance.
Parmenides did not attempt to bridge this gulf, or to suggest how
the two were related. He was admired by Plato, and once again,
his work influenced that of the later philosopher.

His followers tried to solve the problem in a physical frame of
reference, suggesting that the world consists of various combinations, of numbers of bodies each endowed with the properties of
the prime substance and moved or arranged by separate causes or
events. Empedocles of Acragas, in Sicily, a philosopher, statesman and poet, divided the universe into active and passive elements. The passive was represented by the four elementary
bodies, Earth, Air, Fire and Water. The active elements, the
moving causes, were the principle of unification, which Empedocles labelled Love, or Aphrodite, and that of disunity, Strife, or
Ares. The universe was the result of a cosmic process in the form
of an ever-recurring cycle, which began with the elements in
perfect balance; the preponderance of one element over the others
gradually shifted this balance until the universe changed and
continued to pass through a series of changes, returning ultimately
to its starting-point. The central idea of this theory, the insistence
on the perfect balance of nature, was to be of great importance
to the development of Greek medical studies, and to produce a
concept of the desirable harmony of the various forces within the
body which was to carry through to the Middle Ages and beyond.
The concept of a universe which moves through a series of recurring cycles has its parallels in historical thought: it reminds us of
Thucydides and his insistence that events which had occurred in
the past were likely to repeat themselves in the future. Empedocles believed that nature was susceptible to human control, if

the human mind could only develop itself to the right point. This insistence on the value and the power of knowledge led, ultimately, to the inevitable charge of witchcraft. Various stories grew up around him; he was said to have held back the winds by his magic powers, and to have brought rain to end the drought. He met his death, supposedly, in the crater of Etna.

These scientific and pseudo-scientific theories filtered through to the general public. We find the common man using catch-phrases derived from the Ionians and their successors, just as modern popular speech draws freely, but without complete understanding, on the jargon of atomic physics or psychiatry. There was a ready market for popularization. One man who responded to this need was Anaxagoras, reputedly the tutor and friend of Pericles and the friend of Euripides. He held the theory of a number of unchanging bodies stirred up by a moving cause, and his name for this cause was *nous*, or intelligence. He wrote one book, clear, cheap and of popular interest. In the end, like a number of other prominent figures of his time, he was impeached for impiety. The public, ready to go along with the new theories for a time, was in the last analysis resentful of men who seemed to trifle with long-established and deep-rooted beliefs, particularly when the new criticism could be blamed for the disasters of the state. But in the work of these later pre-Socratics (as these philosophers are conveniently if arbitrarily called) there was much of lasting value. The transition had been made from science to pure philosophy; it was possible now to conceive of the prime substance as something other than material. Plato, as has already been mentioned, inherited much of this: the cosmo-logical speculations, the idea of the transitory nature of the world, the concept of *nous* as a moving cause.

We come now to the period of the sophists, a body of teachers whose influence in various fields has been noted throughout this book. By the middle of the fifth century, partly as a result of the new scientific enquiry but also because of other causes, the political, economic and religious foundations of the traditional Greek way of life were beginning to be found increasingly unsatisfactory and insubstantial. The disruption of the Persian Wars had brought changes both inside and outside the city of Athens. There was a growing spirit of disillusion, culminating in the disasters of the Peloponnesian War and the brutalizing of the Athenian spirit. The Ionian spirit of criticism, at least on the level at which it was popularly accepted, was largely negative in its approach. The discarding of previously unquestioned truths and their replacement by scientific and philosophical enquiry had unfortunate effects. Traditional beliefs were fast disappearing; what was there to put in their place? It was obvious that even the scientific investigators did not agree among themselves. In the field of medicine, some turned away from speculation of any sort, and concentrated on practising an art based on immediate empirical observation. What could be seen and measured was seen to be real; there might well be other things, but these were intangible, they could not be easily grasped or perceived. What satisfied in medicine was appealing in other fields of endeavour. There was a corresponding movement among many citizens to cling to the known and perceptible, to abandon speculation and concentrate on the art and business of social living. Success in public life was an immediate goal, and its very immediacy lent it attraction. For this teachers were required, and it is this need that the sophists filled.

The word *sophist*, like the word *tyrant*, does not initially have a bad sense, though it soon comes to acquire one. In its literal use it means no more than 'a follower of wisdom'. The sophists — the term is a blanket one, and covers a wide range of approaches and opinions — were itinerant professors. Their subject was the one most in demand, how to achieve success as this world knows success; how to adapt oneself to the conditions in which one is forced to live, how to make friends and influence people. They were international, they were peripatetic and charged high fees. They were the first professional philosophers. Although they were prepared to teach anything relevant to their main aim, the central subject was, of course, rhetoric. They claimed to be able to teach their pupils to speak persuasively on any theme, and to

o

argue both sides of a case. Some of them were reputable teachers, others were charlatans. Some saw rhetoric as a genuine adjunct to public life and worthy of serious study, others saw it only as a handy tool for working one's own way, and argued that the end justified the means; any dubious tactic, any deliberate distortion of the facts was permissible if it achieved the desired result. Their belief was that the goal of man is the living of a successful and civilized life. This is the standard by which all things are judged. 'Man is the measure of all things', and religion and morality are man-made customs, set up by individuals or groups to satisfy their immediate needs. When the need has departed the institution may be allowed to lapse also. Expediency is the criterion. In Euripides' plays, characters are obsessed with expediency as people in Elizabethan drama are with 'policy'; as the Machiavellian viewpoint was taken up and popularly disseminated in the Renaissance, so was the sophistic approach taken to the heart of the mid-fifth century.

Into this context Socrates was born. He came into the world in 470 and went out of it, sentenced to die by drinking hemlock, in 399. What we know of him is distorted one way or the other, by enemies or by idolators. He wrote nothing, preferring to teach by what has come to be known as the 'Socratic method' — stopping people and engaging them in conversation, leading them by a series of questions into a re-evaluation of their own ideas. He had many friends and disciples who left memoirs of Socrates and dialogues in imitation of his style. Our main sources of information about the historical Socrates are three — Plato's own constructions on the teachings of his master, the more pedestrian and therefore probably more accurate Xenophon, and the caricature offered by Aristophanes in The Clouds. The latter can be dismissed as a serious portrait. The comic Socrates has little in common with the philosopher. He is made up to look like him, he says one or two things which are vaguely reminiscent of the Platonic conversations, but here the resemblance ends. Aristophanes' portrait is a compound of various popular notions of the profession of philosophy, and derives from various sources.

Socrates is represented as a rhetorical teacher of the worst type, which he assuredly was not; his school is given a strong mystic coloration; his language is a mish-mash of pseudo-scientific jargon loosely derived from the Ionians and filtered through a sieve of popular misconception. The horrifying thing is that, from the mere fact of this portrait's being offered, we may be sure that it corresponded to the popular idea of Socrates, and that many people would have thought of him, if they thought of him at all, not as the humane and enlightened thinker whose spirit pervades some of the noblest writings of Greek literature but as a fat, ugly old man who could not hold down an honest job and frittered away his days by wandering through the streets and asking passers-by foolish questions. A legend arose in antiquity that Aristophanes' play contributed to Socrates' death, and had even been sponsored by the men who were later to be his accusers. This is undoubtedly false, but the play does at least reflect the climate of public opinion in which Socrates' death became possible.

Our more important sources are Plato and Xenophon. They give much information about their master's appearance and habits — information that must be treated with care, for fear that it may be influenced by love this time instead of rancour, but which may still be regarded as substantially accurate. Certainly no one attempted to flatter his looks. He was fat, bald and snub-nosed. He was said to look like a satyr; it is interesting to notice, in the busts that later appear of him, how this ugliness is gradually softened, as the cult grows, into a more idealized representation. He had fantastic powers of concentration, and an equally impressive drinking capacity. Far from ascetic, he had great affection for most of the pleasures that the ordinary Greek believed in. The stories that Plato makes him tell about himself reveal a natural and deep-rooted piety; the charges of irreligion and corruption brought against him at his trial were superficial only, covering a more fundamental hostility against him for showing up the weakness of current governmental policies. His pupils were more generally disliked than he was, and Socrates suffered from the odium that some of the more notorious had brought upon themselves. Was Socrates a sophist ? This is a favourite examination question because it is so difficult to answer. In some of the most important ways he was not. He charged no money for his teaching — one of the valid grievances that his wife had against him — and seems to have been content to lead a simple life. Aristophanes represents him with total incongruity as at one moment growing fat from his rich fees, and at another starving through his own inadequacy. It is safe to say that to the material rewards of sophistry Socrates was a stranger. Nor did he criticize for the sake of criticism, or offer easy formulae for success. As represented in Plato, he is constantly emphasizing the difficulty of the studies he recommends, and the unlikelihood of deriving any tangible material reward from them. In his general approach, however, he does partake of the characteristics of his time. He is dissatisfied with traditional explanations, and seeks to lead men to an awareness of their own state. He is contemptuous of orthodoxy unexamined ; and it was for this that the Athenians, in their frightened reversion to orthodoxy after the cataclysm of war, distrusted him enough to order his death.

But what Socrates thought and taught can hardly be disentangled from what Plato thought. This most illustrious of Socrates' disciples was born in 427, and was a close friend and pupil of the philosopher until the latter's death in 399. He travelled widely — to Egypt, to Cyrene, and most important to Sicily and South Italy; hence his contact with Pythagorean thought, which was to be a major influence on his work. In Colonus, the suburb of Athens where Oedipus had died and Sophocles had been born, he founded his *Academy*, legally an institution for the worship of the Muses but in practice a school in which lectures were given and research conducted. As well as this Plato wrote voluminously. He preferred the dialogue form, in memory of his master. Socrates had chosen the oral method because free discussion allowed the argument to proceed in any way it chose, without restraint or inhibition. Plato attempts to recapture this informality on the written page. Most of his works are couched in dramatic or semi-dramatic form, and purport to reproduce an actual conversation. Such is Plato's art that the feeling of immediacy is in almost every case recaptured. It is extremely difficult to place the dialogues in the order in which they were written. The conventional division recognizes three groups. In the first, we have records of authentic Socratic conversations. In the second, although Socrates is still depicted as the main speaker, we have a growing tendency for Plato to put his own theories and opinions into the mouth of his master. In the third, the dramatic element dwindles, and Socrates is no longer the chief speaker. This division is, of course, largely arbitrary, and has been much disputed. In the last analysis it is impossible to say where Socrates leaves off and Plato begins. The retention of Socrates as key figure, even when the ideas expressed were never his, is in accord with ancient practice. To attribute one's own opinions to one's master was to honour both oneself and him. Plato's use of the Socratic *persona* has the same honorific quality as a dedicatory inscription in modern scholarship. In many of the dialogues Plato goes to great lengths to secure an appearance of reality. He scrupulously delineates the setting and the dramatic time. Here is the beginning of his *Crito*, an interview between Socrates and the disciple of that name conducted when the former was in prison (the excavated shell of a small building, brightly floodlit, on the slope leading up to the Pnyx is now pointed out to tourists as Socrates' prison cell; it is merely one of several such buildings that have been given the honour).

SOCRATES. Hey, Crito, what are you doing here at this time of day ? Early, isn't it ?
CRITO. It certainly is.
SOCRATES. What time is it, anyway ?
CRITO. Crack of dawn.
SOCRATES. I'm surprised you got the jailor to let you in.
CRITO. Oh, he's used to me, Socrates, after all this coming and going. Anyway, I've done him a good turn.

SOCRATES. Been here long, or just come?

CRITO. Fairly long.

SOCRATES. Why didn't you wake me up at once, then, instead of sitting there without saying a word?

CRITO. God knows, Socrates, if it had been me, when waking is so miserable I'd rather have stayed asleep. But not you. I've been admiring you ever since I came, seeing you sleeping so peacefully. I didn't wake you up on purpose, so you could have as much rest as possible.[1]

Crito proceeds to the news that Socrates' execution is imminent, and offers plans for his escape. Socrates rejects them, and the dialogue turns on the responsibility of the individual to the community that nurtured him.

The spontaneity induced by the dialogue form has its disadvantages. Plato gives no systematic account of his principal doctrines. To assemble the sum of his thinking on reincarnation, on love, on the nature of the state, we have to work through the dialogues and find a little here, a little there, putting the pieces together as best we can. Much of this work of assembly was done by Aristotle and the later commentators on Plato; Aristotle put Plato's arguments together in as coherent a form as possible because he was concerned to refute them.

In so elementary a survey as this, it is impossible to do more than skim the surface of Plato's work. What follows, therefore, will touch on three main points: first, Plato's theory of Forms, which is fundamental to his philosophy; secondly, his political teaching; and thirdly, his attitude towards the arts, in which he reveals himself to be a true Greek.

Plato inherits from Parmenides the problem of the One and the Many. How can there be a prime substance, eternal and indivisible, and at the same time a world accessible to our sense perceptions which is changeable and transitory? Parmenides had stated the problem but had not attempted to solve it. Plato answers it by postulating a world of Forms, or Ideas, separate from the world of sense-perception and only knowable by the exercise of pure intellect. The Ideas, as Plato conceives of them, are not ideas in the modern sense, formed in the mind; they have an existence independent of anyone who conceives of them. The Forms live in a world of their own, over and above our world. For every class, for every universal on this earth, there is a corresponding Form. This, then, is how Plato attempts to explain the notion of change and decay; the things we see are no more than imperfect approximations to the Forms.

Plato here involves Pythagoras' doctrine of the imprisonment of the soul. He argues that the intellectual and moral personality is the most important part of man. It has always existed and will always continue to exist, after a chain of incarnations in this world. The soul attempts to enter into communion with the world of pure Forms. To do this it must rid itself of the fallacies inherent in the world of sense-perception; it must learn to recognize and avoid the transitory, and concentrate on what is eternal. It can do this by perceiving the ways in which the Forms manifest themselves in this world. Once again, we lean heavily on Pythagoras. Mathematics is the most important study, for here the eternal order is chiefly apparent. After this comes astronomy, and from this one may attain to a knowledge of the Forms themselves.

According to Plato, there is a tripartite division in man. There is reason, located in the head; spirit, the militant force in mankind, located in the breast; and the passions, the carnal desires, located in the belly. All these are equally necessary. Man cannot exist without the satisfaction of his carnal appetites; no more can he fully exist without the satisfaction of his higher desires, the need to associate himself with the world of Forms. The element of spirit provides the impetus to get things done; it is the martial quality in man, without which desires may be formulated but may never be realized. In the perfect individual, these elements are in harmony. Plato's system, in many ways, is akin to the Christian; it was eagerly taken up by the early Christian Church. The concept of a division of interests within the individual was found to correspond to the Christian perception of the war within us; the doctrine of Forms was found to be readily adaptable to the Christian system, if one only allowed that the Forms were ideas in the mind of God. For Plato, however, the Forms represented objective reality; they existed whether the mind could conceive of them or not; they are the objective realities that general terms connote.

In politics, Plato subscribed to the common Greek belief that man could only live a full life in public affairs. His own life was a conspicuous exception to this rule. We possess a number of letters, ostensibly written by Plato. Some of these are considered genuine, some not. The Seventh Letter, held by most critics to be authentic, gives reasons for Plato's dissatisfaction with current politics, and for his absenting himself from state concerns. He was disturbed by the Athenian conduct of affairs in general, and in particular by the treatment which Socrates had received at the hands of the state that produced him. Plato did make some practical effort in politics, but in Sicily rather than Athens. He was summoned to oversee the education of Dionysius II, young ruler of Syracuse, and apparently saw this as his golden chance to put his theories of the education of the ruling class into practice. He was soon disillusioned. His pupil proved recalcitrant, having no liking for Plato's insistence on mathematics as a necessary prerequisite for political studies, and Plato retired in ignominy. A little later he had a second chance with Dion, Dionysius' cousin. Once again Plato tried to put his theories into practice and once again was foiled, this time because of palace politics. Plato was implicated in an assassination plot and had to withdraw hastily from the city.

Although his practical involvement in politics was unhappy, Plato was fecund in ideas. In *The Republic* he sets out his theory of the Ideal State. Put into the mouth of Socrates, it is a theory that springs from the Platonic concept of the make-up of the individual. Political organization is based on the need of one man for another. It gives stability, and lends itself to economy of effort. In primitive society each man does everything for himself. He grows his own corn, weaves his own cloth, makes his own shoes. As society develops it proves easier for these various activities to become specialist functions. One man makes all the shoes for the community, another grows all the corn. Plato sees society as the macrocosm and the individual as the microcosm; the divisions already present in individual man will also be present, on a larger and therefore more perceptible scale, in society. Plato has already argued for the tripartite division of man into reason, spirit and passion. These divisions then will reappear in society; there will be classes of citizens corresponding to these divisions in the make-up of the individual. In Plato's Ideal State there are three classes. The element of reason is represented by the ruling class, whom Plato calls the philosopher kings. Spirit is represented by the warriors; these, together with the philosopher kings, are to be known as the guardians. The passions, or carnal desires, are represented by the working population, the artisans. Their function is to satisfy the bodily needs of the state, to provide the wherewithal to keep the population alive.

For Plato politics is a science. It is not a thing to be treated lightly, or to be apportioned by lot. The philosopher kings must be trained to rule, and ruling must be their main, indeed their only business. Because of this severe restrictions are laid down on the guardian class as a whole. They are to have no private property, for fear this will lead them into temptation and encourage self-aggrandisement. Family life is forbidden. The children are to be reared in common, with no knowledge of their natural parents. Although there is allowance for moving up and down between classes, the distinction between the social orders is in the main to be upheld, and to enforce this in the minds of the populace recourse must be had to what Plato calls the 'Noble Lie' — a deliberately fictional justification for the division of the population, and an argument, expressed in mythic terms, for keeping things as they are. Here Plato draws on the long Greek heritage of political mythology.

All change is to be resisted. Even the pattern of children's toys is to be the same, for in a society so artificially ordered and so rigidly limited the smallest change could serve to usher in other, more important changes until the entire society was disrupted. As this is the ideal society, the only progress can be downwards. We are once again face to face with the cyclical theory, the concept of an original perfection progressively destroyed by a series of changes. Plato sketches what would happen if the pattern of the Ideal State were allowed to break down. First, the communal life of the rulers would be disrupted, and the idea of personal property allowed to appear. Thus the philosopher kings would disappear and power would be concentrated in the hands of the warriors, those who were strong enough to fight for what they wanted and hold on to what they had. Thus would appear a state devoted to physical culture and to war, ruled by a military aristocracy. The love of riches, spreading further, would produce a plutocracy, where status would depend on the extent of one's possessions. The injustices thus created would, in time, cause a revolt of the poor against the rich. Thus would appear democracy, which for Plato represents the complete emancipation of the passions from reason, the artisan class from the philosopher kings. Ultimately, there would be tyranny; a champion would arise from the people who would take it upon himself to rule the state in whatever way seemed pleasing to him. The tyrant, for Plato, is the complete antithesis of the philosopher kings with whom the sequence began.

Plato's Ideal State presents a number of notable features. Although it has never been duplicated in its entirety, various states that have put the common interest above that of the individual have borrowed various parts of it. Sparta, with the idea of a communistically organized ruling class and a large subject population, came close. Nazi Germany evolved ideas of selective breeding which are highly reminiscent of Plato's. Communist China, for some time at least, advocated the breaking-up of family life and the organization of society into more economically viable units. Certainly Plato's picture of the ideal society represents his dissatisfaction with the way things were done in Athens. The military state, of which Sparta was the outstanding example in his time, approximates much more closely to the ideal than does the democratic type, represented by Athens.

In the *Laws*, a later work, Plato attempts to grapple on a more practical level with the problems of political organization. In the *Laws*, however, we see the same hierarchical organism; individuals only live to perform their function in the state. The same fear of change is evident, and because of this, the same insistence on the avoidance of foreign contacts. It is urged that the state be placed as far as possible from the sea, to avoid contamination. Once again Plato takes Sparta as his informing image; once again, there is a modern example in Japan, which until comparatively recent times managed to retain its traditional organization unchanged because of the deliberate exclusion of foreign influence.

Plato's discussion of the arts is involved in his concept of the state. Like any Greek, he saw the purpose of art as primarily educational. A superb artist himself, he must have been unusually aware of the effect that the arts can have on men. For this reason, he feels it doubly important that they shall not be used to disseminate evil influences, or to teach inappropriate lessons. He would have all poetry rigidly scrutinized for immoral tendencies — and his definition of what is unsuitable in art is very wide. Heroic personages must not be represented as engaging in unheroic behaviour. For Achilles to be shown weeping in the *Iliad* is detrimental to the public well-being; the auditors should be offered only illustrious examples for their emulation. Thus, in the Ideal State, the Homeric poems would be subject to strict censorship. Even more so the drama; Plato's censures here are so strict that it is with the greatest reluctance he permits any dramatic activity at all. By virtue of its greater immediacy, drama is even more dangerous as a propagator of false opinions. To show depraved characters on the stage is harmful both to the audience that watches them and to the actors who play them; one of Plato's theories is that one learns by imitation, so to imitate a bad character would imply learning the wrong sort of things. Plato even extends his condemnations to music, a field where the modern reader finds it difficult to follow him. For the Greek, music carried definite emotional connotations. Different musical modes were recognized, each with appropriate characteristics.

Plato would retain the Dorian mode, which is martial and vigorous, but reject the Lydian and Phrygian, which are soft and languorous, tending to enervate those who listen to them. This ideological criticism of music is something still practised in Russia, but fundamentally meaningless to the western listener. It is as if a modern statesman were to argue that only marches should be retained, and the waltz condemned as frivolous. Plato would have agreed with the traditional Chinese saying, that to begin a revolution you have first to change the people's music; he would also have been sympathetic to the objections that our moralists make from time to time to certain popular dances, on the grounds that they are morally decadent.

Plato studies the arts from the point of view of the statesman and educator, and his criticisms are conceived along these lines. He is interested in the arts, not for their own sake, but for their value to the body politic. The social organism is the only important thing, and no standard of value must be admitted which will conflict with this. In his zeal he makes the error that many would-be censors make, in confusing the part with the whole. Because a particular episode in a play or poem shows a character behaving in an unworthy fashion, he would strike it out. He does not seem to realize that, in context, the purport of the scene may be highly moral. When Achilles weeps in the *Iliad*, he shows weakness; but this weakness is part of a grand design that shows the moral degradation and subsequent rehabilitation of Achilles, and so in its entirety has a wholly moral purpose. At the end of the *Republic*, Plato finds other reasons for condemning the arts — or, more specifically, representational art. If we allow him the existence of his world of Forms, perfect exemplars of the imperfect copies that make up this world, then it follows that an artist painting the things he sees about him is working at two removes from truth. Plato suggests elsewhere that art should concern itself not with the depiction of nature, but with pure form — a curious premonition of certain modern schools of art, which has been eagerly seized upon and quoted by the practitioners of those schools.

Plato's successor and chief critic in the world of Greek philosophy was Aristotle, born in 384 at Stagira on the north coast of the Aegean. He was of pure Greek blood, but lived on the outside limits of Greek influence, in the sphere of the rising power of Macedon. His family belonged to the medical guild of the Asklepiadae, 'Sons of Asklepios'; his father was court physician. Thus Aristotle grew up with a keen interest in biology, which was to be for him the key science as mathematics was for Plato. A member of the Academy until Plato's death in 348, he afterwards departed, partly through dissatisfaction with the conduct of the school and partly, no doubt, through professional jealousy; he was not chosen to succeed Plato as the Academy's head. From 343 to 340 he served as tutor to the young Alexander. This connection was to be of great value to him, although the reverse does not seem to have been true: Alexander's career reveals little awareness of Aristotelian teaching. None the less the ruler remembered his former professor and sent him valuable information and specimens from the strange countries to which his armies penetrated. In 335 he founded his own philosophical school, the Lyceum, named after a grove dedicated to Apollo Lykeios. Here was housed a collection of manuscripts, the first important library in Greece; a collection of maps; a natural history museum; and equipment of various kinds for scholarship and research.

Aristotle was a polymath of bewildering accomplishment. His school was devoted to teaching, lecturing and co-operative scientific research, and Aristotle himself worked in and wrote on logic, physics, metaphysics, ethics, political philosophy, psychology, epistemology and aesthetics. In most of his work he reveals a reaction, conscious or unconscious, from the teachings of Plato. He is unable to accept his doctrine of the world of Forms. While agreeing that it is our business as rational beings to know objective truth, he feels that the Forms are so completely cut off from this world that they cannot in any real sense be objects of knowledge. Plato had cited the 'soul' as go-between, but Aristotle seems to ignore this. For him, with his natural scientific bent, the things that we perceive by our senses are the primary realities. Form, far from being something removed from the world of sense-perception, is inherent in the objects of that world: the form of a thing is that which makes it what it is, the intimate inward structure of the thing. Matter is the possibility of the thing being what it is, or something else; this possibility is made actual for the time being by the reception of a particular form. Thus form is the stable element, permanent and scientifically determinable; matter is itself undetermined, but capable of successive determinations. It is thus that Aristotle grapples with the problem of change and permanence, the One and the Many.

In his *Ethics*, Aristotle asks what is the purpose of man. All men, he suggests, aim at well-being, and this can best be attained by activity, not by a docile and passive life. We learn virtue by doing the things appropriate to the sort of person we wish to become, in the same way as we learn the arts and crafts. In his analysis of the various virtues, Aristotle falls back on a familiar Greek doctrine, that of pursuing the mean — the idea of due and right proportion which should be present in all our actions. In striving for the desired quality, we should avoid the twin pitfalls of deficiency and excess. Courage is a desirable quality, but courage in excess becomes rashness, too little is cowardice. Generosity stands between prodigality and avarice. Aristotle gives little pen-portraits of these various types, sketches which suggest a distinct relationship with the stereotyped comedy of the later fourth century and which prepare the way for the character studies composed by later writers. Where Plato regarded all virtues as essentially one, Aristotle demarcates them as much as he can. For him the highest virtue is the contemplation of the proper objects of the mind — the realities revealed to us by metaphysics, by mathematics and by natural philosophy. This activity is the most perfect because it is the least dependent on externals. To practise this desirable contemplation one needs little in the way of material goods, and can go on for longer without wearying.

In his view of politics Aristotle is again more practical and more humane than Plato. He saw politics as the chief of the practical sciences regulating human conduct; for him, as for any Greek, man could realize his fullest potential only by operating within the context of the community. Thus politics, in theory at least, takes precedence over ethics, although in practice Aristotle is fascinated by his ethical studies and treats them in considerable length and with some independence. In ethics, Aristotle had proceeded from the observation of specific cases to the formulation of general principles. In politics he did the same, working from particular examples of constitutions to the science of politics as a whole. A surviving *Constitution of Athens*, attributed by many scholars to Aristotle, is probably one of these individual studies.

If the aim of the individual citizen is to pursue the good life, the function of the state is to help its members to achieve this. Man is naturally a social animal, and the state is a self-sufficient community containing everything necessary for its citizens to find happiness. Aristotle does not fall into Plato's fallacy of making the state something over and above the corporate desires of its individual members. He criticizes Plato's abolition of family life (once again his criticism is slightly unfair, failing to recognize that Plato imposed this restriction on the guardian classes only) and argues that, on the contrary, the family is the nucleus of society. The natural relationships obtaining therein can only be destroyed at the cost of weakening the whole fabric of the state. But, like Plato, he sees the need for adequate leisure if a citizen is to perform his duties satisfactorily. Full-time members of the state must be free for military and legislative duties, and thus the full rights of citizenship are confined to those of independent means. Apart from the time factor, Aristotle feels that the practice of manual labour is ultimately degrading, and makes men unfit for higher duties. Thus agricultural labourers and artisans must be content to be second-class citizens. The state should be of manageable size, smaller than Athens but larger than Sparta. The best type of constitution is a mixed one, combining some features of demo-cracy and some of oligarchy, and retaining power in the hands of the most stable element, the property-owning middle class, who will be least liable to countenance sudden change. Once again the Greek desire for moderation, for pursuing the idea of the mean, manifests itself.

Although, like Plato, Aristotle recognizes the supreme importance of education, and insists that the state must have complete control over teaching, he does not make the same savage strictures on the arts. This is another instance of his reaction against his predecessor. Where Plato had insisted that the arts must be good *for* something, Aristotle argues that they can have a value of their own, independent of their social or educational functions. His *Poetics* is the first work we possess concerned with literary criticism as a subject in its own right. It is a curious and perplexing work. Its value is considerably lessened for us because it is mutilated. Of the original three-part division, dealing with epic, tragedy and comedy, only the central section has survived in anywhere near complete form. Added to this are the difficulties of style. In the form in which we have it, the *Poetics* resembles a set of lecture notes, possibly intended for subsequent expansion which never took place. Thus arguments which might at a later stage of composition have been presented in far fuller form are only sketchily set out here. It is even conjectured that these are not the professor's notes, but a pupil's, and so one remove further from the mind of their originator. Given these problems, the work has still had enormous influence. Aristotle insists that art does not represent individual particulars but universal truths, and thus is a serious study, more useful than history. It comes nearer the truth because the artist may create new happenings in which the pattern of life is clearer than in any particular experience; it does not record what has happened, but suggests what might happen.

In discussing plot-structure, Aristotle evidently proceeds as he had done with ethics and with constitutional history. He has read and studied individual examples. Exactly what he was able to see on the stage is difficult to say. It is important to remember here that he lived long after the great age of the Greek drama. He can have seen little Aeschylus, and is curiously blind to the structural values of Euripides. Sophocles is the author who most pleases him. A play, says Aristotle, must have unity; it must be one story and not several; it must not be so long that the audience forgets the beginning before it reaches the end; the chorus must be well integrated into the action, and psychology must be subordinate to plot. It is this series of dicta which led Aristotle to approve most highly of *Oedipus the King*, and which have helped win that play its title of the most perfect Greek tragedy.

NOTE TO CHAPTER TEN

1. Plato, *Crito*, 1.

Chapter Eleven

The Aftermath of Alexander

As the traveller walks in Athens and inspects the ancient buildings, most of what he sees does not date from the great period, the fifth century, at all. The surviving monuments are predominantly Hellenistic or Roman. The Parthenon still stands, it is true, though mutilated. The Erechtheum, completed in 407 and dedicated to Athens' legendary earthborn king, survives, though part has collapsed and one of the caryatids, pillars in the shape of women, is a modern replacement of the one taken by Lord Elgin with his other trophies from the site. The Propylaia, the great entrance to the Acropolis, is still there, and visitors may now enter the way the ancient processions did, up the main stairway; a few years ago it was necessary to enter almost surreptitiously, by a side-gate. At the foot of the Acropolis, however, it is the more recent buildings that predominate. If you want to see an ancient play in Athens you do not go to the Theatre of Dionysus. The building that Aeschylus and Aristophanes used has fallen out of commission long since, and even the present ruins represent the reconstruction, in the first century A.D., by the Emperor Nero. You go rather to an adjacent theatre built in the century after Nero by the great philhellene and patron of learning Herodes Atticus. It held six thousand spectators in antiquity, fewer now, for some of the seating has been destroyed. It has the semi-circular orchestra characteristic of the Graeco-Roman theatres and what was once a magnificent sculpted scenic façade. Between this and the Theatre of Dionysus lay the Stoa of Eumenes, built by the king of the Eastern monarchy of Pergamon in the second century B.C. Across the modern road to the west of the Acropolis, on the Hill of the Muses, stands a monument to a Syrian prince who held office in Athens, Philopappus; it was erected by a grateful population in A.D. 119, and adorned with statues of members of his family.

In the Agora, the ancient centre of business life, the same impression is given. It is only recently that this area has been uncovered. It was almost entirely built over. One side was cut by the electric railway from Athens to Peiraeus. Five thousand people had to be dispossessed before work could start; interrupted by the war, the excavations have since revealed a number of the fine monuments of later Athens. Most conspicuous now, because completely restored, is the Stoa of Attalus, running along the eastern side. This was another benefaction from an Eastern country, constructed in the second century B.C. Such stoas were prominent features of Hellenistic town planning. They were long rectangular colonnades, often backed by shops. They provided necessary shade, and served as meeting places. One of the most famous philosophical schools of later Athens, founded by Zeno about 300 B.C., was known as the Stoa, and its followers as Stoics, from the fact of its meeting in such a structure.

The Stoa of Attalus has caused considerable controversy. There are always two schools of thought on such matters, those archaeologists who consider it honest and proper to leave ancient buildings in their ruined state, and those who think it appropriate, as an aid for the uninformed public, to rebuild and restore wherever possible. Sir Arthur Evans, in Crete, suffered criticism for his restorations: the issue was not so much the accuracy of what he did, as whether he should have done it at all. Certainly the Stoa of Attalus was restored with exemplary thoroughness. Professor Homer Thomson, who directed the operation, went around searching for 'a millionaire with an interest in ancient philosophy'; stone was fetched from the original quarries; the dimensions were known, and a complete reconstruction of the long two-storied building was made. The shaded terrace now holds statues and the ground floor a museum of objects discovered in the Agora. On the floor above are workshops, shelves lined with pottery fragments awaiting the long slow labour of classification: the work of archaeology is a continuous one, and much of it is drudgery. In one corner of the ancient building a fountain had flowed. This could not be replaced, but the Americans, anachronistically but with thought for the visitor's comfort, inserted an iced water machine. By the time one has made one's way in the burning Athenian sunshine to the Stoa, one realizes why the water was there, and why the Stoa was built at all. It was an exciting experience to be in the Agora while the building was in construction. On every side lay half-finished columns; one had only to close one's eyes, listen to the clinking of chisel on stone, and imagine oneself back two thousand years. The formal opening of the Stoa, though marred by some political unpleasantness, was one of the most stimulating events in archaeology for years.

The visitor stands on the steps of the Stoa and looks across the whole length of the Agora. If all the buildings in front of him were restored on their foundations as the Stoa has been, he would see the site not as Pericles but as the Romans knew it. Not far from the Stoa is a great concert hall presented by Agrippa, aide and confidant of the Emperor Augustus. A statue of the Emperor Hadrian, another of the city's benefactors, stands lonely among the foundations. To Hadrian the Athenians erected an arch which, floodlit nightly, is still one of the city's most impressive monuments. Leaving the Stoa and walking east one arrives in the Roman centre. This is in the Plaka, the old Turkish town, which infiltrates on to the northern and eastern slopes of the Acropolis and is now full of *tavernas*, bright, noisy, open-air restaurants full of the smell of resinated wine and the music of *bouzouki*. Here sits the Roman Agora, much of it still awaiting excavation. Characteristically solid in structure, it boasts an enormous public lavatory and a decree concerning market prices — the whole atmosphere is more stolid, more prosaic. In this area too were Hadrian's Library and the so-called Tower of the Winds, a clever combination of sundial and waterclock ornamented with figures representing the eight winds, designed and built by the astronomer Andronicus in the first century A.D.

This list of donors and monuments is not made idly. It shows the sort of city that Athens became when its classical lustre had

departed. Although its political importance had dwindled to
insignificance, it continued to be venerated as the home of old
glories. Other cities too received benefactions: Eleusis and
Epidauros were cherished for their sanctity, Corinth for its commercial importance. The latter city became even more important
as a centre of trade and industry in the Hellenistic period, but
political involvement destroyed it; caught up in resistance to
Roman invasion, it was sacked in 146 B.C. and its legendary
treasures scattered and lost. In 44 B.C. it was refounded, and the
city one now sees — again excavated by the American School —
is predominantly Roman. There are arched Roman shops,
Roman administrative buildings, a Roman speaker's platform.
Herodes Atticus, the same man who had been so generous to
Athens, let his money flow in Corinth also. The Fountain of
Peirene, largest spring in the city, was enlarged and decorated by
him. It is still possible to see the remains of the ornamental
basins, the decorated arches behind which the water ran, and the
fish paintings, colour still faintly visible on the walls. Yet it was
Athens that remained important and survived as a centre of the
arts and a university town. Many famous men from the Roman
world came to study here. Cicero had instruction in philosophy
and rhetoric at Athens, staying there for his health and for respite
from the hectic politics of Rome. During the Roman Empire
the influx of distinguished visitors was heavy. Athens figured
prominently on the Roman equivalent of the eighteenth-century
nobleman's Grand Tour. Many years after, Cicero Apuleius the
African, mystic, novelist and so-called magician, was resident in
the city for the same purposes. Whatever shifts of power took
place in the greater world, Athens retained its old allure. In this
sense Italy and the west were still what the early colonists had
called them, *Magna Graecia*, 'greater Greece'.

In the Hellenistic world other areas came into political prominence. After Alexander's death his empire was divided into
parts. Macedonia, the old seat of Philip's and of Alexander's
power together with its new Greek extensions, kept its independence until 167 B.C., when it was assailed by the expanding

power of Rome and succumbed. In the east, Syria saw considerable contention between various claimants for the throne. Disputed and divided, it was eventually split up into a number of separate principalities. It was made a Roman province by Pompey in 64–63 B.C. Nevertheless it remained a nursery of Greek culture in the east. In the later division of the Roman world into Greek- and Latin-speaking regions, the Syriac cities preserved much of value from the earlier ages.

Egypt remained the most interesting and the most powerful. When Alexander conquered Syria, Egypt also fell into his hands. To commemorate his conquest and signify the change of rule he had a city built, Alexandria. He was not to revisit it alive, but after his death in Babylon (323 B.C.) he was brought back to the city named for him, in a glass coffin; about this coffin and his tomb many legends have grown up.

Egypt fell to Alexander's general Ptolemy as his share, and the dynasty he founded amalgamated Hellenistic ideas with centuries of Egyptian tradition. His son, Ptolemy Philadelphus, followed the ideas of his adopted country and married his own sister. Such inbreeding was to be common, and to produce its inevitable consequences. The fusion of cultures was symbolized by the creation of a new deity, Serapis — part Osiris, part the bull-god Apis, and in appearance a Greek divinity. The self-deification of the ruler, originated by Alexander himself, was to find a fruitful home in Egypt. When the Roman emperors made themselves gods they had Hellenistic precedent to quote. The women of the Ptolemies were on the whole more lively than the men. There were several Arsinoes and several Cleopatras, the last of whom was to involve herself so fatally with Roman politics and politicians, and at whose death Egypt fell into Roman hands.

Of the great buildings that the Ptolemies constructed in Alexandria, two in particular have lingered in the memory — the lighthouse and the library. The former was completed, probably, in 279 B.C. It was built on Pharos Island, from which it took its name. Such was its reputation that that name has been passed to other languages as a common noun — French *phare*, Italian *faro*, modern Greek *pharos*. It was one of the wonders of antiquity, stood between four and five hundred feet high, and contained scientific marvels which have passed down only as legend and fairy-tale. Standing on top was a statue of Poseidon. The god who had accompanied the first nomads into Greece centuries before now presided over their most cosmopolitan achievement.

The palace complex stood by the great harbour. It was systematically enlarged by various generations of Ptolemies, and abutted on to a more famous structure, the Library, or Mouseion, Home of the Muses. This was the centre of cultural life in Alexandria, and set its stamp on the writing of the age. A powerful system of court patronage prevailed. The scholar-writers were so many Poets Laureate, working to order and bound, if they wished to retain their positions, to offer works which would gratify and be understood by their rulers and be in no way offensive. Some remarks about the nature of Hellenistic writing have been made already, in various connections, in the course of this book. Its lack of vitality, its preciosity, its limpness when compared to the masterpieces of the past, have been noted. Just as diffusion of the Attic dialect simplified it and made it more bland, the wash of Greek culture which now spread over the world was notable for its thinness and lack of profundity. Hellenistic art, both literary and visual, was concerned primarily with the particular. Where fifth-century sculptors had idealized their subjects, the new men exploited them for their human interest. Far more concerned with originality than their predecessors had been, they sought to titillate and shock. Anything that might arouse interest in a public rapidly becoming blasé and over-sophisticated was seized upon and cultivated. Thus the characteristic sculptural form of the new age is the individual portrait bust: the more interesting the face for its own sake, the more it lends itself to this almost theatrical exploitation, the more attractive the sculptor would find it. Or there are the large works designed to overwhelm, to distract the eye in various directions, to draw it to investigate fascinating if irrelevant detail; above all, to draw attention to the artist's cleverness in securing these effects and reproducing the textures of human skin, animal hair and fine silk in microscopic exactitude rather than subordinating such finesse to the larger purpose of the work as earlier artists had sought to do.

So it was in literature. The levelling of cultural aspirations, coupled with the broadening of the potential audience, brought several themes into prominence. In the theatre, as has already been shown, domestic subject matter was paramount. Audiences were presented with what was familiar to them, types and characters known from their own experience. Here is the opening of a mime — a dramatic sketch of everyday life — by the Alexandrian poet Herodas, written about the middle of the third century B.C. The suburban matrons who figure here are drawn from Alexandrian prototypes, but they are so generalized as to be universal. With the addition of a bridge table, the century could just as well be the twentieth, and the locale Wimbledon or Westchester County.

KORITTO.   *Metro, sit down!* (to the servant) *On your feet, you :*
           Get the lady a chair! Do I have to see to everything
           Myself? Won't you do anything unless
           I'm there to tell you? I don't have a housemaid,
           I have a block of stone. Come feeding time you're ready
           And counting every crumb — and if one bit gets spilled
           You sit there muttering the whole day long
           And grumbling fit to crack the plaster. Oh,
           Waiting till now to dust it, are you,
           Just when we need it? You should be locked up!
           Thank your lucky stars the lady's here. If we were private
           I'd have given you the back of my hand, I would!
METRO.   *Darling Koritto, it's the cross we both of us*
           Must bear. All day, all night I'm at them like a dog,
           Snarling at these . . . these . . . well, never mind.
           The reason why I came—
KORITTO.   (to the servant). *Get out of here,*
           Damned good-for-nothing slut. All ears and tongue,
           One long day off, that's all you are! [1]

They go on to gossip about clothes, and the conduct of their neighbours.

So it was with the emergent Greek novel. As history became romanticized, notably with the Alexander cult, the line between fact and fiction grew indistinct. Papyrus fragments show the existence of novelistic treatments of historical or legendary figures. The very existence of such things shows the way public taste was developing. Readers were no longer content to satisfy their appetites on factual accounts, geography, travel books, history. They wanted the diversion of story-writing. When the subject matter is confined, by public taste and enthusiasm, to the particular and domestic, the author is limited in his ways of securing excitement or surprise. Thus there is much use of the arbitrary intervention of chance in human affairs. *Tyche*, luck or coincidence, is the motivating force. Characters are jerked from one incident to another by accident. In such a literature the sea, always looming large in the Greek mind, assumes a new importance. It becomes a convenient metaphor for the mutability of human affairs, an overworked device to bring the stock characters into new relationships.

When the writers depart from the domestic and familiar they do so usually for an escape-world, a pastoral and idyllic landscape suitably populated. The countryside, like the sea, is a recurring theme among Greek writers, but like the sea the meaningfulness of the country changes. Hesiod wrote of the bucolic life, and so, in the Hellenistic world, does Theocritus; but Theocritus' countryside has as much in common with Hesiod's as Marie-Antoinette's Petit Trianon with a Breton farmhouse. An increasingly urban age hankers — or thinks it does — for rural simplicity and the freedom of life without rulers or walls. But the rural life must be delicately packaged and prettified. The Hellenistic Greeks loved the country much as the English love dogs, only when tamed, cleaned and taught a few tricks.

When Homer, in the *Odyssey*, wrote of the Cyclops Polyphemus, he described a monster to fire the imagination. Odysseus' encounter with him is a tribute to the unfailing ingenuity of Greek manhood confronted with the ruthlessness of brute nature. Theocritus shows a different figure, a Cyclops in love:

> There is no other remedy for love,
> No salve or ointment, Nicias, I think,
> Only the Muses, mild for men
> And giving no unease, but hard to find.
> But you are a physician, I believe
> You know this well, for the Nine Muses love you.
> So, long ago, my countryman the Cyclops
> Found this way easiest, when the down
> Clung fresh on lip and cheek, and he was struck
> With love for Galatea ; and his love
> Was not with apples, ringlets or with roses
> But with sheer passion. All things else he let go by.
> Time and again his sheep would wander back unherded
> From green pasture to the fold, while he alone
> On the weed-strewn shore from daybreak serenaded
> Galatea, wounded sore beneath his heart
> Where Cypris in her majesty had struck him.
> But he found remedy, and seated on the pinnacle
> Of rock would gaze across the sea and sing. . . .[2]

So we hear how the Cyclops serenaded his love; how he laments his own ugliness, and wishes that he had been born a fish, so that he might dive under the water to his beloved nymph 'and kiss your hand, if I could not your lips'. There is even a bizarre echo of the blinding from the *Odyssey*:

> There are oak logs here, and banked fire ever burning.
> I'd give my soul to you to burn, and I would give
> This single eye, the sweetest of my treasures.[3]

This is Cyclops sentimentalized, a Caliban sighing for a Miranda. Already the familiar furniture of romantic poetry begins to appear. One of the things we learn about Homer's Cyclops, and Euripides' also, is his oneness with the soil. He has a fierce concern for the well-being of his sheep, even as they depend on him. In Theocritus the sheep, like the countryside itself, have become part of the pastoral backdrop, painted figures in front of which the protagonist attitudinizes.

Polyphemus is in love. Love becomes a standard theme of the age. Barely noticed before in literature, romantic love now emerges as a subject of major importance. This is partly due to the new concern with the domestic, the facts of family life, and partly to the fact that so many themes were now impossible. Apollonius of Rhodes, in his time librarian at Alexandria, wrote an epic poem, the *Argonautica*, on the subject of Medea. It deals, in would-be Homeric manner, with the voyage of the *Argo* and the quest for the Golden Fleece. The language is modelled, at least in part, on Homer, but the thought is Alexandrian. Apollonius is clearly not concerned to use the subject for the searching analysis of motive and morality that Euripides mined from it. Love is a dominant theme. Here is the description of the first meeting between Jason ('Aeson's son') and Medea when the hero has just arrived in Colchis. Eros sends his arrow of love into Medea's heart:

> Then with both hands he strained the bow apart
> And shot Medea. Stupefaction seized her.
> The god flew homeward from the vaulted hall
> Laughing his delight, and in the maiden's heart
> His shaft burnt deep, like flame. She darted
> Glance on bright glance at Aeson's son. The heart
> Within her panted in its anguish, she had thought
> For nothing else, her soul with sweet pain melted,
> And as a peasant woman heaps the kindling round
> A blazing branch — a creature bound to labour —
> So she might make a fire at night beneath her roof
> On early rising, and the flame from little grows
> To great, and burns up all the twigs together,
> So did love entwine around her heart, and burn
> Unseen by human eye. She was distracted ;
> Her cheeks grew pale, and red, and pale again.[4]

It is axiomatic in this convention that when love occurs, it is always love at first sight.

Perhaps the most significant event in Apollonius' life, so far as it concerns the literary history of the era, was not a poem but a quarrel: the quarrel that Apollonius had with his mentor and predecessor Callimachus, who worked in Alexandria until his death around 235 B.C. Callimachus maintained that the age of the epic, the lengthy work, was past: his age demanded brevity with elegance, the short, highly polished poem. 'A long book', he pontificated, 'is disaster.' Apollonius wrote his *Argonautica* to defend his thesis and prove that Homeric techniques were still valid. Callimachus retaliated with a bitter poem called *Ibis*, in which, we are told, he compared Apollonius — using a wealth of recondite and unpleasant allusion — to the bird of that name, a native of Egypt known for its ungainly stance and disgusting eating habits.

The atmosphere of Alexandria encouraged such bickering. Put a number of argumentative and opinionated scholars, most with rather less than first-rate literary talent, into an enclosed and artificial atmosphere, and the results are predictable: rancour, affectation, a fierce desire to outdo one another in erudition, storms in literary teacups. Add to this the pressure of patronage and the necessity of conforming to palace protocol, and it is easy to see how the Library, at its worst, could resemble a nightmare senior common room. Apollonius himself is not wholly typical of Alexandrian poetry — not merely because of the length of his work, but because of his comparative simplicity. For the most part display of learning was a *sine qua non*. The more allusive and recondite the work, the greater the status of the poet. Often the triviality of the permitted subjects needed to be swaddled in learning if a poem was to appear at all. When Queen Berenice, wife of Ptolemy III, lost her hair from the temple where it had been dedicated, Callimachus wrote a poem about it, relating (on the authority of Conon, court astronomer: scientists were not immune from the perils of patronage) how it had been taken up to heaven and fixed there as a constellation. We know the poem mainly indirectly, through a Latin version made by Catullus, but it seems to have combined flattery with obscure erudition to an alarming degree. Here is Callimachus writing his *Hymn to Zeus*.

He desires to establish the fact that when the Father of the Gods was born there was no water to wash him, for the rivers were not yet in existence:

> Broad Ladon was not flowing yet, or Erymanthus,
> The pristine river; not a drop of water ran
> In all Arcadia, though soon it would be called
> Well-watered. Then, when Rhea shed her girdle,
> Iaon's waterway upheld a spreading horde
> Of hollow oaks, carts travelled close on Melas,
> And over Carnion snakes nested by the hundred
> Though it runs with water now. A man could travel
> By foot over Crathis and the pebbles of Metope
> And thirst, though the stream's great bounty lay beneath him.[5]

Take a point and labour it to death; take a statement and turn it into a glossary. That is the Alexandrian way.

When art falters criticism is elevated to the stature of art. That is the only way the age can save its face. So it was in Alexandria. Theocritus, poet in the Alexandrian tradition, could write of the death of his fictional shepherd Daphnis

> For him the jackals howled, and the wolves howled,
> And for his death the woodland lion wept.[6]

No less in the Alexandrian tradition was the scholar who could comment on these lines 'That is, the lion *would* have wept' (if there had been any lions in Sicily!) It has already been noted that the Alexandrian scholars edited and circulated the masterpieces of the past; they also started the mass of critical commentary which has accompanied these works through the ages. Some of it is pedantry at its most trivial, as when a commentator glosses two words in a Greek tragedy meaning 'Oh, oh!' with two others meaning 'Alas, alas!' Much of it was of the greatest value. Aristophanes of Byzantium, head of the Library at the end of the second century B.C., showed Alexandrian scholarship at its best. He was a man of great critical discernment and vast accomplishment. He edited the *Iliad* and *Odyssey*, Hesiod's *Theogony* and the plays of Euripides; he made the first critical edition of his comic namesake; he compiled books of proverbs, dictionaries and grammars. We have the Greek texts in their present state because the Alexandrians interested themselves in their preservation. Many of the treasures here were destroyed by war or accident. When Julius Caesar was in Egypt, in 48–47 B.C., the inhabitants of the city rose against him, and fighting was fierce. Caesar, besieged in the Palace, contrived to set fire to the Alexandrian fleet in harbour. Flames spread to the Library. This fire has been exaggerated and romanticized, notably by George Bernard Shaw, who uses it as a key incident in *Caesar and Cleopatra*. After the Romans, the Arabs are usually blamed for such philistine destruction of the Library. In fact most of the damage had already been done, by Christians, in A.D. 391. The Arabs were sensitive to the vestiges of Greek culture. The Pharos inspired the minaret, the works of Aristotle were translated into Arabic. The feeling of the fusion of cultures which characterized Alexander's foundation continued into the later history of the city. In our own time, when the Greek poet Constantine Cavafy wrote *Waiting for the Barbarians*, and the English Lawrence Durrell *The Alexandria Quartet*, they were both able to draw, in their different ways, on the city's lassitude, its world-weariness, its curiously tainted stock, that had been there from the beginning. Alexander could hardly have sought a more fitting memorial to the good that he did, or the harm that he caused.

It was an age that sought the easy answer, the convenient formula for success; an age that no longer had understanding of, or patience for, the intellectual toughness at the root of Socrates' enquiries. It was ripe for conquest, and the conquest came swiftly, as power shifted westwards and Rome assumed a tighter hold on the Mediterranean. First the Greek colonies in Italy fell, as Rome consolidated her power and moved south. Cumae, oldest Greek colony in the country and home of an imported oracle, became a Roman dependency — without voting rights — in 338 B.C. Thurii, the Panhellenic colony in which Pericles and Herodotus had had a hand, voluntarily joined the Roman side in 282. Taras, the only Spartan colony, called by the Romans Tarentum, fell after some resistance ten years later. It was only a short step to the conquest of Greece itself. The city states, for ever quarrelling internally, still not realizing that the day of such small units of power was over, made the mistake of inviting Roman intervention. Visitor became conqueror. Macedonia was annexed in 148 and the political power of other Greek states speedily reduced.

The weight of the Roman hand on Greece was less heavy than might have been feared. Romans were on the whole respectful and cautious. There were isolated acts of barbarism and brutality, but Greece, though reduced to subject status, continued to enjoy a considerable measure of autonomy. The effect of Greece on Rome was another matter. Rome, girded for war, was still culturally inadequate. In conquering Greece and its dependencies it found itself confronted by a culture already mature and pervasive. By many avenues of trade Rome had been conditioned to the acceptance of Greek art works long before this. The old Greek cities in Italy maintained their national character and cultural independence after conquest. Pompeii had its theatre nearly two hundred years before a permanent stage building was erected in Rome. Greek continued to be spoken in South Italy. Greek words creep into the Latin vocabulary, as technical terms, as slang. Often there are significant changes in meaning. *Logi* in Latin means 'nonsense, idle chatter'. It is nothing more than the venerable and highly reputable Greek word *logos*, meaning argument, debate, the process of verbal reasoning. Greeks come to teach Romans the arts and sciences. Often they come as slaves; in many households the servants were more cultivated than their masters. There is a prevalent adoption motif in ancient Rome which demonstrates the Roman dependence on older cultures. It is told several times, about different people: it tells of an imported slave who demonstrates his literary ability, is set free by discerning masters and goes on to a free and honourable career. It is a type of story that continues, with variations, into the Italian Renaissance. Its purport, surely, is that the Romans, though they might not have the time or energy to be creative, had the *expertise* to recognize those who were. Forestalled in the realm of invention, they reserved for themselves the rôle of patron. One such freed slave was Livius Andronicus, according to tradition taken at the capture of Tarentum and brought to Rome. He went on to be the father of Latin literature, translating Homer into rough native verse forms and, in 240 B.C., giving the first Latin translation of a Greek play in Rome.

Rome follows the Greek models in great things and in small. When Plautus and Terence write their Roman comedies they are frankly imitating specific plays of the Greek New Comedy. When Lucretius writes the curious compound of atomic physics and poetry entitled *On the Universe*, he is writing a defence and expansion of the Greek philosophy of Epicurus. Greek rhetoricians taught their art in Rome. Virgil models his *Aeneid* on the *Iliad* and *Odyssey*. For the Augustan age Alexandrian poetry had a special appeal. Major and minor poets copy the work produced under the Ptolemies. Virgil's *Eclogues* echo Theocritus. Ovid, smarting in his exile and lashing out at the world, writes an *Ibis* in imitation of Callimachus' abuse of Apollonius. Seneca, writing tragedies under the Emperor Nero, takes most of his inspiration from Euripides.

The list could go on almost indefinitely. Roman critics recognized the extent of the debt even while they deplored it. 'Satire at least', states Quintilian, 'is wholly ours.' He was wrong. It is hardly worth labouring a point already sufficiently made : that although the political importance of Greece dwindled to nothing, its cultural importance remained enormous. The Greek-speaking bloc remained a largely self-contained unit within the Roman world, and in the later unwieldy days of empire it was natural for a division between Greek and Latin powers to be made. Constantinople, New Rome, completed in A.D. 330, became the centre of a new Greek world in which much of the old was preserved — a world which spread its influence to the Balkans and beyond; a city which was for Europe in its emergence what Paris was to be in its maturity, the centre of art and elegance, the place of cultural pilgrimage : the centre of the Greek Orthodox Church and home of Eastern Christianity until its defeat by the Turks in 1453. It was the old enemy, the easterner, and the old conflict: the original battle between East and West which has not yet seen quietus.

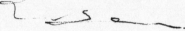

NOTES TO CHAPTER ELEVEN

1. Herodas, *Mimes*, VI. 1.
2. Theocritus, *Idylls*, XI. 1.
3. *Ibid.* XI. 51.
4. Apollonius of Rhodes, *Argo-* *nautica*, III. 283.
5. Callimachus, *Hymn*, 1 (to Zeus), 16.
6. Theocritus, *Idylls*, I. 71.

Q

Index

Index

233

238 AN INTRODUCTION TO THE GREEK WORLD

Siwah, Egypt, 60

Skene, 140

Slavery, 118

Socrates, 66, 126, 155, 157, 187, 198–
202 ; in *Republic*, 15 ; teachings,
198–200 ; sources of information
about, 198–200 ; in *Crito*, 201–2

Solon, 91, 122–3, 171

Sophists, 128, 157, 196–200

Sophocles, 32, 136, 149–51, 152, 200,
213
Antigone, 13, 59, 138
Oedipus at Colonus, 138
Oedipus the King, 71, 138, 149–50,
213
Philoctetes, 150

Sparta, 10, 26, 29–32, 182 ; government, 108–12 ; social structure,
112–18 ; men's life in, 113–14 ;
women's life in, 114–15 ; military
machine, 114–17, 206 ; colony,
115 ; culture, 116–17 ; slavery,
118. *See also* Peloponnesian War

Spartiates, 111

Sphacteria, 174

Stoics, 215

Styx, River, 58

Sunium, 2

Susarion, 135

Syracuse, 30

Tainaron, Cape, 58

Tantalus, 53

Taras (Tarentum), 115–16, 226

Telemachus, 88, 105, 107

Terence, 228

Terpander, 109

Thales of Miletus, 164, 190–2

Theatre design, 138–42 ; festivals,
142–5

Thebes, 3, 26, 120, 138

Themistocles, 28–29

Theocritus, 37, 221–2, 228

Theodosius, Emperor, 63

Thera, 8

Thermopylae, 29, 117

Thersites, 100

Theseus, 25, 43, 119

Thespis, 135

Thetes, 122

Thomson, Professor Homer, 215

Thucydides, 146, 172–3, 195 ; *History*,
31, 71, 117, 129, 173–8 ; qualifications as a historian, 173 ; use of
speeches, 176–8 ; methods, 178–
179 ; religious beliefs, 179–80 ;
views on function of history, 180

Thurii, 167, 226

Titans, 193

Tiryns, 23, 106

Trade, 11–12, 26

Tragedy, 135, 136–8, 145–53

Trapezus, 185

Triptolemos, 69

Troezen, 25

Trojan War, 5, 24, 41, 52, 73, 166.
See also *Iliad*

Troy, 24–25, 83. *See also* Trojan War

Turks, 4, 9, 228

Tyche, 221

Tyrtaeus, 109

Ulixes, *see* Odysseus

Ventris, Michael, 22

Virgil, 76, 85, 228

Wolf, Friedrich August, 80–82, 84

World War, Second, 6

Xenophanes, 64, 97, 164

Xenophon, 126, 127, 181–7, 198, 199
Anabasis, 12–13, 181, 182–6
Hellenica, 181
Symposium, 84

Xerxes, 28–29, 59, 170, 171, 172

Zagreus, 193

Zemelo, 55

Zeon, 215

Zeus, 7, 14, 40, 44, 45–46, 52–53, 57,
60, 63, 65, 73, 93, 104, 107, 148,
193

PRINTED BY R. & R. CLARK, LTD., EDINBURGH